Dracula's Wars

Dracula's Wars

Vlad the Impaler and his Rivals

James Waterson

For Beruška

The old centuries had, and have, powers of
their own which mere 'modernity' cannot kill.
Jonathan Harker's Journal, 15 May
Bram Stoker, *Dracula*

We look on past ages with condescension, as a mere preparation
for us … but what if we are only an afterglow of them?
J.G. Farrell, *The Siege of Krishnapur*

First published 2016
This paperback edition published 2019

The History Press
97 St George's Place, Cheltenham
Gloucestershire, GL50 3QB
www.thehistorypress.co.uk

British Library Cataloguing in Publication Data.
A catalogue record for this book is available from the British Library.

ISBN 978 0 7509 9240 4

Typesetting and origination by The History Press
Printed and bound in Great Britain by TJ International Ltd

CONTENTS

ACKNOWLEDGEMENTS

The Szekelys – and the Dracula as their heart's blood, their brains, and their swords – can boast a record that mushroom growths like the Habsburgs and the Romanoffs can never reach. The warlike days are over.

Blood is too precious a thing in these days of dishonourable peace; and the glories of the great races are as a tale that is told.[1]

I have acknowledged the intellect, passion, humour and numerous kindnesses of two of my former tutors at the School of Oriental and African Studies in the introductions of a total of four previous volumes. I am pleased to once again have the opportunity to express my ongoing debt to Dr Brian Williams and to Dr David Morgan. I thank the former for having set the undergraduate essay 'Discuss Ottoman relations with the Serbs from the Battle of the River Maritz to the fall of Constantinople' and the latter for expounding his theory 'that you just cannot avoid the Mongols' on day one of Eurasian History 101, which has shaped my approach to the subject ever since, and it is a pleasure to once again prove him right; for if the nascent Ottoman state was not the direct result of the collapse of the Mongol-created Sultanate of Rum then I am not entirely sure what it was.

To these superb teachers and academics I would like to add a third and somewhat belated acknowledgement. Dr Colin Heywood introduced me to the later Ottoman Empire and I can give him no higher praise than that given during a review of one of his works on Bosnia by the Bulletin of the School of Oriental and African Studies: 'another example of his versatility and of thoughtful and careful scholarship in both its conceptual and practical aspects, unlike much Ottoman scholarship, Heywood's prose is always a pleasure to read.' It was also always a pleasure to listen to Dr Heywood lecture.

I would like to thank my indulgent Dubai office colleagues, Ian Milburn and Larry Neal, for their genially unimpeachable forbearance at yet another retelling of how Grousset's classic tripartite chronology of Crusade and Jihad in the Holy Land, *L'anarchie Musulmane: L'equilibre: L'anarchie Franque*[2] could be applied *mutatis mutandis* to the medieval and early modern history of the Balkans as a scheme, with Dracula as both an identifiable point in its evolution, and an exemplar of the anarchic response of the medieval Europeans to the challenge of the Ottomans in the fourteenth and fifteenth centuries.

Their restraint and nodding encouragement while I expounded such ideas has led, in no small part, to the production of this volume with its overarching theme of '*L'anarchie Européen: L'equilibre: L'anarchie Turc.*'

One final thank you goes to Dr Anna Vičánková for her always charming and cultured discussions with me that have embraced Hussites, Mamluks, Crusaders, Samurai, Janissaries and Landsknechts.

A NOTE ON TRANSLITERATION, TITLES AND DATES

There are many, many ways of rendering both Turkish and the Cyrillic writings of the Balkans into English. I have generally opted for the most commonly used 'short' forms of names rather than the more scholarly forms, simply because the vast swathe of names that the reader encounters whilst reading any history of the medieval Balkans means that any familiar faces are welcome.

For city and country names I have used the nomenclature of the period. The Balkan cities are given their European names rather than Turkish names unless that change has remained 'permanent' (or has at least lasted down to our day) as this is how they are most commonly denoted in other texts that the reader might be led to review.

Diacritical marks have generally been omitted for the sake of clarity, and uncommon or unique terms have been italicised; for example, *voivode*, a vassal prince or military leader and ruler of a territory.

TIMELINE

1241–42	The Mongols invade Hungary.
1261	The Byzantine Palaiologi retake Constantinople from the Latin Crusaders.
1301	The Ottoman ruler Osman attacks Nicaea.
1307	Beginning of Angevin dynasty in Hungary.
1326	The Ottoman ruler Orhan captures Bursa.
1329	Nicaea captured by Ottomans.
1330	Battle of Velbazhd-Kyustendil, Serbia defeats Bulgaria. Battle of Posada, Wallachia wins independence from Hungary.
1337	Nicomedia is captured by the Ottomans.
1345	Ottoman annexation of the Turkish beylik of Karaysei.
1346	Ottomans form an alliance with John Kantakouzenos of the Morea against the Byzantine ruling house of Constantinople.
1343–52	Serbia conquers most of Byzantine Greece.
1354	Earthquakes allow the Ottomans to occupy Gallipoli, their first European territory.
1359	Traditional date of independence of Moldavia from Hungary.
1361	Ottoman capture of Adrianople (Edirne).
1362	Accession of Ottoman ruler, Murad I.
1363	First Battle of the River Maritza.
1365	Edirne becomes the new Ottoman capital.
1370	The Kingdom of Poland joined with the Kingdom of Hungary.
1371	Battle of Cernomen–Second Battle of River Maritz. Coalition defeated by the Ottomans, beginning of fragmentation of Bulgaria.

1385	Ottomans enter Albania, Ottoman capture of Sofia.
1386	Ottoman capture of Nis.
1387	Ottoman capture of Thessalonica, Ottoman capture of Konya.
1389	First Battle of Kosovo, most of Serbia accepts Ottoman suzerainty.
1393	Collapse of Bulgarian independence.
1396	Crusade and Battle of Nicopolis, Crusaders and Hungary defeated by Ottomans.
1402	Battle of Ankara, Ottomans defeated by Timur Leng. Ottoman sultan, Bayezid I, captured.
1402–13	The *Fitnet Devri*. The sons of Sultan Bayezid make war on each other for possession of what remains of the Ottoman Empire. An alliance with the Despot of Serbia finally brings Mehemmed I to the throne.
1417	Wallachia accepts Ottoman suzerainty.
1418	The Order of the Dragon formed to honour Christian leaders combating heretics and the Ottomans.
1419–36	The Hussite Wars rage across Eastern Europe.
1422	Ottoman siege of Constantinople.
1431	Vlad Dracula born.
1431	Vlad II Dracul is made a member of the Order of the Dragon by King Sigismund of Hungary.
1434–44	Reign of Vladislaus III as King of Poland from 1434 and of both Poland and Hungary from 1440.
1436	Vlad II Dracul takes the throne of Wallachia.
1437	Vlad II Dracul signs an alliance with the Ottoman Sultan Murad II.
1441	John Hunyadi forces Vlad II Dracul to resume resistance to the Ottomans.
1441–44	Hungarian–Ottoman war.
1443–44	John Hunyadi leads a major offensive against the Turks and occupies Nis and Sofia.
1444	Hungarian–Ottoman war concludes with the Peace of Szeged.
1444	Vladislaus III breaks the truce and invades Ottoman territory; he is killed when his multinational Crusader army is crushed at Varna.

1444	John Hunyadi escapes the debacle of the Crusade of Varna and is briefly imprisoned in Wallachia.
1444–47	Interregnum in Poland.
1447	John Hunyadi raids Wallachia. Vlad II Dracul is assassinated in the marshes near Bucharest and his son, Mircea II, is killed. Hunyadi proclaimed ruler before passing Wallachia's sovereignty to his vassal Vladislaus.
1448	Vlad Dracula claims power in Wallachia with the support of the Ottomans.
1448	Second Battle of Kosovo. Vlad Dracula assumes the Wallachian Prince's Crown.
1448	Vladislaus defeats Vlad Dracula; Vlad Dracula flees to the court of Moldavia.
1453	The Fall of Constantinople to the Ottoman Sultan Mehemmed II.
1454–66	Thirteen Years War between Poland and the Teutonic Order.
1456	John Hunyadi defeats the Ottomans at the siege of Belgrade using an army of professional troops and armed peasants. Death of John Hunyadi.
1456–62	Vlad Dracula returns to Wallachia with Hungarian support, Vladislas II defeated and killed. Wallachian nobility, the boyars, punished en masse by impalement by Vlad Dracula for the killing of his brother and father. Vlad Dracula raises lower order men into his personal household and bodyguard.
1456	Vlad Dracula rebuilds Poenari Castle using slave labour. He pays homage to the Hungarian king and the Turkish sultan.
1458–61	Vlad Dracula makes war on the Saxons of Transylvania.
1460	Crusade called against the Ottomans. Mehemmed II occupies Bosnia, Serbia and the Peloponnese. Albania continues to resist under George Skanderbeg.
1462	The Ottoman governor of Nicopolis attempts to ambush Vlad Dracula but is captured and impaled. Vlad Dracula campaigns along the River Danube to the Black Sea with a force comprised extensively of Wallachian and Bulgarian peasants. Vlad Dracula attacks the Ottomans during a celebrated night attack.
1462	Ottoman aggression finally forces Vlad Dracula to flee to Hungary despite a campaign of guerrilla warfare and scorched earth tactics. Mehemmed II's auxiliary cavalry is led by Radu,

	Vlad Dracula's brother. Radu III is recognised as Prince of Wallachia by most boyars and by Hungary.
1462–74	Vlad Dracula imprisoned by King Matthias Corvinus of Hungary.
1463	Battle of the Vistula Lagoon, Teutonic Knights' Fleet defeated by ships from Danzig and Elbing.
1463	Michael Beheim, a *meistersinger*, authors a long poem detailing the cruelties of Vlad Tepes and his victories against the Ottoman Turks.
1466	Teutonic Order becomes a vassal of the Polish Crown.
1467	Skanderbeg breaks the second Ottoman siege of Kruje.
1467	Stephen of Moldavia goes to war with Matthias Corvinus, King of Hungary, over the Black Sea fortress of Chilia.
1468	Death of Skanderbeg.
1469	Matthias Corvinus elected King of Bohemia.
1470	War between Radu III of Wallachia and Stephen of Moldavia.
1471	Montenegro's prince swears vassalage to Mehemmed II.
1473	Stephen of Moldavia defeats Radu III in battle near Bucharest. Radu III dies and is replaced by Stephen's candidate, Basarab III Laiot.
1473	Mehemmed II defeats the vast army of Uzun Hasan in Anatolia with artillery and handguns.
1475–76	Ottoman Turks raid Moldavia but are defeated by Stephen the Great at the Battle of Vaslui.
1476	Vlad Dracula takes a command under Matthias Corvinus. He carries out a massacre in Srebrenica.
1476	Vlad Dracula assumes rank of *Voivode* of Wallachia again with the support of an army of Hungarians, Transylvanians, Moldavians, Serbians and Wallachians.
1476	Vlad Dracula killed and decapitated in marshes near Bucharest.
1480	Ottoman invasion of Italy.
1480	First Ottoman siege of Rhodes.
1481	Death of Mehemmed II. Contest between Bayezid II and Cem for Ottoman throne.
1485	Bartholomeus Gothan prints an account in German, *About an Evil Tyrant Named Dracole Wyda*.

1488	Marcus Ayrer authors a history of Vlad the Impaler, detailing his atrocities.
1492	Moldavia again accepts Ottoman suzerainty.
1497	Vasco da Gama rounds the Cape of Good Hope.
1500	Matthias Hupfuff publishes a pamphlet in German on Vlad Dracula with a woodcut depicting him eating amid hundreds of impaled victims.
1510	Portuguese threaten Ottoman Indian Ocean trade.
1514	Battle of Chaldiran, Safavids defeated by Ottomans.
1517	Capture of Cairo, Mamluk Dynasty extinguished by Ottomans.
1519	Charles V crowned as Holy Roman Emperor.
1520	Accession of Suleiman I, the Magnificent.
1521	Ottoman capture of Belgrade.
1522	Second siege of Rhodes.
1526	Battle of Mohacs, Hungary completely defeated by Ottomans. Hungary effectively dismembered by Ottomans and Habsburgs.
1527	Croatia accepts Austrian–Habsburg rule.
1529	Ottoman siege of Vienna fails.
1543	Antonio Bonfinius authors a detailed version of the later life of Vlad Dracula and his death.
1552	Ivan IV of Russia seizes Khanate of Kazan.
1552	Ottoman control of much of Transylvania.
1565	Failure of Ottoman siege of Malta.
1568	Treaty of Edirne between Ottomans and Habsburgs agrees the partition of Hungary
1571	Battle of Lepanto.
1575	Massive devaluation in silver currency value across Europe with Spanish New World mines' overproduction. Disastrous effect on Ottoman silver coinage.
1580s	'Harem politics' begin to dominate the Ottoman polity.
1580s–90s	Janissary revolts and Anatolian revolts over debasement of coin.
1593–1606	Habsburg–Ottoman war.
1614	Death of Elizabeth Bathory, a Hungarian countess famous for bathing in virgins' blood.

1618–48	Thirty Years War.
1656	Huge revolts over coin debasement paralyse Istanbul.
1657–58	Revolt of Rakoczi in Transylvania.
1667	Ukraine divided between Russia and Polish–Lithuanian Commonwealth.
1669	Crete falls to Ottomans.
1671–72	Polish–Lithuanian Commonwealth at war with Ottomans.
1683–99	Poland, Venice, Habsburgs and Russia at war with Ottomans.
1683	Second Ottoman siege of Vienna fails.
1686	Ottomans lose Buda and large parts of Hungary.
1687	Second Battle of Mohacs, Ottomans defeated.
1688	Ottoman loss of Belgrade.
1688–97	War of the League of Augsburg.
1690	Ottomans retake Belgrade.
1697	Ottomans routed at Senta by Habsburg army.
1699	Treaty of Karlovitz brings peace between Habsburgs and Ottomans.
1897	Bram Stoker authors the novel *Dracula*.
1847	Petar Petrovic Njegos composes 'The Mountain Wreath'.
1989	Slobodan Milosevic reinterprets Serb and Balkan medieval history in a speech on the anniversary of the First Battle of Kosovo, laying out justifications for the launching of the Balkan Wars.

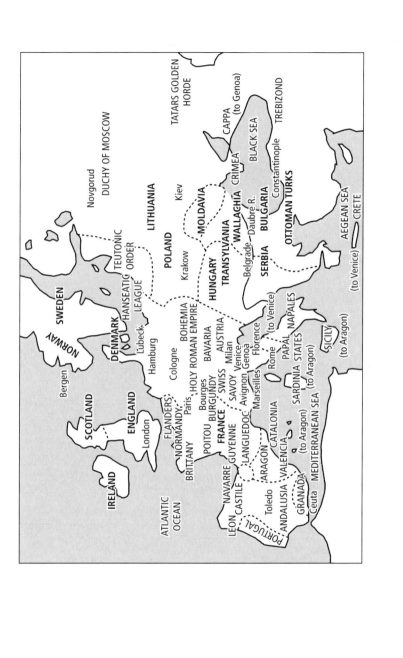

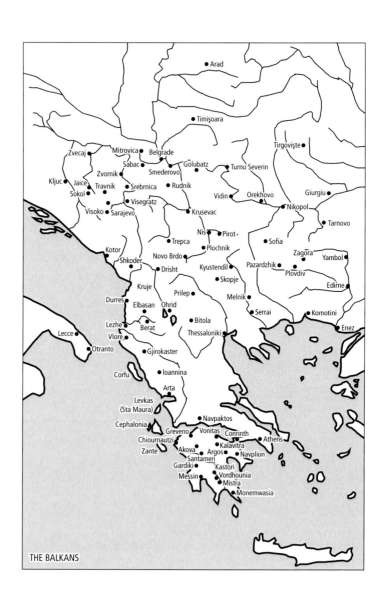

THE BALKANS

INTRODUCTION: WHY DRACULA?

The nosferatu do not die like the bee when he sting once. He is only stronger; and being stronger, have yet more power to work evil. This vampire which is amongst us is of himself so strong in person as twenty men; he is of cunning more than mortal ... he is brute, and more than brute; he is devil in callous, and the heart of him is not ...[1]

Vlad Tepes or Vlad Dracula was, in many ways, a walking shadow and a poor player that did strut and fret his hour upon a stage filled with characters who outshone him by far. His contemporaries included such luminaries as Mehemmed II, John Hunyadi and George Skanderbeg.

So, why review his life and deeds?

The answer to this lies in the very nature of Dracula. He epitomises the petty tyrants that made up so many of his predecessors, successors and rivals and who composed the body politic of the Balkans in the medieval age. Equally, his dubious vassalages to this or that overlord are no more or less complex than those of virtually every other minor Balkan prince of the same period, and can act as a study in the way that Eastern Europe reacted to the rapid incursions and stunning victories of the Ottomans in this same period. His tactics, approach to warfare and the armies that he built are likewise a version in miniature of the military changes that were occurring right across Europe in the fifteenth century.

Also, Dracula's tale is full of feats of daring and ferocity, and that should be reason enough to look at his life. He was also perhaps cursed, as the Chinese phrase has it, to 'live in interesting times' and the action in which he was enmeshed, in order that we can fully comprehend it, requires us to look beyond the Balkans and to other deeds undertaken both in the further reaches of Western Europe and in Asia Minor and the Levant.

Almost continual warfare raged across Europe during the period 1300 to 1500 with France, England and Scotland confronting each other during the Hundred Years War, the Wars of the Roses torturing England, and politico-religious wars blazing across the rest of Europe. The confrontations between Muslims and Christians in the Balkans and in Spain, and between the Ottomans and their Turkish 'cousins' the Mamluks of Egypt and the Turcomen of Iran and Anatolia, as well as the last bitter flaring up of the great Turko-Mongolic conflagrations of the thirteenth century, made the period one of true political and military revolution.

Dracula died an ignoble death, little mourned and apparently of little political contemporary consequence. That he has been heard of since, and indeed achieved an apparent immortality, is of course due largely to his metamorphosis at the hands of Bram Stoker into the vampire count of Victorian horror fantasy.

Like Dracula, the legacy of the medieval age has also reverberated down into the modern world. It has continued to light the way to dusty death for so many in the Balkans, particularly at the beginning and at the end of the twentieth century. This means that the period, the individuals who shaped its history and their deeds remain of vital interest. I have aimed, in this volume, to make sense of the actions of Dracula and his rivals. This is no easy task; it is often hard in the history of the Balkans to discern an intelligible pattern of intent among its rulers or to ascertain reason or morality. Despite this and the sometimes apparently random, chaotic and near-nihilistic acts that these characters not infrequently undertook, I hope I have revealed their acts as being much more than simply 'sound and fury, signifying nothing'.

1

AN OTTOMAN CREATION?

THE EUROPE INTO WHICH
VLAD TEPES WAS BORN

He may not enter anywhere at the first, unless there be some one of
the household who bid him to come; though afterwards he can come
as he please.[1]

The world that Vlad Dracula was born into was one of petty tyrants,
and even today, after the disintegration of Yugoslavia and the collapse of the Communist Bloc in the late twentieth century, we are
once again in a period defined by 'Balkanisation'. Indeed, the history
of the region has, almost perpetually, been defined by fragmentation
with, at best, non-cooperation between neighbours and, at worst,
straightforward hostility.

It was not always so but the progressive disasters that struck the
Byzantine Empire from the close of the eleventh century onwards
through to the Latin–Venetian Crusader conquest of Constantinople
in 1204 and the spectacular implosion of a Serbian successor state
after the Battle of Kosovo in 1389 left behind a prickly assortment
of nationalities, faiths and affiliations with little cohesion, led far too
often by men of narrow vision and debased motives.

The tenuous hold of the Latin emperors of Constantinople, and of
their Venetian allies, ended in 1261 when Alexius Strategopoulos, a general of Michael Palaiologos the Emperor of Nicaea, whilst reconnoitring

in the vicinity of Constantinople discovered that the city was virtually undefended. The majority of the city's Latin and Venetian forces were off besieging an island in the Black Sea, and whilst Strategopoulos did not exactly stroll into Constantinople he was certainly the recipient of a great deal of help and advice from the populace and was unhindered by any defence worth the name by the Latin forces. A small detachment of Nicaeans entered through an undefended portal in the land walls and opened the city to the main army.

Baldwin II, who had been emperor for some thirty-three years, fled and the Latin Empire died quietly:

> By the providence of God the city of Constantine again became subject to the Emperor of the Romans, in a just and fitting way, on the 25th July, in the fourth indiction, in the 6769th year since the creation of the world, after being held by the enemy for fifty-eight years.[2]

The hyperbole of the Byzantine historian George Akropolites notwithstanding, nothing can disguise the fact that Michael had, in fact, gained little more than the opportunity to regain the seat of his illustrious predecessors. No Byzantine emperor would ever again wield the power of a Justinian or even an Alexius and the city was a shadow of its former glory.

Indeed, the events of 1261 presaged much of what was to occur in the Balkans throughout the late thirteenth and fourteenth centuries. Michael's success against the Latins was due largely to his alliance with Bulgaria and a treaty with Genoa, by which he granted it privileges similar to those enjoyed by the Venetians in the former Byzantine Empire. A Genoese fleet ferried the Nicaean army across the Straits to Thrace, and that it did so was no surprise. Bitter rivalry between the two main Italian maritime republics in the eastern Mediterranean was a feature of the entire crusading period[3] and it would continue to damage European attempts to meet the challenge of the Ottomans in the eastern Mediterranean in the fourteenth and fifteenth centuries despite repeated papal interdictions.[4]

Furthermore, the forces of the restored Byzantine Empire remained weak. Improvements in the economic condition and security of

Western Europe in the twelfth and thirteenth centuries appear to have been matched by a downturn in the economy of the eastern Mediterranean. There was a lack of 'external security' in the Balkans following the loss of Byzantium's eastern Anatolian colonies after 1071, and through the incursions of the Bulgars into the Danube valley in the 1180s and the Vlachs throughout the Balkans in the 1190s. In fact the Greek Empire's agricultural production and manufacturing output actually grew over the eleventh century, but there was an economic decline in the empire in the same period that became so acute that the first debasement of gold coinage since the fourth century was made in this period. This economic deterioration was related to a rise in the influence of the Byzantine aristocracy, whose acquisition of lands made the peasantry dependent on local 'feudal' lords and made direct revenue collection by the state increasingly difficult.[5]

The effects of the economic embarrassment of the state can be seen in the empire's naval dependence on Venice in the late eleventh and twelfth centuries, leading to its concession of toll-free passage through Byzantine waters following Venetian ravaging of the Greek coastline and islands in 1125 and a further extension of rights following more Venetian 'gunboat diplomacy' in 1175. By the time of the Massacre of the Latins in 1182 there were approximately 60,000 Venetians in Constantinople.

The Latin Empire's financial woes between 1204 and 1261 are a good indication of what Michael was winning back for the Greeks. It was throughout its brief life chronically short of manpower and money and appears to have been unattractive even to adventurers from the West. By example, during the poverty-racked reign of the last emperor 1,000 Latins were in the service of the Saljuq Turks against the Mongols. Pope Gregory IX even resorted to pleading with the Count of Brittany to crusade for the Latin emperor rather than for Outremer. Henry of Romania neatly summarised the situation: 'there is nothing lacking to [our] complete possession of the Empire save an abundance of Latins.'

Given the above it is not surprising that the restoration of Michael Palaiologos to Constantinople depleted Byzantium's Anatolian border of troops. Between 1204 and 1261 there was a definite lessening in the westward movement of Turkish nomads in Anatolia as the Byzantine ruling elite's enforced Anatolian exile in Nicaea and Trebizond required them to defend the region, and to at least attempt to reduce a rapacious tax regime that had been applied to the peasantry of Anatolia. These crushing taxes had commonly caused desperate peasants to join the nomad Turks.

This partial renascence of Byzantine Anatolia ended abruptly with the move back across the Bosporus of the Byzantine aristocracy. The westward movement of the Turkish war bands that thrived in the hinterland between the Byzantine Empire and the Saljuq Sultanate of Rum began afresh. Later, of course, the Byzantines' internecine struggles for power would even lead to active invitations to these same Turkish nomads to fight in the Greek civil wars.

Byzantium was a hollow shell of its former self. Its territories embraced a corner of north-western Anatolia, Thrace, Macedonia, Thessaly and a smattering of small holdings in the Peloponnese. Most of Greece still lay in Latin Frank hands, and all of the north-western Balkans was lost irretrievably. Venice and Catholic Hungary controlled Dalmatia and Croatia, and even Michael's ally, Bulgaria, remained wary of too close an alliance with the old Orthodox power. That the Latin Empire of Constantinople failed to last in fact had less to do with a renascence of Greek power than a failure on the part of the Latins to ally themselves with the Vlacho-Bulgar states and 'diplomatic ineptitude'[6] in dealings with the native populace. Any actions of the Latin emperor were also hampered by a constitution that favoured the Venetians and fief holders far more than the central authority. A not dissimilar position faced the Byzantine emperors in the late thirteenth and fourteenth centuries. The power of the aristocracy had been enhanced by the simple fact that the emperors needed every ounce of Greek support they could gather, and the empire resembled more and more the feudal entities by which it was now surrounded.

Of course the Latin Empire had failed to gain the support of the emerging Balkan states because of what we might today term confessionalism, but what was to the medieval mind a much more straightforward question of faith, salvation and identity. Identity was a potent concept in the Middle Ages and particularly so in the Balkans. The sometimes vicious attempts to suppress religious dissent in this period, and the lack of a unified and coherent response between Catholic and Orthodox Europe to the Ottoman threat, only make sense as long as we keep this idea of identity in mind. Medieval communities were defined by their religion, and religion also demarcated each community's political allegiances. Leaders who 'switched' their allegiances from Catholic to Orthodox or vice versa risked losing all allegiance from their lords and from the 'peasant base'. It was not for nothing that Thomas Aquinas compared those who slipped from the true faith to counterfeiters, as both eroded the secular foundations of society.[7]

A distinct religious and cultural identity seems to have been arrived at by Western Europeans during the High Middle Ages. This appears as an element of the changes to the Western European mindset over the Crusades period. There was a change from the desire to make pilgrimage to the Holy Places to one of the 'holy right' of the Latins as holders of the only true Christian creed to conquer Christendom and beyond for the Catholic faith. As an example of this, Robert of Clari justified the sack of Constantinople in 1204 by the need to remove the relics from the schismatic Greeks to the safety of the West.[8]

Furthermore, the outlook of Western Europeans appears to have been affected profoundly by a notion of 'universal' Crusades. Helmond of Bosau discussed the attitude of the Second Crusade's participants: 'to its initiators it seemed that one part of the army should be sent to the eastern regions, another to Spain and a third against the Slavs ...' Certainly during the preaching for the Second Crusade there was an alteration in the 'format' of indulgences. There was a distinct change from the notion of a penitent pilgrim to a more formal system of indulgences that were not centred on the Holy Sepulchre. This has been viewed as an attempt by the Papacy to bring the Crusading movement more under its own control in order to use the movement as a tool of its temporal policy.[9]

A distinct shift away from the notion of Crusading as being centred on the Holy Sepulchre was certainly clear by the time of the Latin conquest of Constantinople.[10] The indulgences granted for the Fourth

Crusade differ markedly from those of any previous *expeditio*; the notion of a merciful god who rewards meritorious works was introduced and this allowed for an even greater degree of flexibility in the use of the Crusade weapon. Certainly an extension of the essence of crusading was seen later in this period with the Albigenisian Crusade and the Baltic Crusades,[11] which went as far as the settling of peasants from the Netherlands, Flanders and Westphalia in East Prussia by the Teutonic Knights. There was concurrent success for Western Christendom in Spain and by 1248 only Granada remained to be taken in Spain by the Reconquista.

Of the Catholic world's wooden-headedness towards the 'Eastern question' on both temporal and spiritual matters much more later, but it is enough to say now that the Byzantines had, potentially, in the late thirteenth and early fourteenth centuries the opportunity to cast themselves as leaders of the Orthodox world by simple virtue of once again having possession of the senior Patriarchate of the Orthodox world within the walls of their capital. To this end Michael VIII Palaiologos had both the Bulgarian and Serbian Orthodox churches subordinated to the authority of the Patriarchate of Constantinople in 1272.

The newly restored Byzantine Empire concentrated its efforts during the 1260s and 1270s on bringing the Black Sea coast back under its control and returning Bulgaria to a position of clientage through a 'classic' Byzantine blend of military action and marriage alliance. There were also piecemeal recoveries of the minor Latin principalities in the southern Peloponnese. Michael VIII Palaiologos came to the throne with southern Thrace, Thessalonica, southern Macedonia and a few offshore Aegean islands under his control. Michael was able to establish a Greek district of the Morea and by the first decades of the fourteenth century, Byzantium again controlled most of the southern Peloponnese.

Michael allied himself to Catholic Hungary in the hope that it would act as a counterweight in the north to the rising Orthodox state of Serbia. Ironically, the greatest threat to Michael's ambitions in fact came from the Catholic West. Charles of Anjou had enjoyed papal favour in his usurpation of the Crown of Sicily in 1266 and this meeting of minds seems to have extended to the possible re-conquest of Constantinople and to the extension of Charles' power throughout the eastern Mediterranean. Charles undertook lengthy preparatory work for such a venture by gathering an invasion fleet, and by forming alliances with the Balkan states surrounding Byzantium. He also established cordial relations with the Mamluk Sultan of Egypt and Syria, with the aim of allowing unimpeded operations for his fleet in the eastern Mediterranean.

Byzantium lacked the resources to reconstitute a fleet anywhere close to the empire's navy of the eleventh century and Michael was forced to take on economically disadvantageous alliances with Venice and Genoa, which were granted extensive commercial privileges and resident colonies in Constantinople, in exchange for naval assistance.

Charles made good headway in his plans to restore the Latin Empire of Greece, and by the 1270s Corfu, some of the adjacent Greek coastline and Achaia were in his hands. He then moved against Epiros and drove the despot John Angelos into Thessaly. Charles also proclaimed himself King of Albania, and established alliances with Stefan Uros I of Serbia and even with John of Thessaly.

Michael gained a short-term advantage in the conflict by acknowledging papal primacy over a proposed union of the Orthodox and Catholic churches at the Council of Lyon in 1274. In exchange for agreeing to the union, Michael obtained papal assurances of non-interference as he gathered allies and forces for an offensive against Charles' forces in Epiros and Thessaly.

All the benefits that Michael gained by recognising the Pope as the overlord of the Orthodox church were, however, swiftly lost as the empire's Orthodox clergy, patriarch and a large part of the population rejected the union. Michael attempted, through a fairly vigorous persecution, to stem this loss of support for his cause but soon enough he had lost the Balkan Orthodox states of Bulgaria, Serbia, Epiros and Thessaly to the enemy. Byzantine leadership of the Orthodox world was damaged irreparably, and the ultimate benefactor of Michael's policy was to be Serbia.

The election of a French Pope, Martin IV, in 1281 seemed likely to doom Michael, and the Pope took no time at all to condemn Michael as a schismatic and illegitimate ruler. Charles therefore seemed primed to conquer the Balkans for Catholicism and was prevented from doing so only by Byzantine gold. In a masterful piece of diplomacy, Michael brought to life the revolt against Charles known as the Sicilian Vespers, and also financed the fleet of Pedro III of Aragon during his attack on Sicily and his attempt to take Charles' throne. Charles' challenge was effectively ended by Michael's political skill but the Byzantine emperor had been forced to alienate his own people and any potential Orthodox allies and to denude Anatolia of its forces to meet it. By the turn of the century Byzantium's armies were dependent on Latin, often Catalan, and Turkish mercenaries.

These mercenary forces were, however, still impressive in their make-up and abilities. Turkish mercenaries acted generally as light cavalry skirmishers armed with a bow that was used to lay down harassment fire, a typical technique of steppe nomads. There were also heavy cavalry archers who shot larger composite bows like their contemporaries in the Mamluk armies of Egypt and Syria. Their discipline and ability to lay down rapid, accurate and coordinated arrow-fire would have been similar to that of the famous *Bahriyya* regiments of Egypt.[12] The Byzantine Varangian infantry guard of Anglo-Saxon and Scandinavian mercenaries would have provided both longbow archery and close quarters capability with their war axes.

Michael had, however, also exhausted the treasury and growing financial pressures forced him to hold back on fortifications repair and rebuilding, and also to strip away garrisons along the Anatolian border that faced the increasingly aggressive Turkish nomads.

Michael died in 1282, and that his successors were unable to match his achievements or repair the damage done by his religious policy is not surprising. That they were unable to do so is related partly to the above issues of exhausted finances, heavy taxation in Byzantine lands, Western European threats, and the actions of a Greek aristocracy that made alliance to the empire by other Orthodox states unattractive. What was perhaps more important, however, were the internecine feuds and competition for the imperial purple that wracked the empire in the first half of the fourteenth century and the rise of Serbia, which claimed both militarily and spiritually to be the true successor to the Byzantine state from before 1204. The Byzantine civil wars are of utmost importance in the creation of the world that Vlad Dracula was born into simply because they were the root cause of the Ottoman expansion into Europe, an occurrence that would define the character of and the conflicts within the Balkans for the next seven centuries.

It is also important to any understanding of how the above events brought the Ottoman Turks across the Bosporus and into Europe in the early fourteenth century that the early Ottoman state and its ethos are understood. The 'Turkic drive' across Anatolia in the twelfth and thirteenth centuries has been misunderstood previously by even great and skilled historians, who have seen ideology where there was in fact *realpolitik* in its purest form. It has been a common fault to write of the expansion of the Turks across Anatolia as being related chiefly to a form of *Ghazi* tradition amongst the Turkic peoples, keen to expand the borders of Islam and to extend their religion into the *Dar al-Harb*, the realm of war or more simply those lands which were not, as yet, Muslim. In fact the Turks' push across Anatolia, and into conflict with the Byzantine potentates that existed, tenuously, on its northern coast, was related, rather, to a combination of simple opportunism, changes in the Byzantine society of Anatolia, pressures on the Muslim societies of the near-east in this period and a degree of compulsion related to potential Malthusian crises.

That *Ghazism* has been seen as the main element contributing to both the Turkic expansion in Anatolia and the formation of the Ottoman state is due to a generous application of hindsight and a search for a unifying theme in a period where there is instead a flux of actions by the Turks, some of which, in fact, ran counter to the idea of any expansion of the *Dar al-Islam*. In fact, the theory that a Holy War was being waged by the Anatolian Turks in the thirteenth century[13] was adopted as an elegant hypothesis that corresponded very tidily to the Ottoman ideology of the later fourteenth century.[14] The primary sources do not support such a hypothesis. No Byzantine text discusses

27

the existence of *Ghazis* in the marches of Anatolia.[15] This does not, of course, rule out entirely the possibility of *Ghazi* activity on the border but it certainly detracts from the idea of hordes of fanatical Islamic warriors. The typically fastidious interest in all religious matters of Byzantine writers would have ensured the recording of such a phenomenon. Other Georgian, Syriac and Armenian sources tend to emphasise the impact of the Turkish expansion on the Christian peoples of the region. This gives a very incomplete history and, of course, absolutely no indication of the self-view of the Turkic nomads. In the absence of any written contemporary doctrines for a 'fanatic resolve to war against the infidel'[16] it is hard to countenance an impressively large movement of Islamic fanaticism in Anatolia in this period.

There is, of course, evidence of a long tradition of holy warriors in Islam. This stretched back to the seventh-century *ribats*,[17] fortified religious houses on the borders of Islam from which attacks could be made on the unbelievers' lands beyond and from which *Ghazis* could defend the lands of Islam. Furthermore, among the orthodox leaders of Syria who led the counter-Crusades of the twelfth and thirteenth centuries, *Ghazism* was a central characteristic of their ideology, and this is not surprising. Saladin, though a Kurd, has to be viewed as a product of the religious and political culture centred on cities such as Cairo and Damascus, and the Turkish Mamluks of Egypt and Syria were an urban elite whose cultural and military mores were shaped by long exposure to Arabic civilisation and orthodox Sunnism. Furthermore, an alliance between the military men of the near-east and the 'men of the pen', the religious scholars, was necessary to legitimise the actions of men such as Zengi, Nur al-Din, Saladin and Al-Zahir Baybars,[18] who as often as not were usurpers of thrones and of the levers of power, and to bring the body of Sunnism together as one society into the conflict with the Crusaders. This is a central tenet of jihad.[19]

As a counterpoint to the above, Turkic culture in Anatolia in the thirteenth and fourteenth centuries was one of a pragmatic tribalism, and whilst it is possible that 'wars of the faith', or *Ghaza*, were endorsed by the sheikhs who guided the religion of the Turks, the religion they propagated was very much more akin to the shamanism of the steppes than to 'orthodox' Muslim teaching.[20] Indeed, there is evidence of both mummification and human sacrifice among the nomads of Anatolia in this period.[21] Furthermore, if we apply the example of another steppe people, the Mongols, to the Turkic nomads of Anatolia in this period then a picture of a society with a large degree of religious tolerance emerges.[22] Certainly 'syncretism and latitude' appear to have been the dominant features of religious life in the Sultanate of Rum[23] and it was common for the Sultans of Rum to have both Christian mothers and wives, and for there to be a large presence of Christians at the sultan's court.[24]

The nature of Turkish Anatolian society, which was numerically strongly Christian with a minority Turkic hegemony (William of Rubruck, a contemporary, in fact suggested a ratio of ten to one), is illustrated nicely by the volume of overtly Christian iconography found on Danishmendid coinage,[25] the presence of Christian judges as late as 1340 in Ottoman Bithynia and the complete absence of any forced conversion to Islam within any of the Anatolian states until at least 1354.[26] Indeed, even in the longer established Turkish Sultanate of Persia Coptic and Armenian Church writers praised Sultan Malik Shah for his religious tolerance and policy towards Christians.[27]

Tribalism was therefore the key to the Ottoman state's genesis, and not jihad. To understand fully what this meant in thirteenth- and early fourteenth-century Anatolia we need to look at the nature of Turko-Mongolic tribes. It is valueless to view the tribe as a simple group created through patrilineal descent. The racial make-up of the tribes that have operated across Eurasia right from the times of Attila and before and down through the times of Chinggis and Kublai Khan was that of 'shared interest organisms'. The tribes that operated in Anatolia may very easily have been comprised of Byzantine Greeks, Turks, Kurds and Armenians. For these individuals, fighting on the borders of the *Dar al-Islam* would have been, in many ways, 'a means of livelihood'.[28] Indeed, the Byzantines took advantage of the fighting ability of these men by placing *Akritai*, nomad mercenary warriors, from the Balkans and southern Russia in the Anatolian borderland as a buffer to the border incursions of the eastern Turks in the thirteenth century. These tribes appear to have operated in much the same way as their 'Islamic' counterparts, and it seems likely that 'desertions' from the *Akritai* to warrior groups across the border were common as conditions of service were more advantageous and the opportunity for booty was greater.

Turkish incursions into Byzantine Anatolia showed an upturn in intensity at certain times. These peaks of activity appear to be related to pressures from the east and to internal economic pressures on the Turkish pastoralists of Anatolia. Successive waves of Turkic peoples were set in motion right from the advance of the Kara Khitai in 1141 into Central Asia, the defeat and capture of Sanjar, the Sultan of Eastern Persia, by the Ghuzz Turks in 1153 through to the Mongol invasions that culminated in the Mongol defeat of the Anatolian Turks at the Battle of Kose Dagh in 1243, and their sack of Baghdad in 1258. Equally the chaos of the Mongol Ilkhanate of Persia and Iraq in the late thirteenth and early fourteenth centuries made Anatolia an attractive proposition both to Turkish warriors and to members of the *Ulema*.[29] The *Ulema* were of particular importance as they brought structure to nascent Turkish states and also gave an Islamic 'gloss' to their conquests. It is entirely feasible that the writings of these men were the genesis of the '*Ghazi* heritage' of the Ottomans. An example of their florid prose is given by the historian Oruj:

> *Ghazis* and champions striving in the way of truth, and the path of Allah gathering the fruits of *Ghaza* and expending them ... choosing truth, striving for religion, lacking pride in the world, following the way of the sharia, taking revenge ... blazing forth the way of Islam from the East to the West.

At a more prosaic level, western Anatolia would also have enticed Turkish pastoralists fleeing events to the east due to its fertile river valleys and high ridges.

Inspired tribal leaders would have been a focus for warriors, and it is possible that religious rhetoric would have been used by such men, but this did not have to be Islamic per se, the expounding of a shamanic creed is also possible. Indeed, a 'popular' non-orthodox Islamic culture was present in the Ottoman border state with a strong oral tradition, suffused with the mystical aspects of Sufism. Ottoman rulers and their followers were connected through membership in mystical orders or *dervipes*, fellowships or *ahis*, and even guilds or *esnafs*.

Furthermore, it is as likely that factors such as the success of the leader in warfare and the economic advantages of joining or supporting a clan leader were paramount in potential followers' minds. Booty was certainly the economic basis of most groups operating on either side of the border, and there was almost 'perpetual conflict' in the marches both against 'Christian lands' and, perhaps even predominantly, against Islamic states, as in the conquest of Karacahisar in the last quarter of the thirteenth century by men whom the Great Saljuq chroniclers in fact regarded as 'rebels'.[30]

As noted above, Byzantium had lost much of its free peasantry from which it could recruit both militia and regular troops and even more of its ability to gather revenue from western Anatolia in the late twelfth and early thirteenth centuries. The introduction of mercenary forces as an attempt to shore up the border aggravated these problems as the ferocity shown by these mercenaries towards Catholic and Orthodox Christians alike and the severe taxes of the Byzantine lords who controlled them contributed to an insecure and harsh living for the Greek peasantry. The definitive example of this was the Catalan mercenaries who arrived in Anatolia in 1304. They were effective in that they defeated the Turks on several occasions but they were also rapacious and indiscriminate in their pillaging of both Turkish and Byzantine regions. The Byzantines brought them back to Europe but they caused chaos there too, ravaging Thrace, Macedonia and Thessaly before finally seizing control of Athens in 1311.

It is entirely likely, therefore, that Byzantine Christian peasants often preferred Turkic rule to Byzantine rule because this offered lighter taxes and a higher degree of security. There was certainly acquiescence in and not uncommonly assistance by Byzantine Christians in the incursions of the nomadic Turks.[31]

The grassroots détente seen above was not, of course, the only engagement between Turks and Byzantium. Turkish Princes fleeing from their sultan's wrath often found refuge with the Christian Byzantines rather than with the Muslim rulers of Syria. It is, in fact, almost impossible to find evidence of an ideological confrontation in the region during this period, and this is perhaps why, added to their obvious military ability, the Byzantine princes competing for the throne of the *Isopostolos* turned to the Turks, and to the Ottomans in particular, for warriors.[32]

It was local success in the borderlands and against other local Turkish lords that brought more and more *Akinji*, or raiders, to the standard of Osman, who claimed independence for his *beylik* in 1299 from the Saljuq Sultanate of Rum. Of course, Osman had some natural advantages in that his territories lay astride the main route to Europe and abutted Byzantium's most populous and richest Anatolian territories, but it was his innate talents that made the most of the opportunities that this provided. The fact that these raiders came with their households also gave longevity to what could have become simply a transient warrior band with plunder as its main intent, and the state settled upon a capital, Bursa, shortly after the death of Osman and the succession of his son, Orhan, in 1326.

The Byzantine civil war that erupted in 1321 between Emperor Andronikos II and his namesake grandson lasted seven years, but this first war drew in Balkan powers rather than the Turks. Bulgaria backed the young pretender whilst Serbia took the part of the elder. With Byzantine Macedonia's support finally going to the younger Andronikos, the old emperor was forced to abdicate in 1328 but Byzantium's tribulations were far from over. The empire's European territories shrank once more, with Serbia gaining most from this withering away of the Greek state.

By this time the most successful *beyliks* in Anatolia were the Ottomans in the north-east and the Karaman in the south-west, and the tribes formed around these Turkish families also incorporated Greeks, Kurds and Armenians. Anatolian piracy engaged the attentions of the Venetians and Genoese, and the Turkish port of Smyrna was taken by a force comprised of Venetians, Cypriots and papal troops in 1344 to prevent its use by the pirate emirs.

A second Byzantine civil war ensued upon the death of Andronikos III Palaiologos in 1341 and the accession of the 9-year-old John V Palaiologos under the regency of John Kantakouzenos, Andronikos' closest friend and supporter. Kantakouzenos' opponents in the power-play over the 'will' of the child emperor were John V's mother, who would pawn the crown jewels for 30,000 Venetian ducats in 1343 to support her cause, and the Patriarch of Constantinople. In brief, Kantakouzenos was threatened on all sides by the Serbs, the Bulgarians and the Anatolian Turks, who were now marauding along the Thracian coast, and as soon as he left the capital to deal with these dangers to the state he was ousted from his position as regent. He responded by declaring himself co-emperor with John V.

This second civil war was complicated further by inter-class conflict pitting impoverished peasants against wealthy aristocrats and a split in the Orthodox Church between the *hesychasts* and the patriarch and regency. Kantakouzenos, by default, became the champion of the *hesychasts* and their belief in direct communion with God via meditation.

Kantakouzenos allied with Serbia in 1342 whose *boyars*, or nobility, were keen to pursue further the conquest of lands in Macedonia, but the Serbs reversed their support for him a year later and so Kantakouzenos turned to the Anatolian Turks for assistance. Initially this came from within the 'legitimate' Saljuq Turkish state but soon enough he also obtained the military muscle he needed from the Ottomans. The Ottomans were carried across the Dardanelles by what was left of the Byzantine navy. His new allies turned the conflict around and soon enough Kantakouzenos' apparently hopeless situation was reversed and Thrace was re-conquered. Thessalonica remained beyond his reach, however, and Macedonia was lost to the Serbs. The price for Orhan's aid was the plundering of newly won territories, and to this was added the opportunity for the Ottomans to raid across Bulgaria when Tsar Ivan Aleksandur allied with the Constantinople faction.

The Constantinople regency also called upon Anatolian Turks in 1346 but the scheme backfired as there was nothing left to plunder in lands that the Ottomans had already passed through, so these 'new' Turks turned on their paymasters and raided across Bulgaria and throughout Constantinople's environs. To add to the misery, the Black Death ravaged the city between 1346 and 1349.

Orhan cemented his relationship with Kantakouzenos by marrying his daughter in 1346. At this time probably 6,000 Ottoman *akinji* were at Kantakouzenos' disposal and when he finally took the throne as Emperor John VI in 1347 he was protected from the Serbian threat to his north by his loyal Ottoman allies. By 1348 there were as many as 20,000 Ottoman troops engaged actively in Byzantine warfare and every one of them was needed as in 1352 a new contest began for the Byzantine imperial throne. John V Palaiologos attempted to win back what he had lost in the first contest with Kantakouzenos.

It was this second war that firmly established the Ottomans in Europe. John V Palaiologos turned to Serbia for aid and 4,000 Serbian horsemen battled Kantakouzenos' Ottomans at Demotika in October 1352. The Ottomans were victorious and perhaps gained more from the campaign than Kantakouzenos. After conducting several campaigns in the service of Kantakouzenos, Orhan politely presented a bill of expenses. It called, among other items, for the surrender to him of a Greek stronghold on the European side of the Dardanelles. Like many another foolish and ambitious schemer, the Greek discovered too late that it was easier to summon the Devil than to get rid of him. After vain remonstrations he was obliged to make over the small castle of Cimpe Tzympe to his Ottoman ally in 1354.

Despite the above 'success' Kantakouzenos' cause was damaged severely by the loss of Constantinople in 1354 and by 1357 John V Palaiologos was able to depose him. Kantakouzenos' son Matthew was also ransomed over to John V Palaiologos by his Serb captors.

None of this, however, really impacted on Ottoman gains or their continued belligerency and Orhan's son Suleiman reached as far as Adrianopole with his forces, and also began an investment of Gallipoli. Then, in 1354, an earthquake pulled down Gallipoli's walls and the Ottomans swiftly, and bloodlessly, took occupation of the city. Gallipoli very quickly began to look much more like a permanent acquisition rather than just another staging post on a campaign. Administrators and the fabric of a new 'colony' soon began to appear.

Most of eastern Thrace was overrun by Ottoman forces in the 1350s and colonised with more Turks from Anatolia. The Ottomans were now placed strategically astride all of the major overland routes that linked Constantinople to any potential Balkan or Western European allies. Philippopolis was threatened and tribute was exacted from John V from 1356 onwards.

Soon after Orhan's death in 1360, his successor Murad I won an important victory when he captured Adrianople, the most important Byzantine military, administrative and economic centre in Thrace. Murad transferred his capital there from Bursa, renaming it Edirne in 1361. This was a dramatic statement of intent as Edirne stood directly on the front line between Christendom and the Ottoman state, and its significance was not lost on John V Palaiologos.

The emperor appealed to the West for help, and like Kantakouzenos he held out the carrot of ending the schism between the Byzantine and Latin churches and of submission to the supremacy of Rome. The failure of this policy was not entirely surprising. The Byzantine embassies begging for assistance were sent home by the Pope with nothing, prompting the emperor's chief advisor to state, 'Constantinople will be taken, once this city is taken the Franks will be obliged to fight the barbarians in Italy and on the Rhine.'[33] A Venetian-backed Crusade *was* sent against the Ottomans in 1366 but by 1369 Murad had conquered eastern Thrace. This, added to a series of personal disasters that included the diplomatic faux pas of remaining mounted whilst the Hungarian king Louis I left his mount to greet him, being hauled off to a debtor's jail in Venice in 1369, and then being captured on his way back in Bulgarian territory, brought John V to finally accept suzerainty under Murad I in 1371.

Murad's reign would see an acceleration in the Ottomans fortunes in battle, and before we turn to review the conditions of the other Balkan states that Vlad Dracula would later both ally with and compete against, it is useful to review the reasons for Ottoman success in this early stage of the development of their empire.

The nobility of the steppe and of war are clichés but they hold a kernel of truth. The Turko-Mongolian tribes were places where men rose by ability to lead, as was the case with Chinggis Khan, Timur Leng and Osman, the founder of the Ottoman dynasty. In its early years the Ottoman state was a meritocracy similar to other steppe-tribal confederations, but what also occurred was that the Ottoman rulers started to give this potent force the overlay of a rapidly developing state with all the sophistication that this implies. An element of steppe custom that commonly caused the disintegration of Turko-Mongolic states and which the Ottomans, to a large degree, managed to control – though in a fairly repugnant manner at times – was the problem of the 'patrimonial share', by which all members of the family of a deceased ruler were entitled to something. This, of course, worked against a ruler passing on his territorial possessions whole and to a single successor and a frequent result was civil war among sons that weakened or destroyed the state. Even a fairly well-regulated, if weakly bureaucratic, Islamic state, such as that left behind by Saladin in Syria and Egypt, broke up immediately upon his death as brothers, sons and nephews grabbed at individual cities and principalities.[34] Similarly, the Mongol civil war that began the break-up of the Mongol Empire began over the question of who among his brothers should rule following the death of Mongke Khan in 1259, and how far the writ of the Great Khan or *Khagan* ran over the territories of those over whom he was technically only *primus inter pares*.[35] Give or take a few periods of turbulence when the throne was disputed, the Ottomans managed a smooth series of successions from the fourteenth to the sixteenth centuries and the men who became sultan were, without exception, remarkable individuals.

Of course, the nomad warrior lifestyle also works at odds with the creation of a taxable agrarian base and other basic industries that generate fiscal and economic resources.[36] Ottoman warfare in the age of Dracula was technologically advanced and this would not have been possible without the measures that the early Ottoman sultans undertook to create fiscal stability and an economic infrastructure within the state that was capable of supporting the army's logistic and technological needs.

An early fifteenth-century Greek commentator wrote that the Ottomans' success was related to strict discipline. He also wrote of their well-ordered camps and excellent, and well-maintained, road system.

The support system for the army also seems to have been highly developed with dedicated pack animals that were in the full employ of the state and whose use was optimised by a skilled commissariat department. Later in the sixteenth century other admiring enemies would write of the Ottomans' devotion to war, and how they consistently took the offensive and disdained fortification. Their troops, even in the lower ranks, were well trained and disciplined, and as prudent in the use of resources as were their leaders, and their camps, in an age when 'camp sickness' was a greater killer of soldiers than the enemy, were clean and well ordered with no gambling, drinking or even swearing. The level of organisation even ran to the provision of an official corps of water carriers who did far more than that and also acted as stretcher-bearers and orderlies.

Ottoman archery training manuals require such extremes as bending the bow 500 times in each daily session. Such discipline could not even be expected of steppe nomads such as the Mongols. The nearest equivalent to this level of dedication to the military arts is to be found in the *mamluks* of Egypt and Syria, men whose lives had been purchased by an *ustadh*, or master. Military slavery had a long history in Islam reaching right back to the ninth century and beyond, and it was common for these men to reach up to the highest offices of state. The same thing would occur in the Ottoman state and even in this early period of conquest the Janissaries, manumitted slaves, augmented the Ottoman army's nomad warriors. The *sipahi*, or tribal cavalryman, with all his advantages of speed of deployment and shock value, was counterbalanced by the discipline of the Janissary infantry. Murad I can probably be recognised as the creator of these 'slave-soldiers', or for at least formalising the process of selection for the Janissary corps:

> Of these prisoners that the warriors in the Holy War bring back, one-fifth according to God's law belongs to the Sultan ...
>
> They harvested the young men. They took one in every five prisoners captured in the raids and delivered him to the Porte. They then gave these young men to the Turks in the provinces so that they should learn Turkish, and then they sent them to Anatolia. After a

few years they brought them to the Porte and made them Janissaries, giving them the name *Yeni Ceri*. Their origin goes back to this time.[37]

Yeni ceri means 'new troops' and the Ottomans found more and more 'new men' to bring into the military slavery system as they expanded in the Balkans. Therefore, the sultans were able to use the institution of Janissary slavery to create a distinct powerbase of their own within the more 'democratic' activity of what was essentially a tribal society and confederation. The sultans, as noted above, also used alliances with dervish orders and religious fellowships to hold their state together. The system was not perfect, and as we will see it nearly collapsed along with the Ottoman state at the very beginning of the fifteenth century. What finally signalled the victory of centralisation over the 'tribal' elements in the state took place in Vlad Dracula's lifetime. It was, as we shall also see, the conquest of Constantinople.

The Ottoman state was, therefore, primed with all the requirements for success on the battlefield and in the diplomatic field, for expansion in southern Europe. Standing in opposition to it was the truncated Byzantine Empire and a group of other states, of which a few appeared to be in the ascendant but none of which was built on particularly firm foundations.

The state of Bulgaria had looked to regain past greatness in the twelfth century. For many generations after the crushing of Bulgaria in 1018 by the Byzantine emperor Basil II, the Bulgar-slayer, the Byzantines more or less effectively ruled in the Bulgar lands. Then, in 1186, there was a rising against Greek rule led by two Vlach[38] brothers, Ivan and Theodore Asen. The Vlachs were Romanian-speaking nomads who had migrated into the mountains during the period of Byzantine domination. The Asen brothers raised the standard of revolt with the help of Cuman nomads from the Danube, and they drove out the Byzantines. It is not clear, however, what role the Bulgarians, in fact, played in the struggle. The Vlachs were nimble mountain folk armed with bows and javelins while the Cumans were, of course, horse archers, so the Bulgars may merely have provided administrative and technical skills and a gloss of legitimacy. Indeed, given that the Cumans were a steppe-nomadic people and that the Vlachs were traditionally semi-pastoralists, it seems doubtful that Bulgarian political control over them was anything but nominal. The Slavic form of Orthodox Christianity prevalent in Bulgaria was what seems to have bonded the Vlachs most strongly to the Bulgarian cause in this period. Since the Vlachs' native language was, in fact, Latin based, their ready acceptance of the Slavic liturgy and the use of the Cyrillic alphabet in writing their vernacular speaks for strong cultural ties with Bulgaria and with Orthodox European civilisation in general.

The struggle between the Bulgars and Greeks was indeterminably grim with the committing of atrocities, treason and perfidy being common to both sides and, despite a reasonable degree of success against the Byzantines, the two brothers were murdered by their own followers. This brought a third brother to the fore, Kaloyan, whose epithet 'Roman-slayer' neatly sums up both his success and his methods. His raiding of Thrace and Macedonia caused near-desolation in those regions and his response to the brave defence of Varna by its populace was to drive the captured citizens into the city's defensive ditches where they were then buried alive.

By the middle of the thirteenth century these Bulgarian successes were, however, a distant memory as the Mongols of the Golden Horde raided the east of the region almost annually, eventually forcing Mongol-Tatar clientage on the Bulgars, and political fragmentation took hold as the Hungarians sought to extend their control of the Danube into its lower courses. The *boyars* of Bulgaria ended the Asen dynasty in 1256, the initial instigators being *boyars* from the regions surrounding Belgrade.

The Bulgars then embroiled themselves in an anti-Byzantine policy through agreements with the Mongol Golden Horde and with Charles I of Anjou and Sicily. They were double-crossed by the former, who accepted the bribes of the Byzantines not to invade Greek lands and instead to devastate further tracts of Bulgarian territory, whilst the latter's dreams of a Greek empire never materialised.

Coinage devaluation, peasant rebellions and continued Mongol raiding led to further depositions of rulers. Divisions widened between the common people, who were influenced by the Bogomils' teaching, and an Orthodox Christian military elite maintained by forced labour and the conscription of peasants. The term Bogomil, freely translated, means 'dear to God'. It may have been taken from the founder of the sect, the priest Bogomil, or he may have been given that name by the sect. That the Bogomils were far beyond the pale for both the Orthodox and Catholic churches may well have more to do with their antipathy for ecclesiastical hierarchy, and their resistance to both state and church authorities, than their actual beliefs, which were certainly heretical. They believed in dualism and the creation of the world not by God but by the Devil. Bogomils refused to pay taxes, to work in serfdom, or to fight in conquering wars. They disdained feudal society and the established churches as these were manifestations of the material world, which of course had its origin with Satan's creation. Both churches would also have been alarmed by the apparent popularity of the creed among the lower orders; it spread in various forms across the Balkans, through to the Russian lands, Bosnia, Dalmatia, Serbia, to Italy and then to France, where it evolved into Catharism.

Bulgaria lost territory to both Hungary and Byzantium late in the thirteenth century and a ferocious peasant uprising under a swineherd named Ivailo tore the country apart. Bulgaria had to accept domination by the Mongol Golden Horde and the end of the thirteenth century saw a puppet, Smilets, on the throne whose only really notable achievement was to make a political marriage for his daughter to the Serbian Prince Stefan Uros III Decanski. The Bulgarian maiden would become the mother of medieval Serbia's greatest ruler, Stefan Uros IV Dusan.

Smilets was killed in 1298 and Bulgaria became the battlefield for a contest between a renegade Mongol, Chakak, who looked to take the state away from the control of the Golden Horde and the Mongol Khan, Toktai. Chakak was overthrown by the *boyars* and his head was offered to the Khan as a token of goodwill. Bulgaria entered the fourteenth century very much as a client state of the Golden Horde.

The sultans' exploitation of Bulgaria's political fracturing would be a feature of the Ottoman advance in the fourteenth century and this applied to other Balkan states, too. The Ottoman rulers continually showed a diplomatic vision sadly lacking among many of the region's other rulers, and an informed understanding of the inner workings of their enemies' polities. Opportunities to undertake conquest and subsequently suppress potential revolt in occupied states was commonly undertaken through playing off rivals in a series of temporary and shifting alliances, often sealed by political marriages with women from the subjugated ruling houses.

Bosnia in the fourteenth century was also a religiously fractured state, similar to Bulgaria. Hungary had chipped away at Byzantine Dalmatia from the beginning of the twelfth century, and had absorbed Croatia in 1102. This separated Bosnia from the Adriatic coast and gave it its name, 'Bosnia', the land centred on the Bosna River. Croats and Serbs competed for the area until the 1160s when Byzantine authority was re-established, followed by Bosnian 'independence' in 1180 under nominal Hungarian suzerainty.

Initially Bosnia did well in this period from silver mining and through trade relations with the Adriatic port city of Dubrovnik. This, however, then made the state attractive both to Hungary and to Serbia. The bête noire of Bogomilism was used by the rulers of both these states as a stalking horse for their territorial ambitions. In 1203 the Bosnians announced adherence to Catholicism to avoid a Crusade being called against them but despite this, and almost certainly because the Bosnian church was Roman Catholic in dogma but intentionally detached from papal control, the claims of Bogomil heresy persisted.

Despite the above threats to Bosnia as an independent entity the early fourteenth century saw the state grow and flourish as the Bosnian royalty married into that of Hungary and Serbian invasions were repelled. Territory that gave access to the Adriatic Sea was also gained and mining expanded to bring lead as well as silver to the European market. In the early 1370s the Bosnians began to take advantage of the Ottoman distractions of the Serbs to lay claim to the Adriatic coastline between the Gulf of Kotor and Dubrovnik. The rulers of Bosnia even went as far, in this period, as claiming the royal Crown of both Bosnia and Serbia through maternal Serbian ancestry. Following the death of King Louis I of Hungary in 1382, the Bosnian rulers also gained effective control of much of Croatia and Dalmatia. By doing so they placed themselves directly in front of the Ottoman juggernaut. Their ruler Tvrtko I would discover what that meant in 1389.

A further strand of European weakness lay in feudalism. This was particularly true in the case of Serbia. The feudal organisation of state and society was the dominant fact of medieval history in the thirteenth and fourteenth centuries and every European country was arranged on the basis of feudal land tenure.[39] In these times of fierce struggles and weak central authority the feudal network was the basic unit of security and notions of sovereignty and of citizenship depended on the stipulations of an express or implied contract. The vassal expected efficient protection and in theory if this was not forthcoming the connection to his lord could be severed.[40] In this period therefore it is possible to deduce the basic forms of virtually all Western political organisation and social intercourse from feudal contract theory. The basis of feudalism was an arrangement of society on the basis of contracts, *homagium* and investitures and tenure conditioned by service called the *feudum*, *fief* or *lehn*, which placed duties on both the suzerain and the vassal. The French jurist Beaumanoir described this interdependence succinctly: 'the lord is quite as much bound to be faithful to his man as the latter is bound in regard to the lord.'[41] A 'classic' feudal system would show a society that was comprised of lords and tenants, with the status of every single person being defined by oath and contract. Bishop Fulbert of Chartres, writing in the eleventh century, described the duties of the vassal as being derived from the oath of fealty that was owed by all subjects without distinction of rank. 'The vassal undertakes not to assail his lord, not to endanger the safety of his household or to impede the lord's undertakings.' On a more positive front, the vassal is bound to give his lord advice, faithful obedience, or *fidelitas*, and aid. The central duty of the vassal was military service, regulated according to a certain number of days. Conditions of service extended from the knight into the lesser vassals who comprised the 'army'. Serjeants, archers and garrison soldiers were at the base of a pyramid, the apex of which was the feudal lord. The positive influence of feudalism as a political system can be argued. Having a 'ready-made' government apparatus, however flawed, was an important element in the conquest and early administration of the Kingdom of Jerusalem by the First Crusade, for the Normans in their conquest of England and southern Italy, and for the Serbs during their period of rapid expansion in the late fourteenth century.

However, the basic problem with feudalism in the fourteenth and fifteenth centuries was that the notions of property and the order of society in the medieval age were, in fact, decidedly weaker than the theory could allow.[42] This fact makes the chaos that commonly engulfed the society of medieval Eastern and Western Europe easier to comprehend. In particular, the more 'elastic' nature of vassalage that can be discerned in this period makes the collapse of states such as Serbia in 1389 and the inability of European states to unite for even time-limited enterprises against a common foe easier to understand.

In simple terms, the feudal system 'tied' men to a higher lord but not to the sovereign because, whilst the European sovereigns tried persistently to halt the trend of royally bestowed fiefdoms becoming hereditary, they failed against the strength of the magnates in the West and the *boyars* in the East. Such hereditary estates disrupted the idea of statehood and often led to the formation of numerous political bodies within the boundaries of 'nations'. Those at the bottom of the pyramid fared particularly badly from both the internecine warfare that took place within medieval society and the exaction of forced labour, or *corvee*, which was owed through contract to the feudal lord.[43] The eleventh-century description given by Saint Bernard of Clairvaux of French society applied equally to Eastern Europe in the fourteenth century – serfs were inventoried along with other possessions such as villas and farms.[44] The obligations of the peasant to the lord that tied him to land that might well be unproductive and ravaged by internecine wars meant that the Ottomans, at least in this early period, were not viewed unfavourably as potential new masters by the peasantry and lower orders. Indeed, there is evidence that the Turkish invasions may have actually benefited the peasantry of the Serbian lands. The Ottomans formally recognised the Orthodox Church and there is no evidence of persecution in the fifteenth century. Furthermore, the implementation of the *Kanu i Osmani*, or 'Code of Osman', created a less oppressive tax system than was seen under the Code of Dusan. Under the Dusanic system the peasant was expected to work for the lord for two days a week and six gold francs a year were to be paid, as were hearth taxes. Customs duties on the trade of any surplus and state tithes were also extracted. Under the Ottomans *corvee* labour was reduced to only three days a year. The centralising of the tax system under the Islamic *timar* arrangement (of which more later) also reduced abuses.

The architect of the Serbian state was Stefan I, who carved an independent Serbia out of the collapsing Byzantine Empire following the Latin conquest of Constantinople in 1204. He moved quickly from being a *zupan*, or Byzantine vassal lord, of the principality of Serbia to king of an independent nation recognised by the Pope of Rome and with its own national Orthodox church formed under his uncle, Archbishop Sava. The canonising of Stefan I's grandfather Stefan Nemanja in 1199 had already solidified a strong partnership between state and church in Serbia and this was continued by the Nemanja ruling dynasty. A cult of Nemanja, fostered by his son Archbishop Sava, sanctified the ruling house and bestowed on it a divine right to rule from the Serbian Orthodox Church, though this did not stop Stefan I from accepting a royal crown from the Pope in 1217 for his conquests in the region now roughly corresponding to Croatia. Of course, at this juncture the Latin Empire of Greece was still in existence, and the winning over of the Serbs to the Western Church was an act of vital diplomacy for the Roman Curia. This Catholic coronation was, however, opposed strongly by the Orthodox clergy of Serbia and by Archbishop Sava, who promptly re-crowned Stefan as an Orthodox ruler of Serbia with a crown sent by the Nicaean patriarch.

The ongoing internal disasters of the Byzantines at the end of the thirteenth and beginning of the fourteenth centuries gave Serbia its chance to unseat the Greeks and replace them as the emperors of the East. From 1282 onwards there was a steady attrition of Greek territory and the gaining for Serbia of control of both Macedonia and northern Albania. A treaty was finally negotiated in 1299 with an imperial princess and the city of Skopje to be Serbia's new capital being given to King Milutin of Serbia to seal the agreement.

Princess Simonis and the enormous entourage she brought with her into the Serbian court changed the Serbian nobility enormously, bringing new styles, titles and methods of administrative, as well as legal, and financial institutions. Of these the most important was 'Byzantine style' feudalism, with land tenure based on the condition of military service. This was absorbed into the prevalent Serbian tradition of patrimonial share-out and joint inheritance, and subsequent landholding among brothers. Unfortunately the same thing occurred in Serbia as had taken place in the Byzantine Empire under this system. The land grants, soon enough, became not conditional upon service to the Crown and government, but instead hereditary grants beyond the legal grasp of the state. This was a recipe for fragility almost at the outset and, married to the over-rapid expansion of the Serbian 'empire' that gave little time for consolidation of lands before the challenge of the Ottomans arrived in the region, it took just one hard shock to bring this house of cards down.

King Milutin died intestate and a civil war erupted among his illegitimate son, Stefan Decanski, his legitimate but younger brother, Konstantin, and their cousin, Vladislav. Decanski eventually took the throne as Stefan Uros III Decanski but ground was lost to both Bosnia and Bulgaria, and Byzantium and Bulgaria forged an anti-Serbian accord. Decanski destroyed the Bulgarian army and killed the Bulgarian tsar, Michael Asen, at the Battle of Kyustendil, and this was enough to bring Bulgaria virtually under Serbian political control. Its vassalage was total in all but name and the Serbs then started a conquest of Macedonia in 1331.

Serbia's new king, Stefan Uros IV Dusan, after swiftly overthrowing and murdering his father, occupied Macedonia, Albania, Epirus and Thessaly whilst Hungary was engaged in an ongoing struggle with Venice for possession of the Adriatic coast and Byzantium and Bulgaria remained politically rudderless. He made a powerful political statement when he elevated the Serbian archbishop to the rank of patriarch and established the primate's seat at Ped in Kosovo. Dusan now moved on to having himself crowned tsar by the Serbian patriarch. His lands stretched from the Danube to the Gulf of Corinth, and from the Adriatic to the Aegean coasts. His capital, Skopje, was strategically located and well fortified. It sat astride the important Vardar–Morava commercial route and its large Greek population made it a well-administered economic centre that could manage the wealth generated by Serbia's flourishing mining industries and trade.

In 1346 Dusan had himself crowned emperor of the Serbs and Greeks by the patriarch of Constantinople, who almost certainly performed the ceremony under duress. The Serbian Empire was flourishing and with Stefan's promulgation of a constitution, Dusan's Code, in 1349 Serbia became one of the most developed countries in Europe. The code describes a society led by an autocratic ruler who was dependent on the support of a small but powerful secular and religious landholding elite, who, in turn, dominated, but were themselves dependent on, a mass of free peasants and serfs. It was, in fact, a 'classic' but fragile feudal pyramid.

Dusan invited the Venetians to join him in the conquest of Constantinople after failing at the high walls of Thessalonica for want of a fleet to besiege the city effectively, and gained papal support for the venture through the proliferation of rumours that he intended to re-unite the Catholic and Orthodox churches. The venture was, however, halted in 1354 by Hungarian incursions in the north and by Dusan's death in 1355.

The fractious, fragile and factional nature of the state very rapidly showed itself during the reign of Stefan's son, Urosh, who was too mild-mannered and lacking in character to rule a group of nobles among whom ancient tribalism was still present and to which had been allied the newly assumed rights of feudalism. Perhaps if Stefan had lived, and if his plans for the conquest of Byzantium had come to fruition, there would have been an effective Serbian riposte to the Ottomans' seizure of their first European territory on the Gallipoli peninsula and to their conquest of Adrianople in 1361. But when Dusan chose to support the rebel John V against Kantakouzenos in 1352 he suffered defeat at the hands of Orhan's Ottoman mercenaries and any besieging Serb army attempting the reduction of Constantinople would have had the unsettling thought of the Ottomans of Gallipoli lying on their flank.

As it was, the Serbian *boyars* threw off royal control and the state fragmented. The Greek provinces of Thessaly and Epiros, as well as Stefan Uros IV Dusan's former Albanian holdings, split away and a series of small independent principalities formed in western and southern Macedonia. Hungary threatened from the north, and Uros was only able to hold Montenegro, eastern Macedonia and the central Serbian lands from the Danube down into central Macedonia by accepting their co-rule with powerful local *boyars*. There was constant warfare among these regional nobles and it was only the increasing threat of the Ottomans as they began to envelop the remaining outposts of the Byzantine state and to push into regions claimed, or at the very least sought after, by Serbia, Bulgaria or Hungary that brought an ephemeral unity and a coalition army into the field in 1363 to challenge the new Ottoman Sultan Murad I's army near Adrianople.

The first Battle of Maritsa took place on the banks of the river between what was probably an Ottoman expeditionary force and an allied army of Serbs, Bulgarians, Bosnians, Wallachians and Hungarians. The major Serb leaders were Jovan Ugljesa and Vukasin Mrnjavcevic, and Louis I led the Hungarian contingent himself at the Pope's urging. Whether this venture should really be called a Crusade is hard to say. The Crusade 'weapon' was being used with a fair degree of frequency by the papacy at this time against both external and internal enemies of the Catholic body politic. This said, the numbers were impressive with at least 20,000 men being committed to the cause and it has been suggested that if the Byzantines had also engaged the Ottomans then the Turks could even have been ejected from Europe.[45]

The Ottomans had nowhere near this many men in the field. The sultan was fighting Catalan mercenaries in Byzantine employ at Biga, and the bulk of the army was in Anatolia. An expeditionary force was therefore despatched to at least slow the Christian army until reinforcements could be brought up. The allied army in fact crossed the Maritsa River very easily, meeting little resistance, and made camp near its banks. There was feasting, presumably because the leaders of the army thought that their progress to Adrianople would be an easy one the next day, and few measures were taken to secure the camp.

An Ottoman night attack using light cavalry tore through the camp with each rider holding two torches to give the illusion of greater numbers and to create greater confusion. Panic ensued among troops, who were either drunk or asleep, and a frenzied retreat led to a large number of drownings in the river.

The defeat caused the most damage to Bulgaria. There was immediate payment of tribute to the Ottomans but even this could not prevent the beginnings of a Turkish occupation of upper Bulgaria. Serbian casualties in the battle were heavy and there seemed little chance of the state being put back together.

With the 'unity' of 1363 obviously having been forgotten, in 1365 King Louis I invaded and seized the Bulgarian province of Vidin and the Bulgarians worked so hard to eject him from this north-western corner of their lands that they quickly lost Thrace to Murad I. Whilst a certain Stratsimir was able to proclaim himself the Bulgarian Tsar of Vidin, by 1370 Murad I controlled most all of Thrace and his possessions bordered Bulgaria and the south-eastern Serbian lands of Ugljesa, who was the most powerful Serb regional ruler but also the most exposed to the risk of Ottoman invasion.

It was this that drove Ugljesa to attempt to forge an anti-Ottoman alliance from the Balkan states in 1371. His diplomacy failed, however, because Byzantium could be starved into docility by the Ottomans as they controlled every route in and out of the empire and because Bulgaria was now terminally split between Stratsimir's state of Vidin and Tsar Ivan Shishman's holdings around Turnovo. Shishman's hold on the throne was unsteady, and he was threatened directly by Stratsimir and attempting to keep the Ottomans from undertaking any further aggression against his lands. Of the Serbs, only Ugljesa's brother, Vukasin, joined him.

Ugljesa and Vukasin led their forces into western Thrace in September 1371 and their plan seems to have been, as it had been in 1363, to attack Adrianople, now renamed Edirne and the Ottoman capital. They reached the Maritsa River near the village of Chernomen to the north-east of Edirne and, whilst history did not entirely repeat itself in that the allies were defeated during the day this time, the fact remains that the Ottomans were once again outnumbered and that they launched a surprise attack. Murad I annihilated the Serbian army and both Ugljesa and Vukasin were killed during the debacle.

Such was the magnitude of slaughter that the Ottomans referred to the battle as the 'Destruction of the Serbs'.

The same epithet might equally have been applied to the empire of Serbia, as what was left of the Nemanja state collapsed with the death of its last two guardians at Chernomen. The Battle of Maritza opened up Serbia to the Ottomans and the effective collapse of Serbian resistance that was its sequel in fact makes it clear that this battle was of much greater significance than the far more famous 1389 Battle of Kosovo.[46]

Uros also died before the year was out and so did Greater Serbia. A rump central state endured but no ruler would again hold the title of tsar. Perhaps for this reason Murad I was cautious after his victory. He left much of both Macedonia and Serbia in the hands of local chiefs and allowed them to become his vassals.

Murad I would have used the Western style of vassalage with fiefs for rewards, but for his possessions in Anatolia and to reward his own men in Europe he would have used a system rooted in the Saljuq Turkish Empire and common across the Middle East, the *sipahilik*.[47] In this system, an Ottoman *sipahi* or trooper's *timar*, which was based on the earlier Islamic entity of the *iqta*, bore some parallels to the fief of a Western knight, to the extent that it provided his salary. However, in many ways, the *timar* was more complex, in that it could be a 'share' of an industry, such as the spice trade, a textile production centre or simply a piece of land, and unlike the Western knight, the *timar* holder was not resident on the land from which the *timar* was drawn. Local government officers, often civilians, managed it for him and collected the taxes or rents for him. Furthermore the *timar*, in theory, was not hereditary like a fief, so in some ways it paid for service and not family loyalty. The distribution of *timar* was therefore a powerful means of ensuring loyalty to the sultan and of rewarding his men. The deed of detailing the territorial extent, personal revenues and holder's obligations was issued by the sultan. Needless to say the system had a pro-rata hierarchy. Troopers received a *timar* and *beys*, or higher lords, received *zeamets*, which were commonly composites of several *timars*.

The allegiance of *beys* and *sipahis* could reasonably be expected by virtue of the simple fact that the sultan, in this early period, led the army in person and therefore by example – and he also gave and took away *timars*. Failure to fulfil obligations to the state meant redistribution to another candidate. Both the old lands and the newly conquered European lands remained at least technically, and to a large degree in this early period in reality, the sultan's property.

Murad I revised the *sipahilik* in 1371 and allowed a larger degree of attachment between lands and lords but only in the former Byzantine territories, and this was probably because these holdings were already portioned out as pronoia holdings to powerful Greek military families. There was an easier exchange of loyalties from emperor to sultan if these clans were allowed to simply retain what they already had. As noted above, Serbia had adopted the Byzantine 'system', faulty as it was in many ways, during its years of expansion and the Ottomans therefore applied the same land rules that they used in the Byzantine lands to the Serbs. In fact, the Ottoman actions after the Battle of Maritza have been described as following a well-established pattern for south-eastern Europe.[48] Murad I operated within the feudal system and took defeated princes as vassals. The integration of the Serbian lands and lords into the Ottoman war machine was further increased by the requirement of 1,000 troops from each vassal to serve in the Ottoman forces. Murad I may have actually preferred to bring Serbia under the Ottoman aegis in this way rather than by direct control and incorporation as it afforded him extra contingents of troops and did not over-extend his own resources for garrisoning new territory.

In fact then, the heavily stratified feudal society that had been established under Dusan's code favoured the Ottomans' conquest of Serbia. The Ottomans were able to incorporate this military society into the *timar* system and members of the lesser nobility, or *voyniks* (under the Dusanic system), were incorporated as *askari*. The *voyniks* were exempt from tax and were granted lands in return for loyalty to the sultan. To the lesser nobility this was of huge importance as in the aftermath of the fracturing of Dusan's state the higher magnates and the Orthodox Church had seized much of the revenue-yielding land.[49] This system was undoubtedly successful in maintaining the loyalty of many of the Serbian lords throughout most of the fifteenth century and this is evidenced by the way in which Serbia continued to be governed successfully by the Ottomans up to the sixteenth century by this devolved system and by the actions of Serbian vassals during critical junctures of Ottoman history. Furthermore, despite Turkish migration into Rumelia[50] over the course of the fifteenth century, half the *timars* in Branichera remained under Christian lords.[51] One of the major Christian vassals of the Ottomans at this point was a certain Prince Lazar Hrebeljanovid, who held lands in the north of Serbia under suzerainty to Murad I.

Ottoman raids after Chernomen became almost incessant in Bulgaria and the Turnovo Bulgarian Tsar Shishman accepted vassal status under Murad. His sister entered the sultan's harem and this act of human bondage upon Shishman's sibling had much more to it than simple lust on the part of the sultan. There was a large commercial element to the capture of slaves of both sexes. The Burgundian traveller Bertrandon de la Brocquiere wrote of how he met Turks leading slaves to Edirne for sale from Plovdiv, 'fifteen men and ten women, chained by the neck, inhabitants of Bosnia …'[52] but the reasons for the unpleasant, distasteful and abhorrent policy of forced concubinage were also related to destruction of morale among communities. The sexual use of captive women inflicted shame on the women and on the men who had failed to protect them.[53] The apparently nihilistic quote attributed to Chinggis Khan,

> The greatest happiness is to scatter your enemy, to drive him before you, to see his cities reduced to ashes, to see those who love him shrouded in tears, and to gather into your bosom his wives and daughters,

describes an unpleasant truth and certainly the place of mass rape, an unpleasant evolution of concubinage, in the arsenal of the ethnic cleanser and those interested not just in conquest but in the extermination of a people has been well delineated in the modern world of 'conquest'.[54]

Even the sacrifice of Shishman's sister did not completely stop the marauding across Bulgaria. Chernomen also meant that the Byzantine emperor John V had to accept Ottoman vassalage completely and could only really hope for the survival of his state either through the benevolence of the sultan or through some outside agency. His captive throne was an object of Ottoman meddling from 1371 onwards.

Anatolian affairs then took much of Murad's attention during the later 1370s and into the 1380s. He used the forces of his Serbian vassals in campaigns against Karaman and the other Turkish *beyliks*. The Serb heavy cavalry seems to have been relatively effective in this arena, composed as it was of horse archers equipped in Byzantine or elite Mongol style with composite bows, maces and some horse armour. The Serbians also employed light infantryman with 'old-fashioned' javelins and had a core of well-trained crossbowmen.

Murad I's absence from Balkan affairs in this period allowed Prince Lazar to ally himself with the Serbian Orthodox Patriarchate, which was, even in the post-Nemanjic period, a powerful political player, and with Macedonian and Montenegrin nobles. This brought him control of much of the old central Serbian lands.

Then, in 1385, whilst Shishman of Bulgaria was involved in a small war with Wallachia, Murad I took Sofia and the Ottoman 'front line' now sat at the level of the Balkan Mountains. The Ottomans drove on north-west from Sofia, reaching the Albanian coast in 1385, and in 1386 Nis was captured. Not only was this city a major hub on the Vardar–Morava highway, one of the sources of Skopje's wealth in trade, but it also lay further north than both Skopje and Ped. There was a very real chance that the political heartland of Serbia would be cut off from possible assistance from Hungary and from the Adriatic. Lazar accepted Ottoman vassalage at this point and his decision may have been based on simply not being able to form enough cohesion among the Balkans' Christian leaders to be able to take on the Ottomans, whose advance seemed irresistible at this point.

The Ottomans pushed on into the north-central Balkans and along the old Roman road, the Via Ignatia, into Macedonia. Thessalonica fell to them in 1387. There was then a lull as Murad I returned to consolidate his position in Anatolia. He defeated the forces of Karaman and took Konya from them in 1387.

Murad's absence was taken as an opportunity by his Serb and Bulgarian vassals to breach their vassalage to him. Lazar rapidly formed a coalition with Tvrtko I of Bosnia and Stratsimir of Vidin and refused a call to undertake his obligations as the sultan's vassal. He and Tvrtko defeated a local contingent of Ottoman troops at Plocnik, to the west of Nis, and at this juncture Shishman decided, perhaps rather rashly, to claim independence for Bulgaria.

Murad I's successor would be given the moniker *Yildirim*, or thunderbolt, but the lightning campaign that Murad launched in 1388 makes him just as worthy of the title. Shishman and Stratsimir were forced swiftly back into the yoke of vassalage and tribute was demanded from Lazar. Murad I's detaching of Bulgaria from any league of Christian states was of enormous political importance. As he marched north to take on Lazar he was joined by many sympathetic Serbian nobles. Lazar turned once again to Tvrtko of Bosnia and also to his son-in-law, Vuk Brankovic, the ruler of northern Macedonia and Kosovo, and was also able to convince Hungarian and Albanian contingents to join the campaign.

The two sides met at Kosovo Polje, the 'Field of Blackbirds', on 14 June 1389. A few things are clear about the battle, though much is not and much mythmaking has been undertaken about its aftermath. The Serbs brought bombard artillery to the field and had a long history of deploying it after it was first imported into the Balkans via Dubrovnik in 1351 but this was not enough to give them victory. If there was a victory for the Turks then it was 'a damn close run thing' and the battle, horrifically bloody though it was, was so inconclusive that Tvrtko's emissaries in fact informed the courts of Europe of a Christian victory over the Turks.

That Murad I was killed by Serb or Hungarian knights at some point after the battle seems beyond dispute, and that Lazar of Serbia was executed on account of the sultan's killing after being captured appears equally clear.

In fact, Kosovo Polje *became* an Ottoman victory. The Ottomans' resources of men were not exhausted by the battle, whereas the

Serbs' were. Certainly it is true that in the short term the Turks were decimated by the battle to a point where they could not pursue their enemies, and the new sultan, Bayezid, I also had to withdraw to Thrace in order to quell any opposition from his brothers. But Anatolian troops could replace the Turks' losses; there was no similar reservoir of men for the Serbs. The damage inflicted on Serbia was also enough to bring about its collapse, although the real damage was done by Serbian lords fleeing the coalition after the battle, including Lazar's son, Stefan Lazarevic, who took vassalage under Bayezid I, immediately after the battle. Indeed, Lazar's coalition, upon examination, looks more and more like an alliance of the unwilling and the coerced. Vuk Brankovic, for example, was certainly not pro-Turk but was also decidedly not pro-Lazar, despite his family ties, and there were a number of defections of Bulgarian and Serbian magnates to the Ottomans before the battle.[55]

Further damage was done to the fabric of Serbia by its neighbours. There has been a common idea in modern Serb nationalist thought that Serbia fought against the Turks to defend Europe. Indeed, in 1989 Slobodan Milosevic neatly encapsulated the Serb nationalist interpretation of Serbian medieval history. He stated that Prince Lazar had battled to 'defend Europe from Islam' and that Serbia had continued to his day to be 'a fortress defending European culture and religion'. The actions of the other European states, particularly those of Hungary, would appear to indicate that they were not aware that such sacrifices were being made on their behalf. The Hungarians used the distractions of the Ottoman advance to further their own aims in the lower Danube basin[56] and Stefan Lazarevic's acceptance of vassalage by Bayezid I was at least in part related to the perceived threat of further Hungarian expansion.[57] The view propounded by Milosevic and his followers that this period and the subsequent history of the Balkans was comprised entirely of the clash of two diametrically opposed ideologies is clearly incorrect. It was, rather, a time made up of shifting alliances, political opportunism and the interference of events outside the region. Milosevic's 'Serbian sacrifice for Europe' that he used to justify his civil war was, in fact, predicated on a medieval fantasy.

As discussed earlier, the taking of Christian concubines by Ottoman sultans and in other theatres of war between Islam and Christendom had distinct aspects of plunder, intimidation and triumphalism about it. However, the union between Bayezid I and Olivera Despina, Lazar's daughter and Stefan Lazarevic's sister, was more like a dynastic marriage alliance than any mere addition to the sultan's harem, and this too followed a pattern not unusual in Islamic–Christian relations. Bayezid I was born in 1354 and some sources claim his mother was Greek. The Ottoman sultans, like the Abbasid caliphs of Baghdad and the Umayyad caliphs of Spain, may have preferred marriage or concubinage with Christian women simply because marriage to Muslim women ran the risk of subsequent divorce and the ex-wife's family then being able to claim a dynastic link and even make claims on the succession. Indeed, it is notable how many caliphs and sultans were the offspring of concubines.[58]

Bayezid I had been appointed governor of the newly conquered Anatolian provinces in 1381 and later took control of all the affairs of Asia Minor. His nickname of the 'thunderbolt' was acquired after his swift defeat of the Karamanids in 1386. He was already, at his accession, a competent and experienced administrator and an impressive, if somewhat impetuous, general.

Bayezid followed up on the 'victory' at Kosovo Polje by raiding throughout Serbia and southern Albania. Most of the local princes accepted vassalage, and Vuk Brankovic, the last independent Serb prince, died in an Ottoman jail in 1392.[59]

Bayezid also began the settlement of Yoruk Turks from Anatolia along the southern stretch of the Vardar–Morava highway and looked to use this as a platform for operations aimed at bringing the Adriatic coast under Ottoman control. This, of course, meant that direct confrontation with Venice would occur at some point as the republic's trade depended on control of the cities of the Adriatic coast. The limitations of medieval shipping meant that Venice could never entirely 'control' any part of the Mediterranean. It must be remembered that there was no such thing as naval supremacy per se during the medieval age. In fact, control of the sea meant control of coasts and ports.

No galleys of this period could stay at sea long enough or had sufficient offshore range to patrol the open sea effectively or effect a true naval blockade and thereby claim 'ownership' over the Adriatic. The Adriatic was also a difficult proposition for medieval galleys as there is a strong current that runs from west to east, and the prevailing wind is from the north. The eastern shores were, therefore, a constant danger to vessels of this period; no ship of this time could tack into the wind. Under oar-power these ships could only make an average speed of about 2 knots (2 nautical miles per hour) and the large crews of galleys had to be fed and supplied with water.[60] Therefore, 'control' of the eastern Mediterranean, as noted above, meant control over its ports or islands, thus allowing the Venetian fleet to escort convoys of merchant vessels, and to protect them from piracy, along a chain of naval bases or friendly ports. Indeed, sea battles remained rare and the Venetian navy was most commonly engaged with enemies during its support of land forces, often as a form of close support artillery. Harbours and sea walls could be both defended and attacked by galleys with high turrets that carried catapults and later bombards, and which could swing spars between masts to act as battering rams. Their crews were also armed with crossbows and later again with firearms. The republic's standing ground forces were not inconsiderable and in the fifteenth century it was recorded that Venice deployed 8,000 cavalry and 3,000 infantry to wars in the Italian peninsula.

For this reason, the retention of the coast, Venice had in fact been a major 'land power' in the Balkans since the Fourth Crusade and could not afford to lose the coast to the Ottomans. The republic had little interest in the bleak mountains of the hinterland of the Balkans but she did need access to its forests, from which most Venetian ships were built. Venetian colonisation of the coast was extensive and the cities had well-trained crossbow militias backed by a fleet comprised of more than 3,000 merchant ships, many of which could be readily converted into warships or military transports. Much of this territory had, of course, been acquired in 1204, when Venice carefully selected a number of strategic territories as her price for aiding the knights of the Fourth Crusade. Venice's domination of the Adriatic trade routes came through the chain of islands and harbours that the republic claimed, along with their purchase of Crete for 30lb of gold.

The 1380s were a bad time for the Venetians with the Black Death ravaging the republic to an even greater degree than the apocalyptic devastation seen across the rest of Europe and the Middle East. She could do little more than defend her offshore and coastal possessions in the Balkans, but she did carry a great deal of influence in the region, through her diplomacy but also because of her championing of the Catholic faith. In this respect, her natural 'confessional' ally was the Kingdom of Hungary, a state that had several other attachments to the West that ran beyond religion alone.

The medieval Kingdom of Hungary was ruled by a Magyar minority. The Magyars mostly inhabited the central plains whilst the majority Slavs and Vlachs were to be found in the mountains and forests of the kingdom. The Hungarian royal line was descended from the Angevin kings of Western Europe and retained a strong attachment, culturally, to Italian and French customs. For a brief period the Crown of Hungary was united with the other major Catholic power in Eastern Europe, Poland, with the accession to both thrones of Louis I.

When Louis I died in 1382 Hungary entered a period of constitutional crisis that would hobble its response to the Ottoman threat to the northern Balkans. His death saw the accession of his 11-year-old daughter, Maria, which proved to be extremely unpopular among the nobility. The union with Poland ended and Louis I's distant cousin, Charles III of Naples, was acclaimed as the lawful king by powerful factions within Hungary. To add to the complexity of the situation, Maria was offered by her mother as a bride to Louis, the younger brother of Charles VI of France, but she was, in fact, already betrothed to Sigismund of Luxembourg.

In order to press his claim Charles III of Naples landed in Dalmatia and Mary's jilted fiancé, Sigismund of Luxembourg, invaded Upper Hungary. The queen mother revoked her offer to France and Sigismund of Luxembourg would eventually marry Maria in October, but only after Charles had sat on the Hungarian throne for the first two months of 1386 before being murdered. Sigismund eventually came to the throne in 1387 with Maria as his co-ruler and after her death in 1395 there were further claims against the legitimacy of Sigismund, who was undeniably not Magyar and would later become Holy Roman Emperor, and the king of the Germans. There were numerous rebellions and, though Sigismund was able to put them down, there was a definite falling from the heights of autocracy that Louis I had enjoyed and Sigismund had to operate much more as a *primus inter pares* among a league of senior barons.

The likelihood of a confrontation between Hungary and whatever Balkan and Western allies Sigismund could muster and the Ottoman sultan began to increase when Turkish raiders started harrying Hungary's southern borders in the early 1390s. When Bosnia went under in 1391 Sigismund looked to create a coalition of Balkan states to counter the insidious Ottoman advance.[61] In early 1393 Turnovo Bulgaria's Ivan Shishman entered into secret negotiations with Sigismund and Wallachia's *voivode*, Mircea the Old, and Ivan Stratsimir of Vidin also began to plot with Sigismund against their vassal lord, Bayezid I.

Bayezid must have discovered the *sub rosa* negotiations as he launched a whirlwind campaign against Shishman. Turnovo held out but was eventually captured and Shishman fled to Nicopolis, which also fell to Bayezid I, and Shishman was captured and beheaded. Shishman's fate was enough to make Stratsimir reaffirm his loyalty to the sultan and following this show of force Bayezid I summoned his Christian vassals to a conference during the winter of 1393. The key result of this meeting was that Stefan Lazarevic was recognised once more as Bayezid I's most trusted vassal. Emperor Manuel II, clearly recognising that the antipathy of the Serbs for Byzantium could only spur the sultan on to undertaking the city state's final destruction, left the conference convinced he must seek assistance from the Catholic West if his realm was to survive. Bayezid I next moved against the Morean lords and annexed Thessaly before forcing Ottoman overlordship on Athens. A new Ottoman siege of Constantinople was not long in coming and it lasted for another eight years.

Bayezid had other concerns at this time, too. Ottoman campaigning in Anatolia had caused friction between him and the Mamluk Empire, an admittedly fading but still potentially very dangerous opponent, and with the Ak-Koyunlu, a Turcoman tribal confederacy that had taken hold of lands in northern Iraq and north-western Iran following the collapse of the Mongol Ilkhanate. Of even greater concern for the sultan was the appearance of Timur Leng in the Middle East. In 1393 Timur Leng campaigned in west Asia against the successor states to the Ilkhanate and against the Golden Horde, whom he later defeated in a three-day battle near the modern city of Grozny, just north of the Caucasus Mountains, in April 1395. Despite these developments in Asia, Ottoman pressure on the Danube frontier increased and there were major confrontations in Transylvania in early 1395.

Mircea I of Wallachia had built the powerful Danube island fortress of Giurgiu in the late 1380s in reaction to the growing expansion of the Turks and his son Vlad II Dracul is recorded as having said that 'even the women of Wallachia armed with their spindles would be able to conquer the Turkish Empire', but Giurgiu was lost to the Turks in 1390 as the Danube became the new border. Mircea I conducted a series of raids across the Danube into Ottoman territory. In retaliation, Bayezid I, along with Serbian troops led by Stefan Lazarevic and Kralj Marko, attacked Wallachia but they were defeated at the bloody Battle of Rovine in May, and Kralj Marko was killed. Wallachia staved off Turkish occupation for now, but Mircea I could see the writing was on the wall. He accepted vassalage under Bayezid I and the Ottomans annexed Dobrudzha and all of Mircea I's territory lying south of the Danube. Bayezid also began supporting a pretender to Mircea I's princely Crown.

The disasters in Transylvania and Mircea I's flight to his court led Sigismund I to redouble his efforts in wooing Western Europe. He confirmed treaties with France, Venice and several German princes, as well as with Manuel II and Mircea I. A break in hostilities and a four-year truce in the Hundred Years War between England and France also sat in Sigismund's favour and Richard II of England was encouraged by King Charles VI of France to set out for the East with him as 'brothers'. The French king's ambition did not stop at the Balkans, however; he also envisaged freeing the Holy Land from the Mamluk Turks. Duke

Philip of Burgundy was a major sponsor of the Crusade and he probably saw it as a vehicle for avoiding further involvement in any renewed Anglo-French hostilities and for demonstrating Burgundy's independence of action.

Bayezid may have aided the Hungarians in their diplomatic efforts with the West if he really did claim, as was reported, that he intended to conquer Hungary and Italy and to water his horse in the altar of St Peter's. Certainly Boniface X, the Pope in Rome, was enthusiastic as was his rival Benedict VIII, the Antipope in Avignon.

By September 1396 a force comprising Hungarians, French knights and troops and contingents from the Holy Roman Empire had reached the city of Nicopolis after a march from Buda and a crossing of the Danube River that took some eight days. Vidin had been taken fairly bloodlessly and Rachowa somewhat more violently. The Venetians had also carried Knights Hospitaller from Rhodes into the Sea of Marmara. The sultan's army had not been seen and when part of the Hungarian army veered away from the main body of the army in order to gather Transylvanian and Wallachian forces these regions responded enthusiastically and with little apparent fear of Bayezid I. The approximate strength of the army with its Bulgarian and Wallachian allies totalled about 12,000 to 16,000.

Nicopolis was located atop a limestone cliff and comprised two well-supplied walled towns. It was under the governorship of Dogan Bey, who was certain that Bayezid would come to his aid and was therefore prepared to resist the Crusaders to the utmost. The city was an uninviting challenge to an army that boasted no siege engines. The Crusaders therefore settled in for a siege and two weeks passed before any word was heard of the approach of the sultan, who was making a forced march from Edirne through the Shipka Pass to Tirnovo. There he met with Stefan Lazarevic and was also spotted by a force of Hungarian cavalry, which reported his army's presence to the Crusaders at Nicopolis.

The French lord Coucy, with 500 knights and 500 mounted archers, ambushed a large force of Ottomans approaching Nicopolis through a nearby pass. This initial success may, however, have been detrimental to Crusader unity in the later battle as the other lords D'Eu and Nevers apparently felt that their honour was stained by Coucy's success.

More division appeared among the Christian leaders in a war council of 24 September. A plan was presented by Sigismund for Mircea's troops and Hungarian mounted archers to meet the Ottoman vanguard and dispatch the skirmishers usually found there, before the heavily armed French knights rode into meet the Janissary infantry and regular Ottoman troops, whilst the Hungarians protected their flanks from the Turkish *sipahis*. This plan was rejected out of hand by the Constable D'Eu and by Marshal Boucicault. The nominal leader of the French contingent, Nevers, the 19-year-old son of the Duke of Burgundy, who had never held military command before and who had never faced the Turks in battle, readily supported them.

It was a pity for the Crusaders that they did not listen to Mircea I as the Ottomans regarded him as the most courageous and shrewd among all the Christian princes. It is certain that the *Voivode* of Wallachia was appalled by the Western Knights' conception of war as some kind of sport. He knew from bitter experience of the discipline and application to the task of 'real' war of the Ottomans and he knew too that the coming battle was, for his little state, most certainly not a sporting contest but a dire necessity. Mircea I's advice was probably rejected because of Wallachia's misleading record of cooperation with, and acquiescence in, the Ottomans' operations in the Balkans. What the Crusaders would have failed to recognise was that such 'bending with the wind' was, in fact, the key to Wallachia's survival. Mircea I's treaties with each of his powerful neighbours were all designed to ensure at least the autonomy if not the independence of his principality.

Wallachia had experienced Bulgarian, Hungarian and Tartar overlordship in the past and would always be weaker than the states that bordered it. Submission at crucial moments to the will of the most powerful neighbour and then revolt against it when oppression was too strong, or defection from any alliance to the side of another state, was a constant of Wallachian 'foreign policy' that had existed long before Mircea I and would be continued by Vlad Dracula's father and by Vlad Dracula himself.

So Mircea I was ignored. The French stated that they would ride at the Ottomans head on and be the first to engage the enemy. With his allies evidently set on a death or glory charge, Sigismund had little else to do except to organise his own army's battle plan. Word then came that the sultan's army was only six hours' march away and this apparently caused confusion in the Crusader camp, which seems surprising given that Coucy had already engaged Ottomans in the region and that an active siege was under way. Turkish prisoners from Rachowa were executed at this point for 'want of men' to guard them during the expected battle.

The dawn of 25 September saw a fatal division within the French ranks. Sigismund had sent to Nevers that the Ottoman vanguard had been sighted and that within two hours he would have concrete information on the sultan's dispositions and intent. He asked that they postpone their charge and, whilst the proposal was supported by the Admiral of France and Coucy and the younger lords, Nevers and D'Eu, both refused to countenance any such thing and also virtually accused the admiral and Coucy of cowardice.

Accounts of the battle from this point on are confused but it seems that D'Eu led the French vanguard in a charge towards the Ottomans, who were still deploying on the hills around Nicopolis, and his rank as Constable of France would suggest this to be correct. Nevers and Coucy commanded the main body of knights and mounted archers. Sigismund's Hungarians, along with the Knights Hospitaller, Germans and other allies, were formed up as a second wave.

There was initial success as the French vanguard cut through the Ottoman skirmishers of the first line and struck the regular infantry and Janissaries. Ottoman archery and rows of sharpened stakes among the Ottoman positions took down a considerable portion of the French cavalry and the French were funnelled by ravines on either side of the field but the Ottoman infantry line was broken. It seems that the rout of the infantry was taken by the French as the defeat of the whole Ottoman army and they set off in pursuit of the stragglers, even though this meant an uphill ride for those still mounted and an exhausting trudge for the half of the force that had lost its horses but remained in heavy armour. At the top of the slope the French then found themselves facing a corps of *sipahis* that Bayezid I had concealed along with the Serbian cavalry among the ravines and reverse slopes.

A charge from the *sipahis* was enough to break any remaining order in the French forces and during a pell-mell retreat the admiral, de Vienne, was killed and Nevers was captured. At this point there was a collapse in resistance among the knights and the Wallachians and Transylvanians deserted Sigismund.[62]

The collapse of the French centre then allowed the Ottoman cavalry to move out to the flanks of the battlefield, from where they attempted the encirclement of the Hungarians, Hospitallers and Germans. In fact, Sigismund and his heavily armed Hungarians were nearly able to turn defeat into victory at this point. The more lightly armoured Ottoman nomadic horse archers had many advantages over European knights in terms of their speed and fluidity in the battle zone, and certainly when knights were fighting in a disordered mass as the French were by this stage of the battle, the *sipahis* had the upper hand. However, when faced by a well-ordered heavy cavalry the *sipahis* were distinctly outgunned. The Hungarians engaged the *sipahis* and were on the point of pushing them from the field when Stefan Lazarevic's Serbian cavalry entered the conflict with 'fifteen-thousand men and many bannerets'[63] and overwhelmed the Hungarians.

Sigismund and the Master of the Hospitallers managed to escape via a fisherman's boat to the Venetian ships in the Danube. Many others tried to swim to the boats in the Danube and drowned, others boarded small skiffs that then sank from the excessive load. France had lost much, Hungary more but even the victor Bayezid I was distressed by the degree of slaughter his army had suffered in the battle. He had come to the field with, probably, a force roughly equal to that of the Crusaders but he had in fact lost more men on the field. His ire was heightened by the discovery of the massacre of the prisoners from Rachowa. On the morning of 26 September the sultan ordered an assembly of the French and Hungarian prisoners and, after separating the chief nobles from the rest, he forced D'Eu, Coucy and Nevers to watch the execution of up to 3,000 captives, an act that took until late afternoon to complete.

Sigismund, for fear of the Wallachians or Transylvanians capturing him and selling him to the Ottomans or worse, in fact sailed to the Black Sea and Constantinople before making his way home by sea. His ship passed the tower of Gallipoli, where the Ottomans lined their captives from the battle along the shore in order to taunt the king.

The most immediate consequence of the battle was that the Ottomans took complete control over Stratsimir's state of Vidin. Bulgaria was therefore completely subsumed into the Ottoman Empire and ceased to exist. Bayezid I raided Hungary, Wallachia and Bosnia and took Albania into the empire, making vassals of its northern lords. Constantinople was also besieged again until Manuel II agreed that the House of Osman would confirm all future Byzantine emperors.

The Crusade of Nicopolis was Bayezid I's greatest victory and was won by the discipline of his troops and by the loyalty of his Serbian allies. The reverse was obviously the case among the Christian army. The independent-minded French nobles, jealous of their own positions and status and competing with their peers, could not match such unity of purpose or battlefield cohesion. All such unity would soon enough desert Bayezid I's forces, however, in his contest with Timur Leng.

By 1402 Bayezid had brought Constantinople, by a process of encirclement on land and blockade on the seas, to such a condition that its surrender to him seemed unavoidable. Arguably Byzantium and the rest of Eastern Europe was saved from greater disasters resulting from the debacle at Nicopolis by one of the most appalling characters ever to arise in Asia (though the competition for such a title is pretty fierce and extends into the twenty-first century). Marlowe showed an acute understanding of the character of Timur Leng when he gave him these words:

> I that am term'd the Scourge and Wrath of God,
> The only fear and terror of the world,
> Will first subdue the Turk ...[64]

Timur Leng was from the eastern half of what had been the Mongol Chagatay Khanate, but his army was Turko-Mongolian and he spoke Turkish. He was Muslim and claimed the heritage of the Khans through marriage to a princess of the Chinggisid line. In the power vacuum that was Central Asia after the collapse of the Yuan Dynasty, Ilkhanate and Chagatay Khanate, he quickly gathered a large confederate army around him. He started out as a mercenary but before long his extraordinary generalship allowed him to begin conquest in his own name. It was fortunate for Bayezid I's successors that, whilst Timur saw himself as a new Chinggis Khan, he and his descendants did not have the administrative ability of either Chinggis or Qubilai Khan; the empire he carved out was therefore somewhat ramshackle and he spent a lot of time re-conquering lands that had already been subdued once.

As discussed earlier, Bayezid I had already antagonised the Mamluk state of Syria and Egypt with his manoeuvres in western Anatolia and on the borders of Mamluk Syria. By 1400 the Ottomans were hard up against the Mamluk lands as western and central Anatolia came under the sultan's control. A distant outpost of the Mamluk Sultanate in the far north of Syria, Malatya, was demanded by Bayezid I from the Mamluk Sultan Barkuk in 1399. To Bayezid I's mind this had more to do with consolidating his position against the Ak-Koyunlu than a direct attack on the Mamluks. Sultan Barkuk was both surprised and angered by the demand but died before he could take action, and the city fell to the Ottomans after a two-month siege during the period of political stasis that always attended the succession in the Mamluk Sultanate.[65]

Timur began his campaigns in the Middle East again in 1399, despite the fact that he had only just completed a bloody one-year campaign in India. Bayezid I's response was to send to the Mamluks to seek an alliance against Timur but the senior Mamluk emirs responded, 'now he's become our friend. When our master Barkuk died he invaded our country and took Malatya. He's no friend of ours. Let him fight for his country, and we'll fight for ours.'[66]

Timur moved against Sivas, the gateway to Anatolia, in August 1400. He besieged the fortress city and the 3,000-strong garrison surrendered after three weeks under terms that their blood would not be spilt and Timur Leng was true to his word – they were buried alive. There was no Ottoman response to Sivas' fall and the Mamluks were paralysed by internal wrangling, but the slaughter visited upon Sivas should have been a forewarning to both of what Timur was about to commit in both their lands. His letter to al-Nasir Faraj, the boy Mamluk sultan, confirmed his intent towards the Mamluk state and the same was certainly to be expected for the Ottoman state:

> The Sultan your father committed many odious crimes against us, among them the murder of our ambassadors without cause ... Since your father has surrendered his life to God, the punishment of his crimes must be brought before the divine tribunal. As for you, you have got to consider your own survival and that of your subjects ... lest our furious soldiers fall upon the people of Egypt and Syria in a cruel slaughter, burning and pillaging their properties. If you are so stubborn as to reject this advice, you will be responsible both for spilling Muslim blood and for the total loss of your kingdom.[67]

Timur then swept into Syria and halted before Aleppo in October 1400. There he defeated the Syrian Mamluk armies of Damascus, Antioch, Homs and Hama after drawing them out to fight by the simple expedient of making it appear that his army was not going to press the siege of the city. Then in an abrupt *volte-face* that would become characteristic of his 'strategy', Timur left Syria and moved on Baghdad. By the time he had finished punishing the people of Baghdad, in the summer of 1401, for their faint resistance to his army the city was surrounded by 120 towers of skulls and its river, the Tigris, was red and bloated with corpses.

He then moved slowly west to challenge Bayezid I. The Ottoman sultan failed to live up to his title of *Yildirim* during this period. This may have been because he was expecting the imminent collapse of Byzantine resistance and Constantinople's surrender to him under the pressure of his siege or because he felt he had time given that Timur's army had undertaken almost continuous marches and battles in India, Georgia and Anatolia in the last year; exhaustion of morale and logistics was to be expected. Perhaps Bayezid I also underestimated the political abilities of his adversary but Timur had been in communication with the Byzantines and his approach no doubt stiffened their waning resolve.

Bayezid I took a large number of vassal soldiers out of the Balkans across to Anatolia with him, including Stefan Lazarevic's Serbs,[68] but was still heavily dependent on large numbers of Turcomen and Tatar troops from Anatolia and beyond to bring his army up to the size of Timur Leng's forces.

Timur began siege operations against Ankara's Byzantine walls in late July 1402 and Bayezid I was still two days' march away from the city when Timur's troops were already scaling the walls. Bayezid I's troops arrived in poor order after a forced march only to find Timur had poisoned the only source of drinking water in the region. The Ottoman army was therefore in no state to challenge Timur's forces, or to take advantage of the fact that they were deployed for a siege rather than a field battle. Timur had ample time to organise his battle lines.

On 28 July 1402 the two sides met. The Battle of Ankara was the greatest battle that either Bayezid I or Timur Leng had yet fought. The day started well for the Ottomans with the Serbs on the left wing making inroads into their opponents, but a massive defection from Bayezid I's army of his Tatar levies to his opponent sealed the sultan's fate. Essentially ethnicity and the tribal affections that the sultans had worked so hard to dissolve had resurfaced as among the Ottoman ranks many of the Anatolian contingents had a greater affinity for their kith and kin than for the aegis of the House of Osman. This problem would not in fact be fully resolved until the reign of Mehemmed II with the victory for centralisation over the tribal elements in the Ottoman state being fully realised only after the conquest of Constantinople.

The presence of Serbian and other Christian contingents in Bayezid I's army may also have handed a propaganda coup to Timur's agent provocateurs but Stefan Lazarevic's Serbs were also the last defence of the sultan as his army was attacked both by Timur's troops from the front and flanks and by their own Asian levies from the rear. Lazarevic's Serbs hung on until forced to retreat and attempted to cover the withdrawal of Bayezid I and a loyal corps of Janissaries. Bayezid I was eventually captured as he fell from his horse while trying to flee under the cover of darkness at the end of the day's battle.

What was left of the Ottoman army was, somewhat surprisingly, saved from annihilation by Byzantine merchants who shipped them across the Bosporus to safety, undoubtedly for extortionate fees.

Bayezid I died in captivity a year later and it appeared that the Ottoman Empire was at an end. It was saved, largely, by Timur's desire to emulate Chingghis Khan the World Conqueror. By the spring of 1403 he was already re-crossing Anatolia, moving towards Samarqand, from thence to begin his conquest of China. He died on his way to challenge the Ming emperor in 1405. He had set up a motley assortment of petty principalities in Anatolia before leaving. His control of the area was very loose and all he really expected of his vassals was tribute. Under such a shaky settlement Bayezid I's sons Musa, Mehemmed and Suleiman were not only able to fight out a nasty and protracted civil war amongst themselves but also to rebuild the Ottoman state.

Marlowe gave Bayezid this speech delivered to his mocking Scythian conqueror after the defeat at Ankara:

> For though the glory of this day be lost,
> Afric and Greece have glories enough
> To make me sovereign of the earth again.[69]

The simple substitution of Rumelia for 'Afric' in fact brings this speech within the realms of truth. It seems unlikely that the Ottoman Empire would have survived the chaos following Ankara without the resources of their European lands. This said, Stefan Lazarevic's behaviour in the post-Ankara period is at first glance difficult to correlate with a continued loyalty to the Ottoman cause – he became a vassal of the Byzantine emperor.

However, this must be viewed against the chaos into which the Ottoman Empire had been thrown by the death of Bayezid I and the ensuing ten-year civil war. This was a period of semi-independence for all the vassal Christian Balkan states, and it seems most likely that Stefan was looking to secure his lands from the encroachments of the Hungarians following the apparent collapse of the major power in the Balkans.[70] It is notable that he also made immediate agreements with Suleiman, who had fled from Ankara to Rumelia.

The entire history of the Ottoman civil war, or *Fitnet Devri*, requires a volume of its own to describe all its twists and turns, but the part played by Stefan was important enough for a senior historian of the Ottoman state to comment that the alliance between the Despot of Serbia and Mehemmed I was vital to Mehemmed I's final victory over Byzantium, Wallachia and Venice in this period.[71]

Initially the Ottomans were forced into vassalage under Timur Leng and his successor Shah Rukh but, as noted above, the power structures of the Timurid Empire were fragile and poorly applied. The start of the civil war saw Suleiman holding the Ottoman capital of Edirne. He proclaimed himself ruler, but his brothers Musa and Mehemmed refused to recognise him. Suleiman swiftly concluded an alliance with Byzantium, by which Thessalonica was returned to the Greek state, and with Venice in 1403 to bolster his position and to be able to guarantee his communications with the European provinces. Serbia soon turned against Suleiman, probably as a result of his pressuring his vassals for more funds and troops. In 1410 he was defeated and killed by his brother Musa, who had secured the support of the Byzantine emperor, Manuel II, despite the emperor's previous pacts with Suleiman. Musa also secured the loyalty of Stefan Lazarevic, Mircea and the sons of Stratsimir and Shishman. Musa, however, then repeated the mistakes of Suleiman in his dealings with the Christian vassals as he became increasingly suspicious of their growing independence, and his younger brother Mehemmed, having finally freed himself of Timurid vassalage, mobilised the forces of Ottoman Anatolia. By 1412 the Balkan Christian states and much of the European Islamic bureaucratic and commercial classes in the Balkan lands had turned to Mehemmed. He invaded the Balkans, swiftly took Sofia and Nis, and united with Stefan Lazarevic's Serbs. Stefan's machinations against Musa and his collusions with the Byzantine emperor to introduce a certain Orhan as another pretender to the Sultanate whilst Mehemmed was weaker than his brother was of enormous value to the eventual victor in the civil war.[72] In 1413 Mehemmed killed Musa after defeating him south of the Iskar River. At this encounter both George Brankovic and a Serbian contingent were present among Mehemmed I's forces.[73]

Mehemmed I thereby, and by virtue of being the last man standing, reunited the Ottoman state. However, by this point his Serbian, Wallachian and Byzantine vassals were virtually independent and Albania, Bosnia and Moldavia now lay, once again, beyond the grasp of the Ottomans.

To add to his problems Mehemmed I faced internal difficulties related to policies in fact put in place by his brother, the former sultan, Musa. In 1416 a popular revolt of Muslims and Christians broke out in Dobrudzha with the clandestine support of Mircea I of Wallachia. The revolt had a religious element to it with its senior cleric, a certain Bedreddin, preaching a merging of Islam, Christianity and Judaism into a single faith, but there was also a strong revulsion against the bureaucratic and professional classes of the Ottoman state. The nomadic tradition was rearing its head in the European provinces, as it had in Anatolia. Mehemmed I crushed the revolt and punished Wallachia in 1419, by occupying the Danube fort of Giurgiu and forcing vassalage upon the *Voivode* of Wallachia once more.

Wallachia was a small foe and Mehemmed I generally avoided conflict with more powerful enemies as he sought to re-establish the Ottoman state in the Balkans. Raiding was used extensively, however, to bring Albania back under control and to force Bosnia back into vassalage, and a short war was conducted, without any real gain for either side, against Venice. Despite this cautious approach, by 1417 the phoenix-like Ottomans were at least the par of any power in Anatolia and in the Balkans. By 1421 reconquest had begun and the empire of Timur Leng, which had nearly finished the Ottomans, was already in decline. Mehemmed I was also responsible for the beginnings of a policy of extending 'Turkification' throughout conquered Balkan lands.[74] This policy was further extended by his successor Murad II.[75] By 1425 Turkish garrisons and law courts were present in Pristina. Turkish customs officials were also placed in Kosovo by 1426. It is likely that these moves toward greater control in this region and the Ottoman invasions of Serbian lands in 1427 were related to concerns over the succession to the Serbian Despotate and the fact that, in 1425, the good relations that had existed between Murad II and Stefan had deteriorated among accusations that the Serbian prince had been colluding with the Hungarians. If Stefan was indeed in league with the Hungarians then it would not be a surprise as the Ottomans were certainly preparing for conflict with the Hungarians over territorial claims in the region and control of the vital centre of Belgrade.[76] Stefan's lands sat right between the two rival states.

Murad II was only 16 years of age when he was called to the throne in 1421, but like so many of the Ottoman Sultans he had already undertaken senior roles within the empire. His inauguration took place in Bursa and appeared, at first, to be a smooth one with the loyalty of the whole empire quickly being sworn to him. Unfortunately Manuel II, already under pressure from the Turks in his isolated capital of Constantinople, hoped to extend the *Fitnet Devri* and to re-ignite factionalism within the Ottoman Empire. The Byzantine emperor had been harbouring a pretender to the throne in the form of Mustafa Celebi, another of the sons of Bayezid I. Manuel II now released Mustafa upon the empire and even went as far as to supply him with galleys to carry his forces between Europe and Asia. Mustafa was well received by Turks who had become disaffected by the centralising policies of Mehemmed I and Murad II and he defeated an army sent against him by Murad II before taking Edirne, declaring himself the Sultan of Rumelia and crossing the Dardanelles to Asia. By this point Mustafa had assembled a large army but Murad II's military skill and the skills of agitators among Mustafa's army were the deciding factors when the two met in battle. Mustafa's allies abandoned him and he escaped to Europe once more. Murad II pursued him in hired Genoese vessels and soon captured him. The pretender was hung in 1422.

It had taken Murad II a year to consolidate his position. He then turned his attentions to a sixth Ottoman siege of Constantinople in 1422. Revenge for the release and assistance of Mustafa by the Byzantines seems the most likely motive for the siege. Mircea of Wallachia had also aided Mustafa, and so Murad II also then raided Wallachia. He also took advantage of Venice's capture of Thessalonica from Byzantium to force the republic to pay tribute on its newly won city. Murad II also used a coercive diplomacy so typical of the Ottoman sultans when he gained both treaties and tribute from Hungary,

Byzantium, Wallachia and Serbia in 1424. Venice could not afford to give away its commercial predominance in the eastern Mediterranean and therefore persisted in a long war against Murad II until 1430 that only ended with its loss of Thessalonica and the Republic's recognition of Ottoman Macedonia. This was Murad II's price for continued Venetian access to the Black Sea. Murad II cranked up the pressure on the Venetians and showed them the vulnerability of their Balkan coastal ports when he forced the independent city-republic of Dubrovnik into paying tribute. In terms of Anatolia, the 'Mustafa affair' was fatal to many of the *beyliks* that had been plotting constantly against Murad II; Aydin, for example, was annexed and henceforth became part of the Ottoman Empire.

As discussed above, Murad II seems in this period to have been working towards what he may have felt was an inevitable confrontation with Hungary. With this in mind his actions in Wallachia, Bosnia and Serbia seem to have been directed at eliminating Hungarian influence in the lower Balkans. This strategic aim was made easier for the sultan in Serbia after Stefan Lazarevic died in 1427 as he left no direct heir. Lazarevic had designated George Brankovic, the senior noble or *boyar* of Kosovo, who had fought for Mehemmed I, as his successor but as soon as Brankovic took the throne Murad II invaded Serbia. In response Sigismund occupied the fortress city, and capital of Serbia, Belgrade, and Brankovic, finding himself between a rock and hard place, chose neither the sultan nor the king and set up the new Serbian capital in a newly built fortress named Smederevo on the Danube River to the south-east of Belgrade. Contemporary Ottoman texts indicate that Brankovic was in fact more fearful of the Hungarians than he was of the Ottomans at this time: 'Brankovic took over responsibility for the Hungarians, so that they could do no harm to the Muslims.'[77]

Murad II almost certainly looked approvingly at the chaos into which the Wallachian succession had fallen following Mircea I's death in 1418 and his son, Michael's, fleeting reign of only two years. Control of the principality changed hands between Dan II and Radu II some nine times before Alexander I Aldea was placed on the throne by his Ottoman overlord.

Sigismund responded by arranging for Alexander I Aldea's overthrow and the succession of Vlad II Dracul in 1436. Ottoman suzerainty over Wallachia was renounced immediately by Vlad II Dracul, a man whose membership of the Order of the Dragon would have supposed him to be a new champion for Christian Wallachia, but Balkan politics was, of course, never so clear cut as to allow for such a thing.

2

THE DRAGON'S SON:

VLAD II DRACUL'S DEEDS AND
THE YOUTH OF DRACULA

'Fools, fools! What devil or what witch was ever so great as Attila,
whose blood is in these veins?' He held up his arms. 'Is it a wonder
that we were a conquering race; that we were proud; that when the
Magyar, the Lombard, the Avar, the Bulgar, or the Turk poured his
thousands on our frontiers, we drove them back?'[1]

Vlad II Dracul was born sometime before 1395 and was the illegitimate son of Mircea I of Wallachia. In fact, of the many sons born to
Mircea only one, Mihail, was conceived in the marriage bed. He ruled
between 1408 and 1418 as co-ruler with his father. Romanian custom,
which 'allowed' for concubinage, meant that Vlad II Dracul's bastardy
would not impede him from claiming the throne. Another one of the
illegitimate offspring of Mircea, Alexander, ruled between 1431 and
1436 as Alexander I Aldea. Vlad II Dracul was born into a Romanian
elite that still held the real power in Transylvania despite the infiltration
of nomads and other non-Vlach groups from Saxony and Hungary.
Orthodox Christianity was the dominant religion among the Vlachs
but conversions to Catholicism were not unusual and, of course, several rulers in the Balkans in this period including the Byzantine emperor
were not averse to claiming degrees of allegiance to Rome for political
and diplomatic reasons.

The Vlach aristocracy was a warlike collection of *voivodes* that had evolved out of older tribal systems present in Transylvania. It seems that the early Vlachs raised cattle and lived a semi-nomadic existence travelling between temporary winter dwellings and the high mountains. They most likely rode small ponies as they shepherded their flocks across the Carpathian Mountains and were undoubtedly a tough race. Indeed, they had to be so, given that they were squeezed between the powers of Hungary, Greater Serbia during its zenith and the various overlords of the Ukraine ranging from the Golden Horde in the thirteenth through to Poland and Lithuania in the fourteenth century.

The *voivodates*, or governates, the building blocks of Vlach governance, had developed in the high valleys during a period of Hungarian rule as Vlach tribalism was replaced by a simple form of feudalism under local *hospodars* or 'lords'.

Wallachian feudalism was not like that found in Serbia or Bulgaria, as it had fewer social tiers. There were 'free' peasants and *boyars*, and then a prince. There was, therefore, not the level of complexity seen in these other Balkan societies. In some ways this was an advantage in the face of an aggressor – there was less likelihood of the state splitting apart under its higher lords as had happened in Serbia when the Ottomans invaded and in particular after the Battle of Kosovo in 1389. It might be a little simplistic to state that the Wallachian *boyars* understood that they could only stand if they stood together but it does sum up how cohesive Wallachia was as a state and we will see this in its longevity despite enormous Turkish pressure.

The first Vlach or Wallachian 'state' was formed on the River Olt in the Carpathians as a refuge for higher Vlach lords fleeing Hungarian–Catholic forces during the thirteenth century. The nascent state proved strong enough to survive, albeit under Hungarian suzerainty, and had as its bulwark the citadel of Curtea De Arges. This was the seat of the patriarch of the Romanian Orthodox Church, which consistently acted as a strong partner to princes of Wallachia. Though linked to the patriarchate of Constantinople since the conversion of the country by missionaries of the Eastern Orthodox Church during the ninth century, the Romanian church was practically autonomous under the metropolitan of Ungro–Wallachia and exarch of the Plains – meaning Wallachia and Transylvania. There were a number of wealthy monasteries at Tismana, Govora and Snagov, and the capital, from 1385, of Tirgoviste was just to the south of Curtea De Arges. Wallachian princes sometimes even resided and held their treasuries in the monasteries so the faith was very well plugged into the politics of Wallachia.

There were also a few Roman Catholic abbeys belonging to the Dominican, Franciscan, Cistercian, and Benedictine orders, and whilst there was an ingrained suspicion of the church of Rome among the Wallachians, the influence of Hungary was such that these communities were not directly in danger from their Orthodox cousins and Vlad II Dracul would find the presence of Catholic orders in Wallachia to be of help when he usurped the Crown.

The population was mixed and included Turks as well as Mongols, Saxons and the Hungarian–Catholic ethnic group of the *Szekels*.[2]

Wallachia weighed in for Bulgaria against the expansionist Serbia of Stefan Uros IV Dusan in the 1330s and also defeated the Hungarians, a victory that led to a shaky independence from the Hungarian Crown.

An alliance with the Muslim–Mongol Golden Horde against Hungary saw Wallachia grow in the first half of the fourteenth century, even reaching the Black Sea coast, but ground was then lost again to the Hungarians and Wallachia again accepted Hungarian suzerainty in 1368.

The Vlach principality of Moldavia grew out of the demise, in the twelfth century, of Kievan Rus. Moldavia had a larger Qipchaq Turk population than Wallachia, with Slavs and Vlachs making up the rest of the population. The Vlachs appear to have been the military elite of the state and the riches of the trade routes that ran across Moldavia from the Black Sea to Central Europe funded a well-equipped army with extensive weaponry.[3]

Hungarian Szekel armies drove the Mongols out of Moldavia in the 1340s and Hungary annexed the territory. Moldavia was contested between Poland and Hungary during this same period with a Polish army placing a *voivode* on the Moldavian throne. Thus, a pattern of Moldavia oscillating between suzerainty to Hungary and to Poland was set and even the semi-legendary *Descalecat*, or 'founding' of the state, in 1359 by the Transylvanian *Voivode* Dragos of Maramures after the intrepid lord had led his followers over the Eastern Carpathian Mountains was, in fact, part of an action by Dragos to put down a rebellion for his Hungarian suzerain. By 1365 Moldavia was autonomous but under Polish suzerainty.[4] By the end of the fourteenth century Moldavia had well-established access to the Black Sea and River Danube, and to the trade wealth that went along with this. It was also, in many ways, a bystander to the struggles against the Ottomans that Wallachia was enduring. Greater Moldavia covered approximately what is contained within the boundaries of Romania and Moldova today.

As noted briefly above Mircea I, the Old, of Wallachia had defeated the Ottomans in 1394, or rather, had thwarted their attempts to bring Wallachia under control through a series of *razzia*, or raids, but had finally been forced by their incursions to join the ill-fated Crusade of Nicopolis in 1396. It is a credit to him that he continued to resist the Ottomans' creeping advance into his lands following Nicopolis and he managed to defeat Ottoman raiders again in 1397, though the terrain of Wallachia certainly favoured the defender and not the invader. The year 1400 saw some respite as Bayezid I was caught up in Anatolian affairs but Mircea still had to make a spirited resistance to the Ottomans as support from the other Christian states was minimal. In 1408 there were renewed attempts by the Turks on Wallachia despite the ongoing Ottoman *Fitnet Devri* and civil war between Bayezid I's sons.

By 1417 Wallachia had to accept Ottoman suzerainty as it was fast collapsing into anarchy.[5] Mircea I, the champion for so long of resistance to the Turk, was old and would be dead by January 1419. His death led to the chaos described at the end of Chapter 1. Vlad II Dracul came to the throne of a state that reflected neatly the fractured and exhausted condition of Eastern Europe. Furthermore, any Wallachian prince could only rely on a very small contingent of personal forces, including his personal guard and the garrisons of his fortresses. Unless he could unify the *boyars* under him, a Wallachian prince had very little power.

Unfortunately for Vlad II Dracul and for the other princes of disunited states and the greater monarchs of the Balkans, they were facing an increasingly unified, centralised and powerful foe. In 1421, with the accession of Murad II, he faced one of the greatest of the Ottoman sultans.

In Chapter 1 we discussed how the *Yeni Ceri*, or Janissaries, were built as a loyal corps of elite troops from young men captured in European lands by Murad I. As mentioned earlier, one in every five prisoners was sent to the Porte. The significance of the Janissaries, however, went beyond their martial skills. In simple terms the advocates and 'organs' of a formal and centralised Ottoman state were the sultan and the army of the Porte. This centripetal force was in opposition to the desires of the forces of the frontier *beys*. These attempted consistently to maintain an Empire of Osman that would continue to be constructed around tribal affiliations and the power of emirs, who maintained a share of power within the state and who could frustrate unpopular policies. Murad I recognised that salaried slaves could create the absolutely loyal military force necessary to balance the warrior class. This was not a new discovery in Islam: a tradition of slave-soldiers stretched back to at least the ninth century and one of the most successful polities of the medieval world was the slave-soldier Mamluk dynasty.[6] Just as manumitted slaves were turned into superb soldiers by the Mamluk dynasty, so Murad I trained 'his men' in Ottoman tactics and organised them into military units under his direct command. Just like a Mamluk's *ustadh*, or master, the Ottoman sultan owned his men but also paid, fed, clothed and armed them.

Centralisation triumphed because of the peculiar nature of the Ottoman Empire – it was, by the fifteenth century, very much *not* a Turkish state. The *devshirme*, since its informal inception and especially after Murad II formalised the process, was a powerful weapon for the sultan's attempts to create a power base that was both entirely dependent on, and loyal only to, their person.[7] This process of building a state within a state began before the reign of Bayezid I and it became the central plank of his policy for the unification of Anatolia. He greatly expanded the numbers of his slave-soldiers to some 7,000 men and created a large, centralised military government. He also replaced

Anatolian aristocrats with slave-soldier bodyguards, or *ghulams*, whose loyalty to him was without doubt.[8] His over-rapid application of this policy was undoubtedly a major reason for his failure at Ankara and the desertion of a mass of his troops to Timur Leng. The 'steppe traditions' of the Turks were not yet ready to tolerate this attempt to direct their affairs and the desertion of Bayezid I's army was a result of the appeal of Timur's loose confederate state against that of the direct control of the Ottoman sultan.

Bayezid I's previous creation of *defters*, or surveyed records, of *timars*, however, contributed significantly to the state's restoration after 1402 as *timar* holders had a 'vested interest'[9] in the state's survival. This is not to suggest that upon his troubled accession Mehemmed I inherited a state that could be governed entirely by recourse to the *kuls*, or 'slaves', within the Ottoman state and *timar*-holding *sipahis*. Indeed, his final victory in the *Fitnet Devri* was based around the successes and support of the *akinje*, or tribesmen, of Anatolia and the desertions of his brother and then sultan, Musa, by the senior Anatolian *bey* Chandarli and by the Sufi-like sheikh Bedreddin. These men were, in fact, the effective leaders of the frontier element in the Ottoman state. Sultan Mehemmed I fully realised the shift in power that had occurred in the empire from the central powers to the *akinje* during the time of troubles. Mehemmed I therefore put the centralisation project on the back-burner during the *Fitnet Devri* and relied instead on leading Turcoman supporters for his military command and for his civil government. He did not, however, ever show any inclination for dismantling it.

Mehemmed I exiled Sheikh Bedreddin in 1413. He then had the sheikh judicially murdered in 1416 following Bedreddin's preaching of his new faith containing elements of Islam, Christianity and Judaism. Bedreddin had certainly been guilty of acts of *lèse majesté* and he was an alternative focus of power within the state for *timar* holders who had been dispossessed by Mehemmed I. His destruction indicates that Mehemmed I was actively and doggedly engaged on a programme to re-centralise the Ottoman state. This said, Mehemmed I may simply have been forced to respond as the actions of Bedreddin and his follower

Borkhuse and the doctrine of their new creed, which invoked 'common ownership', appealed directly to the nomadic elements within the empire. The revolt of Bedreddin was a massive threat to the fabric of the empire and Mehemmed I was compelled to act despite his undoubted misgivings over his support within the state at this time.

Of course, the highly technological nature of Ottoman warfare and the nature of the economy that grew up to meet the state's military needs, as alluded to in Chapter 1, drove the centralisation process. What also occurred was that there was an effective blurring of any distinction between the state and the sultan.[10] This process was virtually complete by the end of the reign of Murad II.

The reign of Murad II was highly significant in the move toward a centralised state. He began rebuilding it soon after ascending the throne. Once again 'slaves' occupied higher military-administrative positions and were appointed to central government offices. It is notable, however, that the grand wazir, the sultan's deputy, and the head of the treasury remained freeborn Turks. Murad II widened the *devshirme* and his wars in Rumelia and against Hungary saw a heavy investment in firearms and artillery. Much of this hardware was obtained from the expertise of captured and bribed Christian gun-makers, and gun-runners from Dubrovnik and other Venetian colonies also supplied artillery to Murad's army despite papal bans on supplying arms to the Turks. At the siege of Constantinople in 1422 Murad II had cannon capable of firing cannonballs of excessive size and weight, and the cannons were cast on the spot.[11] Firearms had also improved enormously in the early fifteenth century and their dissemination across the Balkans[12] required that the Ottomans, in order to maintain their dominance in the region, make full use of these weapons. This was particularly notable after the contests between Hunyadi and Murad II in the 1440s as the Ottomans experienced, very much at first-hand, how devastating the massed musket fire of their enemy could be. The Janissaries had long been the core of the state, especially if we consider that in the Ottoman empire the army *was* the state, and their influence increased enormously with the need for a highly trained, standing army that could deploy firearms effectively. This new technology brought success against the

Western powers, but perhaps just as importantly it ensured the triumph of the centralised state over the polity of the frontier *beys*. The technology was expensive and this restricted its dissemination among the Turcomen. Furthermore, the Porte appears to have actively restricted the spread of firearms within the empire. The *reaya* were allowed no weapons of any kind and even the *derbenci reaya*, or highway militia, were restricted to conventional weapons such as bows and swords.[13] The attitude of the *akinje* and traditional steppe warriors to firearms perhaps also favoured the sultan in his attempts to restrict the advantage of these weapons to the *kapikulu*, or military-slave administration. Firearms were the antithesis of the traditional ethics and symbolism of the Turcoman military class[14] and it is notable that in both 1473 and 1517 the Ottomans were able to crush vast Turcoman and Safavid armies that did not effectively employ firearms.[15]

The price tag of the new technology also required that the state's economy was strong enough to maintain their use. The empire was based chiefly on an agricultural economy. During Murad II's reign cultivated land was taken from European feudal lords as the sultan rejected the use of vassalage for his Balkan Christian rulers and undertook outright annexation of their territories, which then became *timars* of the state. Lands that were formally held by the Byzantines were, of course, already organised in this way. Conquered territories were considered as *miri*, or imperial lands. Villagers leased land from the state – this ensured that all revenue from such lands entered the state treasury – without diversion to feudal lords. Craft industries and the production of goods for export also became significant under Murad II. There was an active silk industry and the production of velvets and 'export quality' cotton is recorded at Bursa.[16] All this required powerful central control, both to create the production and trade system and to keep it functioning.

Central control was relatively easy to maintain because, as discussed above, the army was the state and the state was the army. This is evident when we look at Ottoman civil administration under Murad II. All ruling members of the elite were from the *askeri*, or military. The Porte was a mobile capital that served both as an administrative centre and as the military headquarters of the sultan. The provinces were, likewise, structured as military units first and civil units second. Each territory from the *kaza*, a small township, to that of the *eyalet*, or province, retained a set number of *sipahi* based on its territorial size and each territorial unit was governed by an officer with absolute authority in both military and civil affairs. Even the representation of these territories was militaristic in its nature. The *sancak*, or banner, was the basic building block of each province. Each *sancak* was created around a city or large town that billeted a regiment of Janissaries and also managed the civil needs of the *sancak* in that the *qadi*, or religious judge, and the offices of taxation were also to be found there.

Murad II's widening of the *devshirme* after 1438 was significant in that it increased markedly the number of individuals within the state who were entirely dependent on the sultan. Indeed, it has been suggested that the central institutions of the Ottoman state in the fifteenth century were direct extensions of the sultan's household.[17] The *kuls* of the household were the central agencies and the Janissaries were paid directly by the sultan. The drawing of these men from the sultan's European conquests and their youth effectively avoided any conflict with pre-existing tribal loyalties that would certainly have occurred with Anatolian followers. A contemporary Ottoman source describes how 'the absolute power of the ruler rested upon his having slaves in his service in the army and administration'.[18] During Murad II and his son Mehemmed II's reigns the sultan truly became the *sine qua non* of the empire's organisation. Consistent military success transformed the office of sultan from being a *primus inter pares* in the steppe tradition to being a *pantocrator*, an absolute, autocratic emperor in the Byzantine style. The sultan became the protector and owner of the state, the head of the Islamic community, and the sole repository of the law.

The Christian states of the Balkans, as we have seen, could claim no such unity of purpose. Only the unifying weapon of the Crusade was really available to the religious and secular leaders of East and West Europe and even that was decidedly double edged. One of the major problems with a call to Crusade against the Ottomans was that such projects had always been, and continued to be, short term by their very nature. The Christian states of Outremer had discovered this from the Second Crusade onwards. Western kings and higher lords often answered the call to Crusade but they rarely, if ever, listened to the council of the Palestinian barons or, as at Nicopolis, to the lords and kings of Eastern Europe. They were also only effectively interested in conquest and not in defence – Outremer benefitted far more from the long-term commitment of a French regiment, a gift from Louis IX, and from the formation of the Templar and Hospitaller Knights than it ever did from the adventures of kings and emperors. Rulers, such as Richard I of England, soon enough discovered that they could not leave their realms for too long. The nature of the war against the Ottomans, with its raiding and scorched earth warfare and with an enemy sitting within the territory of Europe, required a long grinding war, not some form of swashbuckling adventure. Furthermore, in this period the Crusade had become a diverse and highly unspecific venture.[19] The infidel was as likely to be identified as those lying to the east of Prussia or those within Catholic Christendom who rejected orthodoxy. The proclamation of a Crusade with the task of exterminating all Wycliffites and Hussites and other heretics in 1420 was a particularly pertinent example.

The disunity that existed among the Christian states may have been one reason why the Order of the Dragon was formed by Sigismund of Hungary in 1408. Certainly there was a large element of fighting against heresy, seen as a major cause of political fracturing, within Christendom attached to the order. Indeed, the order was formed after the Battle of Dobor fought against the Bosnian Bogomils. The order adopted Saint George as its patron saint, and he was an obvious choice given his association with crusading and with martial valour.

The statutes of the order specifically listed schismatics and heretics as enemies and obliged members to undertake war on foreign enemies of the faith. An obligation of loyalty to the Hungarian king and to his issue was made and the obligation of the king to give royal protection and offices to the members was also explicit. Vlad II was admitted into the order in 1431, and this may be the origin of his sobriquet Dracul as the order's members seem to have had identifying dragon motifs on both clothing and banners. The order was a distinctly Catholic one and antagonistic to the Orthodox faith. The populace that Vlad II Dracul was to try to rule in 1436, after Sigismund had placed him on the prince's throne of Wallachia, was predominantly Orthodox. Perhaps his reputation as a cruel and oppressive tyrant began among his own people.

We know very little of Vlad II Dracul's early life before his admission into the order. He was probably born before 1395 as he went as a hostage to Sigismund's court in Buda before the Crusade of Nicopolis. Mircea had signed a treaty of alliance with Hungary in 1395 and guarantees of his good behaviour were, of course, required. Vlad II Dracul spent much of his youth in the Hungarian capital and in Nuremberg. Mircea's death in 1418 meant that Vlad II Dracul was not required to remain at the court of Buda but he stayed on as a page to Sigismund. He seems to have been treated as any other young Hungarian nobleman would have been and travelled with Sigismund to Prague and Rome. The court was a cosmopolitan place and Vlad II Dracul might have been exposed to both French and German high culture, with their emphasis on chivalry and the knightly way, and the social and moral obligations of the nobility.[20]

Vlad II Dracul may also, however, have found Sigismund's court an ultimately frustrating place. The king's ambitions largely centred on the Holy Roman Empire, which he would eventually rule between 1433 and his death in 1437. Vlad II Dracul's attentions would also have been drawn to the throne of Wallachia after the death of his half-brother, Mihail. As other illegitimate sons circled there was also a claim from a cousin, Dan II, the legitimate son of Vlad II Dracul's uncle, to be concerned about. The origins of the long-lasting Dracula–Dnesti feud began with Vlad II Dracul and Dan II. As we have noted above, control of Wallachia oscillated between Dan II and Radu II some nine times in this period as their Hungarian and Ottoman puppet masters pulled the strings.

Vlad II Dracul left Buda in the spring of 1423. He attempted to ride to the court of the Polish–Lithuanian king, Ladislaus II Jagiello, at Krakow to offer his service. Sigismund, apparently angry at this act of ingratitude, sent a troop of cavalry in pursuit and Vlad II Dracul was captured at the border. Sigismund also confirmed Dan II as Prince of Wallachia.

Vlad II Dracul was, despite the above, sent on a mission to Venice in 1423 to greet the Byzantine emperor John VIII. He remained, however, on the edge of great events rather than being a shaper of them. As noted above, Vlad II Dracul entered the Order of the Dragon in 1431. It was certainly a prestigious honour as there were only twenty-four first-class members inducted and all the candidates came from the royalty of Europe. Among these luminaries were King Alfonso of Aragon and Naples, Stefan Lazarevic of Serbia, Prince Witold of Lithuania, and King Ladislaus Jagiello of Poland. In addition to the dragon cloaks and banners of the order there also appear to have been other insignia including golden collars carrying medallions of the dragon hung dead upon a cross bearing the order's mottos, *O quam misericors est Deus* and *Justus et Pius*.[21] The medallion, so the stories go, was to be worn at all times until the member's death, and after death it was to be interred with the wearer's body.

A mock tourney took place between the candidates and allegedly Vlad II Dracul performed so well that a golden buckle was thrown down to him by a mysterious lady. The tale goes that this buckle was found in 1931 in the tomb of Vlad Dracula.[22]

In 1431 Murad II threw his weight behind Vlad II Dracul's half-brother, Alexander I Aldea, and Dan II was unseated from the throne of Wallachia for the fifth and final time. Sigismund responded by making Vlad II Dracul military governor of Transylvania. He was the ideal candidate as he was guaranteed to watch both jealously and dogmatically the movements of Alexander I Aldea. Vlad II Dracul made the fortress of Sighisoara his headquarters as the hillside fortress, with its thick defensive walls, would be able to withstand the field artillery of the Ottomans and it was located in the centre of the borderlands. It had also just been rebuilt with each of its towers bearing the name of the guild that had paid for its construction and upkeep.

It seems likely that Vlad II Dracul's marriage to Cneajna, a princess of the house of Alexander the Good of Moldavia, in 1425 gave issue to Vlad Dracula in 1431 in Sighisoara. His eldest legitimate son, Mircea, had been born in 1428 and a third boy, Radu, followed in 1435. Its connection to the Moldavian ruling family would be of enormous value to the House of Dracul later.

Sighisoara had a prosperous German mercantile community that supported several Catholic orders including Benedictines, Cistercians, Premonstratensians, Franciscans and Dominicans. Vlad II Dracul, of course, as a member of the Order of the Dragon was sworn to protect Catholicism but given that the wealth of Transylvania lay with the trade and industry of its German, or more correctly Saxon, subjects he also knew that the key to consolidating his power in Transylvania was gaining the financial and military support of nearby German Catholic cities such as Brasov and Sibiu. As briefly noted above, such courting of an alien faith and culture could very well lead to the politically dangerous alienation of his Orthodox Romanian subjects. And in the fifteenth century every prince in Europe did well to realise what a potential powder keg religious disaffection was.

Heretical rejection of orthodox Catholicism was a massive problem for Hungary, and distracted the major Christian power in the region at this time from the Ottoman advance. The Hussite wars raged across Eastern Europe from the first defenestration of Prague in July 1419 through to 1436.

The preaching, complaints and creed of Jan Hus and the Hussites need not overly concern us here. However, the bloody and cruel persecutions of Hussite communities, which went as far as exhausting executioners to the extent that adherents were simply tossed down the shafts of silver mines by government troops, might either lead us to temper our criticisms of Vlad Dracula's later atrocities, or alternatively to be even further appalled by the fact that he stood out to the authors of the period as the doer of particularly repugnant deeds.

What was more significant about the Hussite wars for the evolution of warfare in Eastern Europe and for the 'innovations' that Vlad Dracula would bring to his warfare against the Turks and his neighbours and internal enemies were the tactics and make-up of the Hussite forces that protected the movement. The majority of the troops within the first Hussite armies consisted of peasants and townsmen who were, ostensibly, untrained in the use of weapons and unacquainted with the requirements of the battlefield. Religious fervour more than made up for the lack of military experience, just as revolutionary fervour later led Napoleon to the observation of his French armies that 'the moral is to the physical as three to one'. We should also not underestimate the martial skills of peasants and even townsfolk in the late medieval age – the carrying of side arms and the use of agricultural tools as weapons by local militia was the rule rather than the exception. As we shall see, Vlad Dracula made extensive use of peasants in his wars and he also imitated the greatest hero of the Hussites, Jan Ziska, who early in his campaigns decreed that a defensive guerrilla war was the only way to match an enemy who was superior both in numbers and in weaponry. Vlad Dracula's famous night raid was a classic Ziska-like attempt to avoid engaging the army and Janissaries of Mehemmed II in a pitched battle.

Jan Ziska may also have been the inspiration for Vlad Dracula's use of armoured wagons; the war-wagon was certainly a revolution that did not pass unnoticed by the greatest Christian war leader in the Balkans theatre in this period, John Hunyadi.

Ziska was not the inventor of the armoured wagon but his application of it to the battlefield was his greatest contribution to battlefield tactics and to the evolution of warfare. He recognised that his lightly armed foot soldiers, who were often armed only with modified agricultural tools such as threshers and flails, would never stand against the shock of an armoured cavalry charge. Even when Ziska could obtain enough horsemen to form a cavalry of his own he deployed them in reserve and dedicated them to attacks on the enemy's flanks and not to challenging the opposing cavalry for the heart of the field. Indeed, if the number of horsemen available to Ziska was very small then he would place them within the *waggonberg*, the classic mobile fort formed of a ring or rings of war-wagons for which the Hussites are renowned. Vlad Dracula would also use his cavalry, small as it was on many occasions, judiciously against the large numbers of *sipahis* that Mehemmed II could bring to the field and use wagon defence to protect it until it was needed on the field.

The Hussites also serve another purpose for military historians in that much of their armour and arms, like their tactics, may be the nearest 'match' for those carried by and used by Vlad Dracula's men.

Essentially, we know a lot more about the Hussites than we do about the Vlachs. A broad-brimmed helmet, 'typical of the Germanic lands,'[23] was worn along with leather over cloth or mail. Swords would have been of many differing lengths and quality; there was no centralised armoury available to the Hussites or to Vlad Dracula. The flail was a common weapon used by the Hussites and we can be fairly confident, given the make-up of Vlad Dracula's press-ganged infantry, that this weapon and others with their origins in agriculture such as pitch forks and long-handled blades or hooks would have been used by the peasants either drawn to or conscripted into his forces.

Of course, long weapons are an obvious choice if one is going to fight from within a *waggonberg* and morning stars, long spiked-clubs, spears and lances were ideal both for keeping the enemy at a distance and for stabbing and slashing movements across the weapon's field. There is also evidence of hooks being used to pull attacking cavalrymen from the saddle. The Hussites had access to firearms and so would Vlad Dracula's army. As discussed earlier, firearms were well disseminated over the Balkans by this period. This said, it has been suggested that crossbows far outnumbered firearms in the Hussite armies and this again would be expected in the Vlach armies of Vlad Dracula. So effective was the crossbow, particularly when time to reload was afforded to the user by the protection of his war-wagon against even plate-armoured knights, that its use, no doubt under pressure from the chivalry of Europe, was condemned by the second Lateran Council in 1139 'as being hateful to god'.[24]

Ziska's wagons were not simple carts turned on their side as a defensive wall but were rather constructed to be independent defensive units that when pulled together gained further strength. Four horses were required to pull these wagons as heavy extra planking was fitted to the sides to add protection for the troops within, and the wheels were protected by braces when the vehicle was stationary. Approximately fifteen to twenty men could crew each war-wagon and it has been suggested that the complement would be six crossbow men or hand-gunners with the rest of the troops handling flails or lances.[25]

The Hussites also supply us with some idea of the kind of artillery Vlad Dracula would have been using against the Ottomans. It seems likely that his field artillery would have been of a wrought iron 'hoop and stave' construction strengthened by metal bands. Vlad Dracula had no industrial base the like of his opponents, the Ottomans, of whose impressive cast cannons more later. In fact, for field artillery this did not place him at a great disadvantage. In hoop and stave cannon construction long strips of iron were bound together by hoops that were heated white-hot and then allowed to cool in place, thus binding the strips tight enough to produce a near gas-tight tube that was muzzle-loaded and perfectly capable of firing the type of ordinance used in the fifteenth century for field artillery.[26]

These were the types of weapon and these were the tactics that John Hunyadi would bring to the battlefield to fight the Ottoman armies of Murad II, but the first clash between the two, which would see Vlad II Dracul fighting *with* the Ottomans, did not come until 1438. Murad II's progress in his campaign to bring all of Eastern Europe under his sway in the period between 1431, the year of Vlad Dracula's birth, and 1438 began with attacks on Hungary's allies.

In 1432 Murad started raids against Transylvania. Hungary was torn by rebellions and was still reeling from the debacle of the 1431 Crusade against the Hussites, which ended in total defeat for the king at the Battle of Domazlice. Peace negotiations with the Hussites began in January 1433 but the humiliating defeats inflicted by the heretics had eroded the Hungarian Crown's majesty. The one small positive to arise out of the failure of the Crusade, which had been largely a creation of the Holy Roman Empire, was that the Habsburgs of Austria persuaded their diet to pay for a standing army of 1,000 knights to guard their borders. This was a move away from the feudal armies that had fought for Christendom and which were difficult to hold together or even to gather and a move towards a responsive, regular force that would fight day in, day out – the kind of warfare that the Turks were undertaking against Eastern Europe. This force could be seen as the beginning of the *Militargrenze* of the sixteenth century, of whose effectiveness against the armies of Suleiman the Magnificent we will read more later.

The year 1436 saw the end of the Hussite Wars and perhaps Sigismund of Hungary might have felt that his situation was improving as in addition, and as noted above, he had been able to place his candidate, Vlad II Dracul, on the throne of Wallachia.

In truth Vlad II Dracul had probably been aiming at the throne of Wallachia from the very moment he had been appointed governor of Transylvania. He had minted coins in Sighisoara, bearing the Dragon of the Order on the obverse and the Eagle of Wallachia on the reverse. He had to wait until 1434 to get the nod from Sigismund, who had been advised by the grand master of the Teutonic Order to give Vlad II Dracul his head and to unseat Alexander I Aldea. Vlad II Dracul gathered an army composed of *boyar* exiles, Romanians from Transylvania and mercenaries. By 1436 Alexander I Aldea was, in fact, on his deathbed but Vlad II Dracul had to beat off attacks from Ottoman light cavalry and to secure the Danube against invasion by the Turks before he could lay claim to Tirgoviste in December 1436.

In 1437 Vlad II Dracul attached himself to the sultan's cause. Perhaps we should not be too harsh on the *voivode*, however, as his newly 'won' state sat directly on the Danube frontier of the Ottomans' Balkan conquests. It was entirely likely that Wallachia would become the warzone for any conflict between Hungary and Murad II, with all the attendant destruction that this implies. Furthermore, Vlad II Dracul's feudal lord, Sigismund, was now dead and his feudal obligations, outside of those he had sworn as a member of the Order of the Dragon, were negotiable to say the least. Under his agreement with Murad II, Vlad II Dracul and 300 of his *boyars* were received in Bursa to give their official act of submission and to pay a 10,000-ducat tribute.

In 1438, the year following the great Transylvanian Peasants' Revolt, of which more later, Vlad II Dracul acted as a guide for Murad II on an incursion into Transylvania, a province of the king to whom he owed his position and to whom he had pledged allegiance through the Order of the Dragon. The chronicler Brother George of Hungary recorded how:

> Murad Bey invaded this country at the head of a powerful army. He had, it is said, three-hundred thousand horsemen with him and he was intending to devastate all Hungary. But since divine intervention

had caused a river to flood, the flooding of the country presented an obstacle to the realisation of his project. So he directed his army against the province which extends beyond the mountains, and which is known by the name of Seven Forts [Transylvania]. He pillaged and destroyed with the utmost cruelty, and without meeting any resistance from anyone in front of him.[27]

The raids of the Ottomans were very damaging, with plundering and burning being undertaken on a large scale. Whether Vlad II Dracul's presence ameliorated the damage wrought to some degree is a debatable point. Certainly some towns looked to surrender to him rather than to the Turks in order to reduce the inescapable looting and damage but the fact remains that 70,000 prisoners had been hauled off to captivity by the Ottomans by the end of the campaign.

Murad II's opponent in 1438 might have understood Vlad II Dracul's actions but he never showed any signs of condoning them. John Hunyadi was a Magyarised Romanian from Transylvania. He was bought up as a noble and may well have acted as a page to Filippo Scolari, who was charged with the defence of the southern border; he would therefore have been exposed not only to the ideals of chivalry but also to the realities of hard grinding warfare. One of his numerous, and often contradictory, biographers wrote that Hunyadi was accustomed to both heat and cold from early in his military career. Hunyadi was also present at the court of Stefan Lazarevic and would have heard accounts of how the Serbian despot had been betrayed by Murad II after Stefan had done so much to ensure Murad's father Mehemmed I's victory over his brothers in the *Fitnet Devri*. In 1427, when the despot was dying, the Ottomans were making serious incursions into Serbian lands. Hunyadi also married into the inner circle of Serbian nobility in 1429 and entered into the service of Sigismund of Hungary, accompanying the king to Italy in 1431 and then serving for two years among the mercenary armies of Milan.

The above youthful experiences were, no doubt, important in the formation of the adult Hunyadi. He remained fiercely uncompromising towards the Ottomans his entire life and applied methods of warfare in his conflicts with them that owed a great deal to the techniques he would have witnessed in Italy in combination with the tactics of the Hussites from his own region. He also attracted a great deal of affection and loyalty from all the lords he served as a young man and this continued into his adulthood too, with loyalty from his men and knights also becoming a Hunyadi *leitmotif*.

Upon Sigismund's death in December 1437 Hunyadi took up the defence of the southern border. Ottoman raids had been increasing in volume, possibly in response to the news of the king's declining health. The Transylvanian Peasants' Revolt, a tax rebellion that was in fact led by a petty Hungarian noble, Antal Nagy de Buda, and made up from elements of every strand of Transylvanian society, was also raging.

Sigismund's death saw the revolt's end as the Brotherly Union, a compact between nobles, Szekelys and Saxons, was formed to return the peasants to their miserable standing, to return Transylvania society to its *status quo ante*, and to meet the threat of ongoing Ottoman incursions. The Union attacked and destroyed the peasant army in the closing days of 1437.

The Ottomans had made extensive inroads into Serbia by 1438 and began to dismember the country. It will be remembered that George Brankovic had not allied with Sigismund as the king had taken Belgrade from him, but had rather attempted to resist both Hungarian and Turkish pressure from the fortress city of Smederevo. Murad II laid siege to the city and, though it was briefly relieved by Hunyadi's troops in 1437, in June 1439 George Brankovic fled to the court of the new Hungarian king, Albert of Habsburg. The slaughter in Serbia is recorded as being particularly extensive. The Ottoman chronicler, Asikpasazade, wrote of how the horses of the Turkish raiders 'walked on infidel corpses'.[28]

Meanwhile, Vlad II Dracul, as an ally of the sultan, was continuing on with his own plundering in Transylvania. Hermannstadt and Alba Iulia were both ransacked as well as numerous smaller towns and villages. The sacking of Hermannstadt was perhaps the first of the Dracul clan's atrocities committed against Saxons living in Transylvania. There would be many more. The 'Saxon problem' for the rulers of

Hungary and Transylvania and Wallachia was one that went back to the Hungarian kings' conquest of Transylvania. The land was sparsely populated but fertile and they sought colonists to take on the challenge. Saxons responded enthusiastically and there were massive migrations during the twelfth and at the close of the thirteenth centuries. As colonists tend to do they formed privileged, self-governing communities, with their Catholicism, language and German culture being more than enough to mark them out from the Vlachs and Romanians who, despite being the majority of the population of Transylvania, enjoyed no definable rights.

The Saxons' industry and cohesiveness gave them a powerful voice in Transylvanian affairs and they were even identified as a nation within the nation ruled by the governor of Transylvania. They did not always fall into line with Hungarian policy and their heritage, particularly with the rise to prominence of the Habsburgs, always made them slightly dubious citizens who were often suspected of intrigue by their Hungarian rulers.

The new Hungarian king's call to arms had fallen largely upon deaf ears among the higher nobility, perhaps because he was Sigismund's son-in-law and not his direct descendant, and Hunyadi and his brother often found themselves to be the only men resisting the Ottomans through their raids on the siege lines surrounding Smederevo. Albert rewarded the brothers by making them Barons of the Realm shortly before he died in October 1439.

Hungary's problems only worsened with the death of Albert as his widow, Elizabeth, crowned her infant son, the posthumous issue of Albert, on 15 May 1440 despite the fact that the higher lords had already offered the Crown to Vladislaus, the King of Poland. Vladislaus was crowned in July 1440. A civil war ensued during which Hunyadi threw his weight behind the claim of Vladislaus. He also continued to defend the southern border and to engage the Ottomans and Vlad II Dracul in Wallachia. He was well rewarded with estates by Vladislaus and the fact remains that Hunyadi's dedication to the care of the frontier probably ensured Hungary's survival at this juncture. He was also a decisive influence in bringing the civil war to a successful conclusion for Vladislaus after his crushing defeat of a Habsburg army in early 1441. His reward from the king was the governate of Transylvania, command of Belgrade and the castles along the Danube.

Hunyadi was a conscientious administrator of these new acquisitions. He pacified Transylvania and cleared out the remaining Habsburg partisans, and he made strong representations at court for the nobles of the border region that would have increased their loyalty to him and also bound their fortunes to his. He also repaired the walls of Belgrade, which had come under attack by the Ottoman artillery over the last few years and had been severely battered in 1440 during a tight siege, and was even able to take the offensive against the Turks. In the autumn of 1441 Hunyadi led troops into Ottoman-held territory to the south-west of the River Sava and Belgrade. He met the garrison commander of Smederovo, Ishak Bey, in battle and defeated him. Hunyadi had brought his personal forces and troops recruited in Transylvania into the field in an attempt to break the grip of the Ottoman troops, who had raised the siege of Belgrade but who continued to raid in its environs. Unable to make contact with the enemy, he then started to move with his forces across Transylvania but was cut off by Ishak Bey. In the battle Hunyadi seems to have deployed his heavy infantry in the centre flanked by archers and light infantry. At the extreme flanks he had knights and mounted crossbowmen. Hunyadi also had a reserve of knights with him behind the infantry line. The scanty evidence suggests that the reserve of knights finished the battle with a charge that broke the Ottomans and put them to flight.

It was the first of a series of successes that undoubtedly gave heart to eastern Christendom after so many reverses. Following this victory Hunyadi demanded that Vlad II Dracul renew his pledge to the Order of the Dragon and his oath to fight the Turks. He may also have cajoled Vlad II Dracul with talk of a Crusade that would sweep the Turks away not just from Transylvania but also from Wallachia. The claims that Pope Eugenius IV had achieved the reunion of the Roman Catholic and Eastern Orthodox churches at the ecumenical council held in Florence on 4 July 1439 had, in the eyes of many Eastern European Catholics, laid the foundations for such a Crusade to take place.[29] The Pope himself had stated that, 'by the inspiration of God, we intend to prepare a fleet and land force ... to snatch the Catholic flock from the yoke of miserable servitude'.[30]

Murad II was distracted from the Transylvanian front as he was taking advantage of Venice's war with Genoa to strip Albania, Epiros and the Adriatic coastline away from the republic, but in the spring of 1442 he committed two armies to a direct attack into the heart of Transylvania. Vlad II Dracul allowed the armies of Mesid Bey of Vidin and Shehabbedin Beylerbey of Rumelia to pass through Wallachia unmolested. This time, however, he had put his money on the wrong side.

Hunyadi assembled a force of Hungarian, Transylvanian and Saxon forces rapidly to meet the threat. Unfortunately his 'regular' army had recently disbanded after the Serbian campaign and Hermannstadt had to be defended as it protected one of the few routes that could be traversed by large armies through the Carpathians. Hunyadi also had Polish troops available to him, possibly as a result of the union of the Crowns that had taken place with the accession of Vladislaus III. The formidable Bishop Lepes, the man who had triggered the peasants' revolt of 1437 with his rapacious tax collection, led the vanguard and engaged the Turks on 18 March. The numbers involved in the battles are not clear but it seems that the Hungarians were outnumbered by Ottoman troops and a figure of 2,000 men under the bishop and a further 8,000 under Hunyadi's direct command has been suggested, as have figures of 17,000 men for each of the Ottoman armies.

Lepes' forces met Mesid Bey's near Santimbru in the valley of the River Mures. The Ottoman forces filled the valley with their right flank resting on the valley heights and their left meeting the river. The Ottomans may also have held a large reserve of their troops in Santimbru. Lepes, with Hunyadi supporting him, launched an attack against the Ottoman left but this was repulsed by the Ottoman reserve. Meanwhile, the Ottoman centre counter-attacked and the Hungarian centre was routed. The bishop was captured and later executed and Hunyadi was forced to retreat to the fortress of Alba Iulia. The Ottomans failed to pursue the defeated Hungarians and would soon enough rue their error.

Hunyadi regrouped near Hermannstadt and received more troops into his army. Szekels and Saxons arrived with Anton Trautenberger, and Transylvanian Wallachians of the *boyar* Basarab, a potential candidate for Vlad II Dracul's throne, also responded to his call.

Battle was rejoined on 25 March as the Ottomans were retiring from their pursuit of his forces. Several tales of the battle are told, possibly to embellish the facts, of which there are few verifiable ones. A Hungarian spy has been credited with overhearing the Ottoman plans for battle and how this involved a concentration of forces aimed directly at killing Hunyadi. The story goes that Hunyadi then swapped armour with a loyal lieutenant, Simon Kemeny, and that Hunyadi's banner was also carried by the decoy. Kemeny purportedly took the banner to the right wing of the army with his knights and Hunyadi rode out to the army's left wing with the heavy cavalry. The heavy infantry made up the centre and a detachment of Hussite-style war wagons was deployed on an extreme flank of Hunyadi's cavalry.

Kemeny led the Hungarian centre and right in a general advance but was killed during a concerted Ottoman counter-attack on the banner, during which the Ottoman reserve was committed. Mesid Bey then ordered a general attack at this point as he believed the battle was won. At this point Hunyadi unfurled his personal standard, charged the weak Ottoman right wing and enveloped the Ottoman army. The war wagons were also deployed against the Ottoman right wing and the gunfire and crossbow fire from them caused its disintegration. A break-out of captives from the bishop's army at the rear of the Ottomans is also credited for completing the Hungarian victory. Mesid Bey was killed in the battle along with his sons whilst Shehabbedin Bey escaped the battlefield with the remaining Ottomans. We are also told that Hunyadi exchanged Mesid Bey's head for that of Lepes with the Ottomans.

Hunyadi pursued the Ottomans back into Wallachia and took care of a little outstanding business by removing Vlad II Dracul from his *vovoidate* and replacing him with Basarab II. Vlad II Dracul fled Hunyadi's wrath and sought sanctuary with the Ottomans. The sultan's price for offering refuge was high. Vlad II Dracul was considered by the Ottomans in much the same light as Hunyadi viewed him. He was not to be trusted. In fact, Mircea II, Vlad II Dracul's son, managed to get himself recognised as Prince of Wallachia for a short time before Hunyadi was able to install Basarab II, but Vlad II Dracul's other sons, Dracula and Radu, accompanied him on his flight to Gallipoli. As he reached the city's gates, Vlad II Dracul was seized by guards and bound in chains. His two young sons were taken away to the distant mountain fortress of Egrigoz in eastern Anatolia. Vlad II Dracul remained a perhaps unwilling guest of Murad II for a year in Edirne. He earned his release by giving up his 11- and 7-year-old sons as hostages and through guaranteeing tribute of 10,000 gold ducats and 500 boys for the *devshirme*.

Murad II had also, in fact, decided that Wallachia should cease to exist as an independent princedom and would become a dependent territory. Vlad II Dracul agreed to be his puppet. To this end Shehabbedin Bey was sent back to Wallachia and Transylvania with an army of some 80,000 men in early September 1442. The forces of Basarab II could not hope to stand against such a large force and he retreated to the mountains. This required Shehabbedin Bey to use some of his forces to pursue the Wallachians and to contain any guerrilla activity that Basarab II might undertake against his rear. He was, however, still able to move ahead with a sizeable force up the valley of the River Ialomita. Hunyadi and Basarab II met the Ottomans at a narrowing of the valley. The sources tell us that the Hungarian–Wallachian forces numbered no more than 15,000 men so the narrowing of the valley and the precipitous climbs at each of its sides were of enormous strategic advantage to Hunyadi, especially given the Ottoman penchant for flanking with light cavalry.

The war-wagons were placed to the flanks of the infantry and also drawn up at the rear of the line. The cavalry sat at the extreme right and left. Perhaps surprisingly given the difference in numbers between the sides and the naturally defensive position of the narrow, Hunyadi chose to attack.

The battle was bloody and long. The war-wagons seem to have been deployed in support of the infantry advance. Their firepower might have been of considerable significance seeing as the fight seems to have been one of simple attrition. The Ottoman army did not break until dusk and it is possible that Hunyadi used a feigned retreat to draw them into the fire of his war-wagons. Their losses were appalling if the records are to be believed. Some 20,000 Turks, 200 standards and 5,000 animals were strewn dead across the field at the battle's close.

The Hungarians were distracted from a pursuit of the main body of the Ottoman forces by the need to chase down the dispersed units that Shehabbedin Bey had sent raiding across Wallachia. Shehabbedin Bey was therefore able to retire in fairly good order across the Danube with his remaining troops.

There was no doubt that the Ottomans were now on the back foot in the Balkans. Murad II also faced a number of Anatolian problems, particularly with the Karamanids, and his presence there in 1443 enticed the Albanian lords, who the sultan had thought would be quiescent now that Venice had been neutralised on the Adriatic coast, to throw off Ottoman authority completely.

Murad II's absence was also seen by Hunyadi as an unmissable opportunity. He appealed to the sovereigns of Western Europe to join him in a rolling Crusade against the Ottomans but, despite the support of Pope Eugenius IV, the response was poor. The Hundred Years War had flamed up again with eventual French success at the long siege of Dieppe, and despite the best efforts and apparent success of Cardinal Giuliano Cesarini in reconciling the Habsburgs to their loss of the Hungarian throne, the fact remains that Frederick III, the Holy Roman Emperor at this time, was the first Habsburg to obtain the imperial throne. That he was less than enthusiastic to assist any venture that might profit Vladislaus III of Hungary would not be surprising. This said, there was a response from the chivalry of Europe with considerable numbers of French and German knights joining as independent Crusaders. The army was also heavily supplemented with mercenaries, who were now in plentiful supply as the Czech Hussite armies were disbanding. These men brought a hard edge of professionalism to an army that also contained numerous irregulars mustered from the local peasantry.

The *Longum Bellum*, or long campaign, as it became known also had a long preparation time. These had begun at the close of 1442 and the news that Murad II had been defeated badly in Anatolia added impetus to the planning. Hunyadi ordered wagons, gunpowder and artillery from the Transylvanian towns and money began to flow from the pockets of higher lords. The Serbian despot George Brankovic was particularly generous in adding to the coffers of a campaign directed against his father-in-law.

By the start of the campaign Hunyadi had raised some 10,000 to 12,000 men, mostly Czechs, German, Poles, Serbians and Transylvanians. There were, in common with the Hussite armies and the armies that Vlad Dracula would fight with, also peasant soldiers and probably 600 war-wagons. This 'new army' when added to the troops of the king's household, Serbians serving under George Brankovic and independently led Wallachian troops gave a total of 35,000 men for the campaign.

Hunyadi entered Ottoman territory in September 1443. The campaign was delayed by vehement opposition to the truce between the Habsburgs and Vladislaus III by Jan Jiskra, the most effective supporter of King Albert's widow, Elizabeth. This postponement of the campaign from the summer may, however, have actually worked in Hunyadi's favour as it seems its launch late in the year surprised the Ottomans. The Ottomans retreated quickly from Serbia, burning villages as they went. Hunyadi advanced quickly and his units crossed the Danube and regrouped near Sofia, from where the army marched westwards towards Nis through countryside that had also been scorched by the Turks. Ishak Bey of Smederevo tried to delay Hunyadi's advance at the River Morava but he was forced to retreat across the river under a furious Hungarian assault. Hunyadi went ahead of the main army with some 12,000 cavalry and seized Nis on 3 November 1443 after defeating three Ottoman detachments in three separate engagements. Nis was important to both sides as it acted as a conduit for Ottoman troops moving through to the Belgrade front. News then came that Murad II had re-crossed the Dardanelles from Anatolia and was at Edirne mustering troops. It was at the Battle of Nis that a certain Iskander Bey, or

Skanderbeg, deserted the Ottoman army and led 300 Albanian troops away with him. We will hear much more from Iskander Bey later.

Hunyadi returned to the main army and overwhelmed an Ottoman army that had been cobbled together from fresh reinforcements and the scattered remnants of the detachments defeated around Nis. This latest success led many Serbs in Ottoman-occupied territories to throw off the Turkish yoke and to join the Hungarians. A small Wallachian force under Mircea II, acting for Vlad II Dracul, also arrived to join Hunyadi. Vlad II Dracul was playing a dangerous double game as he had regained the throne from Basarab II with Murad II's support, but was now betting on the Hungarians to be the victors in this latest turn of the game.

On 20 November Hunyadi defeated Shehabbedin Beylerbey of Rumelia. Ottoman losses in the battle were about 2,000 killed and 4,000 captured but the losses to the retreating army were far greater as Serb and Bulgar villagers took their revenge on their former occupiers. Hunyadi reached Sofia and took the city without meeting any further resistance. This is not perhaps that surprising, however, given that Hunyadi had threatened the local population with the enslavement of their wives and daughters if they did not provide food and act as guides on the march into Sofia. Murad II had also ordered the city burnt, apparently to his own great regret, and the Holy War Chronicles of the Ottomans record how 'not a straw was left in Sofia or in its surroundings'.[31] The Metropolitan of Sofia led a Christian service for Hunyadi's men in the Siyavus Pasha Mosque – which had been a church before the Ottoman occupation.

The metropolitan was later to be beheaded by the city's Ottoman governor and his followers were blinded in revenge for the insult to the sultan and the faith. Things then got even worse for the Bulgarians as Murad II issued a decree ordering the execution of any individual assisting the invaders. Ottoman troops took this as a licence to commit murder on the local populace, to enslave their children and to loot. 'The populace of Radomir and Sofia were crushed beneath horses' hooves, and whoever brought a head to the sultan received five florins' bounty.'[32]

Murad II called a council of war in Edirne in early December. The Grand Wazir Halil Candarli remained in Edirne to manage the deployment of the reserves from Anatolia that were arriving and the sultan went with the army to Plovdiv. Murad II had stated that the Rumelians were unreliable and recalled how they had double-crossed both Musa and Mehemmed I during the *Fitnet Devri* and sided with the pretender Mustafa. He now poured men from Anatolia into the fight but still offered *timars* and positions in the Janissaries to any Rumelians who volunteered to fight for him.

The Hungarians then attempted to force a crossing over the Balkan Mountains in the dead of winter. Murad II reinforced all the detachments holding the mountain passes. Hunyadi headed east, presumably in an attempt to find a minor forgotten or at least lightly defended pass away from the major routes to Edirne and Constantinople. Murad II had, however, been thorough in his deployment and on 12 December Hunyadi failed to break through the Ottoman forces defending the pass at the village of Zlatitsa. An Ottoman army under the Grand Wazir Halil Pasha was waiting for him. He had erected palisades and had dug in awaiting the Hungarians' arrival. The Pasha, perhaps encouraged by the thought of the hard march that the Hungarians had undertaken to get to the battlefield, decided to go on to the offensive. He attacked but was repulsed, although Hunyadi was unable to puncture the Ottoman defensive line. The Hungarians were successful in pushing the Ottomans back behind their palisades but were unable to make any further headway. Hunyadi withdrew but over the next few weeks he stayed close to Zlatitsa and sent probing units out to find any way around the army of Halil Pasha. None was found.

On 23 December Murad II arrived at Zlatitsa with additional troops. This and the fact that supplies were running low forced Hunyadi to order a withdrawal. Sometime over Christmas Eve and Christmas Day the Ottoman vanguard made contact with the retreating Hungarian army near the town of Melstitsa. Hunyadi, probably in a cavalry charge, defeated the Ottomans again. From this point on Murad II tracked the Hungarian army but made no attempt to confront it during the long retreat. This was certainly related to Hunyadi's impressive generalship and to the Hungarians' discipline despite their severe supply problems and the loss of most of their war-wagons and horses.

Murad II, having failed to break the Hungarians, switched to a pursuit of the army of George Brankovic. The Ottomans caught the Serbs strung out on the march near Kunovitsa. They swiftly organised an attack and broke the Serbian army. Hunyadi then, however, arrived on the field with his troops and caught the Ottoman vanguard just as it was celebrating its victory. He captured Mahmud Celebi, Murad II's brother-in-law.

The *Longum Bellum* had been an arduous and difficult campaign and had cost a great deal in terms of men, horses and materiel. However, it had done enormous damage to Ottoman prestige as well as the physical damage it had inflicted on Murad II's armies. It had spent four months in Ottoman lands and had given hope to the populations of the hinterlands and the occupied regions. The campaign was seen as a glorious success in Western Europe and Hunyadi returned to a hero's welcome in Hungary in February 1444.

In March Murad II opened negotiations for a truce through his father-in-law George Brankovic and may have used his wife, Mara Brankovic, as his initial intermediary. Murad II offered George Brankovic the return of all his lands if he organised a truce between Hungary and the Ottoman Empire. Brankovic first approached Hunyadi. He offered Hunyadi his own Hungarian estates if Hunyadi agreed to convince the king that peace with the sultan was worthwhile. Vladislaus III signed a treaty guaranteeing ten years of peace with Murad II, but whether he was genuine about peace and then the idea of a Crusade was planted in his mind by Cardinal Cesarini, or if the truce was no more than a ruse from the outset, we shall never know.[33] Of course, the idea that any agreement with a non-believer had no validity had a long history in Christianity, so breaking the truce or making a false peace would have been of little import either way.

The truce was proclaimed at Szeged by Vladislaus III and at Edirne by Murad II. Captured fortresses were returned to the Serbs and hostages were to be freed. George Brankovic received his blinded sons back under the terms of the treaty but there would be no freedom for Dracula and Radu as Vlad II Dracul joined the Crusade of Varna in 1444.

Hunyadi's success had sent the papal advocates of a Crusade into a frenzy of diplomacy and preaching for a Crusade to finally push the Turks from Europe. At the Hungarian diet in April 1444 Cardinal Cesarini announced the formation of a grand coalition against the Turks. Pope Eugenius, King Vladislaus III, Philip the Good of Burgundy, and the republics of Venice and Genoa had all pledged their support for the alliance. The diplomacy was solemnised with the taking of a Crusader's oath by King Vladislaus III that he would lead a Crusade by the end of the year. Pope Eugenius' efforts to raise a pan-European Crusade, however, failed because of the continuing rivalries among the leading Western monarchs.

The plan was fairly simple and also overly complex. The Crusader army would follow the line of the Danube. That was the simple part. What was overly ambitious was the expectation that Burgundian, Venetian and Genoese ships would close the straits and deny the Turks reinforcements from Anatolia and that the Greeks of Constantinople would launch diversionary attacks in the Peloponnese. Given the speed, or rather lack of it, attached to medieval communications the odds on coordinating these three separate but interdependent operations were poor at best. Added to this was the fact that both the Greeks and Genoese had a track record of what might at best be called *realpolitik* and at worst duplicity when it came to any dealings with the Turks. In a further flight of fantasy, the Crusade placed the complete expulsion of the Turks from Thrace and Bulgaria and the saving of Constantinople and the restitution of Jerusalem to Christendom among its objectives.

The land army was nominally led by King Vladislaus but was actually commanded by Hunyadi. The Crusader army consisted of Hungarians, Serbs and a large contingent of German and French knights. Vlad II Dracul sent a force of 7,000 Wallachians under the command of Mircea II. He was once again playing both ends against the middle. His involvement certainly threatened the safety of his two hostage sons and it has been suggested that the declaration of the Crusade changed the way the two young men were treated by the Ottomans. From experiencing a comfortable imprisonment in a fairly well gilded cage and being treated almost as guests who were encouraged to learn Turkish and involve themselves in the martial exercises and pursuits for which the Ottomans were famous, it seems that Radu became the sexual plaything of the sultan or of his son, the future Mehemmed II. Whether Dracula was ever exposed to rape is a matter of conjecture but scrappy documentary evidence exists for his brother's violation. That an adolescent boy would have been profoundly affected by what had become a distinctly unpleasant captivity seems obvious.

The Christian army planned to advance along the Danube, rather than to penetrate deep into Balkan territory as they had done before. Wallachian knowledge and participation would be extremely valuable. Vlad II Dracul agreed to meet Hunyadi at Nicopolis during the Crusade's progress down through Bulgaria to discuss his force's role but did not offer to participate in person.

So the Wallachians were at least present, but what of George Brankovic's Serbs? The eventual failure of the Crusade had several causes but it was certainly in part due to the refusal of the Serbian leaders to participate or even allow the Crusading army to cross their territory.[34] George Brankovic, who had, of course, enthusiastically joined the *Longum Bellum* of 1443 and who had brokered the ten-year truce, had also negotiated a separate peace with Murad II. In holding back from participating in what would become a debacle the Serbian lords were in good company with many other Polish and Hungarian nobles who had also obtained favourable terms from the sultan in 1443.[35] How crucial the Serbian non-participation was in the conflict is indicated by the Venetian senate's assessment of the problems that Murad II faced at this juncture. The senate suggested that the timing for the Crusade was 'propitious'[36] as there were Janissary pay riots in Edirne, uprisings in Albania led by Skanderbeg and now serious attempts by the Byzantines to re-establish themselves in the Peloponnese as the despot of the Morea rebuilt the famous Hexamlion or 6-mile wall that defended the Corinth Isthmus and released yet another pretender to the Ottoman throne. Another strange and apparently serendipitous occurrence at this time was the abdication of Murad II in favour of his 12-year-old son, Mehemmed II. Quite what triggered this hiatus in Murad II's rule and his retirement is largely a matter of conjecture. It is possible that the years of endless warfare and the dogged determination of his enemies – Hunyadi and Karaman – had left him with a determination not to engage in warfare any more. Unfortunately the sultan, like Vlad Dracula, is not available for psychoanalysis.

The Crusader army numbered some 16,000 men but was short on infantry with only a few hundred Czech mercenaries to act as hand-gunners and around 100 war-wagons. There was therefore a preponderance of heavy cavalry and of nobility in the army that bode badly for command and control on the field and for the army's ability to soak up Ottoman attacks. Having no infantry meant there was no platform from which the cavalry could group, and regroup between charges. A cavalry charge is a mass movement, requiring men moving as one – the shock is dissipated if members of the unit arrive piece-meal. Usually knights would withdraw slightly from the front line, usually behind the infantry, to line up before sallying forward. Even this manoeuvre was difficult if the knights were unused to fighting together; indeed it has been suggested that the European charge was a development of the First Crusade that was only possible because the Crusaders fought together over such a protracted period.[37] The knights of the Varna Crusade would not have the advantage of the infantry line or of organisation based on familiarity.

Hunyadi crossed the Danube on 20 September and advanced on the town of Varna, on the Black Sea coast, to break the Turkish ring around Constantinople and to link up with the papal-sponsored fleet. The advance was rapid as fortresses were bypassed and the Ottomans refused to give battle. At Nicopolis on 16 October the Wallachians of Mircea II joined the army. Vlad II Dracul, as we have seen, rode to Nicopolis but then left the Crusade again. The Wallachians partici-pated in the siege of Petretz in Bulgaria and used cannon to destroy the city's walls.

Varna was reached on 9 November. It was an unpleasant surprise to Hunyadi to discover a massive Ottoman army encamped only 4,000 paces to the west and south of his position. His army was trapped with its back to the sea and heavily forested hills and marshes to its north. A council of war was called and Cesarini, backed by several nobles, called for the army to fortify itself in a war-wagon laager and to wait for the papal fleet to arrive. Hunyadi argued for an immediate attack on the Ottoman army and won the support of the king and the majority. It was decided that battle would be offered the next day.

The Venetian–Burgundian fleet had failed to close the Dardanelles due to high winds and the Genoese transported Murad II, who had not retaken the throne but who acted as commander in chief for his son, and a huge number of reinforcements across to Europe. The Byzantine emperor John VIII did not go as far in duplicity as the Genoese, who were probably bribed by Murad II, but he stood aside from the coming conflict for fear of wrecking his delicate relationship with the sultan.

Hunyadi deployed his army in a crescent between the Devina Lake and the Frangen Hills. He may have done this in order to allow the right of his line to face both the Anatolian Ottoman army that made up the left of Murad II's line and the light Ottoman forces that the sultan had sent on to the Frangen Hills. To his rear Hunyadi placed the Wallachians as a reserve, and further back the war-wagon laager and his Czech mercenaries.

Hunyadi stood in the centre with about 3,500 men comprising the king's Polish and Hungarian bodyguards, and Hungarian mercenaries and nobles. Command of the mercenaries was given to the young Stephen Bathory. The left of the Hungarian line faced Murad II's Rumelian troops and was commanded by Michael Szilagyi, Hunyadi's brother-in-law. This was comprised of about 5,000 men, mostly Transylvanian troops and German mercenaries, with some men of the higher Hungarian lords. Hunyadi placed his main strength on the right. Six thousand men were placed under the command of Bishop Jan Dominek of Varadin. Cardinal Cesarini commanded a contingent of German Crusaders, and the Bishop of Erlau and Talotsi, the governor of Slavonia, commanded their own men.

Murad II had 15,000 to 20,000 *sipahis* on his right, another 15,000 on his left and his centre was comprised of some 10,000 Janissaries and other infantry levies well dug in and behind barricades on a small hill. He pinned the peace treaty of 1443 above his tent as evidence of the Hungarians' perfidy. As noted above, he was also able to spare light horses and archers for the Frangen Hills. If, as the chroniclers have reported it, Vlad II Dracul truly did say to Hunyadi and Vladislaus that even the sultan's hunting party contained more men than the crusading host could ever hope to muster, then he showed a prescience sadly lacking among his contemporaries.

A sudden wind blew up and knocked down all of the Christian banners except that of Vladislaus III and then Murad II began his attack on the left and from the Frangen Hills. The bishops of Erlau and Varadin lost control of themselves and their troops and plunged into the attacking Ottomans. This immediately exposed the centre's flank. The bishops were also rapidly surrounded. Talotsi led his men to their aid and into the melee.

Murad II then sent his right wing of *sipahi*s against the Hungarian left but Hunyadi countered this with an attack he led personally against the Ottoman right from the centre. He effectively flanked the Ottoman right and the Rumelians fled before the onslaught. Parts of the Hungarian left penetrated so far behind Murad II's line that they were even able to enjoy some looting. Hunyadi's action and the filling of the gap left in his centre by the Wallachian reserve seemed to have turned the battle back to the Hungarians' advantage but the right wing was in fact near collapse and only Talotsi was able to extract himself and his troops. They withdrew to the war-wagon laager from where they would have seen the rest of the Hungarian right wing fleeing the field and the Wallachians deserting it. They stopped only to loot the Ottoman camp before riding back to Wallachia.

Despite the above, and due to Hunyadi's energy and bravery, the battle remained winnable. Hunyadi led part of the Hungarian left and centre across the battlefield again to attack the Ottoman left. The Royal Guards joined him and when the Beylerbey of Anatolia was killed the Ottoman cavalry broke. Murad II had only his Janissaries and infantry levies left on the field.

Victory was snatched away from Hunyadi by Vladislaus III. Hunyadi warned the king to wait for the whole army to reform before engaging the Ottoman centre. Vladislaus III was, however, swayed by nobles in his bodyguard who were jealous of Hunyadi's reputation and who wanted their sovereign to claim the glory for the victory. He charged the Janissary line. Murad II's troops were hard pressed but their withering fire destroyed the king's cavalry and killed Vladislaus III. What remained of the Polish and Hungarian army fled the field. There was, of course, no infantry line to hold the field and to give time for the cavalry to regroup.

The Ottoman losses were enormous and far larger than the 10,000 that the Hungarians lost. Murad II is quoted with having said Wellington-like after the battle, 'may Allah never grant me another such victory'. He had technically beaten Hunyadi as he held the field, but his army was too exhausted to capitalise on their success and there was no pursuit of the Hungarians for a day.

The Hungarians had lost their king and Cardinal Cesarini also fell on the field. Both deaths were disputed, with the Curia in Rome refusing to believe that Cesarini was dead and a myth growing up about Vladislaus surviving the battle but taking his shame at having lost the battle with him on a pilgrimage to the Holy Land before ending up in Madeira, where he denied his identity until his death of old age.

The Hungarians' major commanders, Hunyadi, Szilagyi and Talotsi, all survived the battle. Hunyadi was captured by a Wallachian lord during his return to Hungary and handed over to Vlad II Dracul.

Vlad II Dracul had been busy in the weeks after Varna. He joined the Burgundian–Venetian fleet that had failed to stop the Ottomans crossing the straits as it sailed into the Black Sea and along the Danube searching for Hunyadi and also aiming to besiege Nicopolis. Vlad II Dracul supplied the fleet and took part in assaults on Turkish garrisons, on one occasion with such enthusiasm that he wrecked a bombard by firing it too frequently and not allowing it to cool properly between shots. He also proposed an ambush on Ottoman troops after offering them a fake guarantee of safe conduct. The galley commanders were apparently appalled by any such suggestion. He also managed to take the fortress of Giurgiu and several other towns along the Danube. Giurgiu was taken after wood was piled up against its walls and then lit, firing the wooden turrets of the fortress. Vlad II Dracul also recognised one of the garrison as a man who had taken his father into captivity in Gallipoli on the sultan's orders. He beheaded the man at once.

The fleet also took along a pretender to the Ottoman throne, a man named Savci who claimed to be Murad II's older brother. He was shown to the Turkish garrison of Silistra but their only response was to fire on the galley on which he was making his speech to them.

Vlad II Dracul and Mircea II demanded Hunyadi's execution on a charge of wrecking the Christians' chances in the Crusade by a refusal to listen to Vlad II Dracul's counsel, but the higher lords of Wallachia refused to countenance this and Hunyadi was released, much to Vlad II Dracul's chagrin. Hunyadi's mind must have been made up for him about the Prince of Wallachia by Vlad II Dracul's acts. He had to go.

The Crusade of Varna was the last concerted attempt by the medieval Christian West to drive the Ottomans from Europe. Its defeat effectively sealed Byzantium's fate and the rest of the Balkan Christian states were left to fend for themselves. George Brankovic reaffirmed his vassalage to the Ottoman sultan shortly after the battle. His resistance to his father-in-law seemed over; he had lost much by his previous resistance including the ravaging of his lands by Ottoman regular and irregular troops and the blinding of two of his sons whilst they were in the 'care' of the Ottomans as hostages for his good behaviour. It is reported that their sister, Murad II's wife, had pleaded for the punishment not to be carried out but her protests fell on deaf ears. In 1446 Vlad II Dracul also accepted Ottoman suzerainty, most likely for fear of Hunyadi's revenge.

The years that followed Varna were marked by a severe and unsurprising deterioration in relations between Serbia and Hungary. Brankovic consistently refused to support any of Hunyadi's endeavours against the Turks and, as in 1444, even refused to allow Hunyadi to march troops through Serbia to the front. Brankovic and the Serbs concentrated instead on trying to eject the Venetians from Zeta and on fighting with the Bosnians over Srebrenica and its lucrative mines.

Murad II resumed his retirement after Varna but, once again, it was temporary. Mehemmed II, surprisingly given his later achievements, was incapable of controlling his high officials, and in 1446 a coup by the young sultan's grand wazir required Murad II to return to the throne once more. The old sultan returned to the field with surprising aplomb.

The Morea was ravaged in retribution for its support of the Crusade of Varna and vassalage was forced from its rulers. Practically all of mainland Greece was conquered and in 1447 Murad II undertook an arduous campaign against the Albanian partisans of Skanderbeg.

Hunyadi became regent of Hungary upon the death of Vladislaus III. King Ladislaus Posthumous, now Ladislaus V, was raised to the throne by virtue of the agreement of 1442 that ended the civil war but was only 5 years old. Furthermore, the Habsburgs would not allow Ladislaus to return to Hungary and he remained in the care of his guardian, the Holy Roman Emperor Frederick III.

As noted briefly above, Vlad Dracula had also by now had 'guardians' in the form of the Ottomans for several years. Before that point his childhood had, in fact, been fairly pleasant. He went with his mother and two brothers to his father's newly acquired capital in 1437. At Tirgoviste he began his training as a knight. He would have been taught how to fight with the sword, and the rudiments of jousting, archery and horsemanship. Apparently he was a skilled rider even from a young age.

He also received instruction in Italian, French and Hungarian. He would have learnt the Cyrillic alphabet for reading the Church Slavonic, in which chancellery documents of the Wallachian court were produced, but also Latin for international diplomacy. Despite Wallachia's almost single-tier nobility there would still have been in the court of Tirgoviste a distinct understanding instilled into all that they were blue-bloods, men of destiny and God's anointed.

It is likely that both Dracula and his brothers were confirmed in the Catholic faith by their parents but they would have been exposed to the Orthodox faith simply because so many individuals at court would have been followers of the Romanian church and because conversion to Orthodoxy was a legal necessity for any future Prince of Wallachia.

The education that Dracula and Radu would have undergone in Ottoman Anatolia would also have been based around the precepts of producing princes but, of course, young hostages were also supposed to be released back into the world as vassals, and loyal vassals at that. There was no forced conversion to Islam; such a thing would have been counterproductive in the moulding of future vassals to rule Christian lands in the name of the sultan. Dracula would certainly have had contact, perhaps even sustained, with the future Mehemmed II, later to be his most deadly enemy.

To the languages he had been exposed to as a child Vlad Dracula now added Turkish, in which he seems to have been fluent. It has been suggested that he was not an easy pupil to teach and as a youth he was prone to temper tantrums, for which he was whipped frequently.

Radu appears to have had the more attractive personality of the pair and soon had many admirers, both female and male at the court. An intense hatred also seems to have developed between the two brothers at this time.

As noted above, the situation of the two princes took a turn for the worse in 1443 with Hunyadi's successes and Vlad II Dracul's association with the Hungarian warlord – however unwilling it was. Their confinement became more unpleasant but, whatever happened to Radu in the chambers of the fortress the two brothers were kept in, the fact remains that he also became the Ottomans' favoured candidate for the Wallachian throne, over and above his older brother. Even after Vlad Dracula was sent to claim his dead father's throne, Radu remained at the Ottoman court and did not leave until 1462. He was also raised to the rank of *sipahi* in the sultan's guard in 1447.

Dracula appears to have been much less favoured by his captors and turned inward to gain an adamantine hardness as he learnt the age-old lesson of every prince – that you can trust no one.

The two boys were no doubt a bargaining chip in the negotiations between Murad II and their father in the summer of 1447. Under this treaty the usual tribute and *devshirme* was required of Vlad II Dracul, but he was also expected to give up the fortress of Giurgiu.

Hunyadi started a war of words against Vlad II Dracul, portraying him as a turncoat who secretly supported the Ottomans. Then in November 1447 he came in person to meet with his candidate for the Wallachian throne, Vladislaus. Hunyadi then crossed the Carpathians to invest Tirgoviste. Vlad II Dracul prepared for a siege but a *boyar* revolt led by followers of the Dnesti clan took place in the city. Mircea II was captured by the citizens of the city and buried alive.

Vlad II Dracul succeeded in fleeing the city and headed for the Danube. He was, however, caught and killed in the marshes of the village of Blteni close to Bucharest. Hunyadi initially proclaimed himself ruler of Wallachia and then passed the Crown to Vladislaus II. In early 1448 the Ottomans released Vlad Dracula, a man who would outdo his father in terms of his lack of chivalry and in the cruelties he would inflict on his enemies.

3

TO CATCH A SULTAN:
DRACULA'S FIRST REIGN

He can, when once he find his way, come out from anything or into anything, no matter how close it be bound or even fused up with fire-solder you call it. He can see in the dark – no small power this, in a world which is one half shut from the light.[1]

The general history of this period is one of ephemeral alliances that were made for short-term gains. The fluctuation of the Serbs, Byzantines and other Balkan powers between union with and animosity towards the Ottomans appears at first sight somewhat bizarre. Vlad Dracula's actions both as lord of Wallachia and during his time off the throne are the perfect example of a pattern that ran right through the Balkans in the post-Varna period. The action of this time must also be viewed against the feudal nature of the Balkan states in which power was often devolved to lesser lords. These petty despots had as their chief aim of policy the survival of their own territories; Dracula again was an exemplar of this principle. Higher politics and ideologies were largely forgotten. Furthermore, it had become by this time a 'standard practice' in Balkan diplomacy to make alliances with a potentially threatening force in the short term against other enemies. Indeed, it has been suggested[2] that the Ottomans were successful in the Balkans in the second half of the fifteenth century because they were the only power following a consistent policy. Furthermore, as the Balkans remained fractured and disunited the Ottoman Sultans' 'project' of creating a centralised state with all power flowing from the Porte was completed by Mehemmed II. It was made possible by his conquest of Constantinople.

At the outset of his regency Hunyadi had been faced by a major crisis born of the feudal system. Early in 1445 the Ban of Slavonia died. His brother was killed in the fighting that ensued and, as he was the Prior of Vrana, his enemies took the opportunity to also place their own candidate for the Bishopric of Zagreb in place. This Croatian emergency distracted Hunyadi from Vlad II Dracul, who as we have seen was not chased from the Wallachian throne until 1447. Hunyadi sent an army against Croatia. His forces plundered large areas of Croatia and forced the counts of Celje to relinquish the towns and forced a settlement on the disputants. He also appointed John Szekely, a Hungarian, to the newly created position of vice ban of Dalmatia, Croatia and Slavonia. Despite the loss of prestige that Hungarian arms and Hunyadi might have suffered after Varna, the Croatian settlement makes it clear that Hungary was still the dominant power in the Balkans in this period and Hunyadi remained the strongman of the Christian East.

Serbia, however, remained unafraid of Hunyadi, or perhaps more correctly George Brankovic was more afraid of Murad II than he was of the Hungarians. In 1448 Hunyadi demanded Serbian participation in a new Crusade. Brankovic refused and also rebuffed the demand for safe passage for the Hungarian army through Serbia. Hunyadi may very well at this juncture have threatened Brankovic that if he defeated the Ottomans his very next act would be to seize Serbia and place a more worthy prince upon its throne.

Meanwhile, in Albania, the career of one of the truly great heroes of resistance to the Ottomans in the Balkans was just beginning. We need now to go back a few years to see how George Kastrioti, who served the Ottomans loyally until his desertion at Nis in 1443 as Iskander Bey, began a career of resistance that would span some twenty years.

Albania existed as a vassal of the Ottoman Empire in Skanderbeg's youth. He was sent to the Ottoman court in 1423 possibly as a noble hostage. He underwent military training in Edirne, converted to Islam and took Iskander Bey as his Muslim name. He was granted a *timar* near to the territories controlled by his father, John. This apparently worried his father, who suspected that the sultan might well order the son to take over the lands of the father. John Kastrioti also had other worries – squeezed as he was between the Venetians on the coast and the Ottomans in the plains. The delicate diplomacy this required is indicated by the letters he sent to the Venetian senate apologising for his son's actions against the Venetians in the service of Murad II. In fact, John Kastrioti did later lose almost all of his lands – not to his son but to the Ottoman governor of Skopje.

Skanderbeg was first summoned home by relatives when the Albanian lords George Arianiti and Andrew Thopia organised a rebellion against the Ottomans in 1432. He, however, remained loyal to Murad II and continued to rise through the ranks; he was now a *sipahi*. The revolt was finally put down in 1436 and in 1437, for a brief time, Skanderbeg was appointed as a governor. He returned to 'line service' in 1438 with the command of a cavalry unit of 5,000 men.

Skanderbeg's father died in 1437 and he and his brother, Stanisha, claimed and were given the same standing as their father had enjoyed with both the Republic of Ragusa and the Republic of Venice. This was despite the fact that Skanderbeg was fighting during this time against the forces of Hunyadi, and Ragusa 'technically' recognised the Hungarian king as its suzerain. In 1440 Skanderbeg was appointed as the *Sancakbey* of Dibra. This brought him back into close communications with the population of his father's former lands and also with other Albanian noble families. Whether this or the growing successes of Hunyadi against the Ottomans caused Skanderbeg's defection can only be conjecture. As noted above, in early November 1443 Skanderbeg deserted during the Battle of Nis.

Skanderbeg arrived at the city of Kruje in central Albania at the end of November. He handed the governor a forged letter purportedly from Murad II and gained control of the city. He quickly gained control of his father's lands and abandoned Islam. He raised his standard, with its red background and black double-headed eagle on it, essentially the modern-day Albanian flag, in rebellion, or rather joined a rebellion that was already taking place.

In August 1443 the Arianiti had again revolted against the Ottomans in central Albania. Skanderbeg's first achievement was, in March 1444, to bring all the Albanian princes together. This took place in the city of Lezhe and the league they formed was named after the city. The Arianiti also became allied with the Kastrioti and Skanderbeg married Andronike Arianiti.

The first challenge for the League came in the summer of 1444, in the Plain of Torvioll. The League's newly united army, under Skanderbeg's command, faced the Ottoman general Ali Pasha and his army of 25,000 men. Skanderbeg had 7,000 infantry and 8,000 cavalry under his command. Three thousand of the cavalry were skilfully placed, undetected, in a forest to the Ottomans' rear. The Ottomans found themselves surrounded by the Albanians as the 'phantom' cavalry emerged on to the field. Ottoman losses may have been as great as 10,000 killed or captured. Similar victories followed in October 1445, when the Ottoman garrison forces of Ohrid were decimated, and at the Battle of Otonete in September 1446.

At Otonete Murad II had sent a force of 15,000 cavalry under Mustafa Pasha into Albania. In fact, the Pasha's army and the war of pillage Murad II had planned was only part of a larger venture designed to challenge Hunyadi. Mustafa Pasha split his forces, presumably to extend the range of their destruction, but Skanderbeg took advantage of the Ottomans' reduced forces at Otonete and also completely surprised them. As his troops charged through the camps they slaughtered nearly all the Turks. Five thousand were killed and only 300 prisoners were taken. As a result Mustafa Pasha could do no more than protect the border and the flank of the main Ottoman army. Skanderbeg had saved Albania from plunder and destruction and was becoming famous all over Europe.

The problem was that he was also soon enough becoming infamous in the eyes of the Venetians. At first the republic viewed Skanderbeg as an effective buffer between their Adriatic towns and the Ottomans; indeed the city of Lezhe was even in Venetian territory. The Venetians' view changed, however, as Skanderbeg looked increasingly likely to lead Albania into independence under himself and not just free of the Ottomans but also of Venice and Ragusa. A dispute over border fortresses led quickly to the Albanian–Venetian War of 1447–48. Rewards including pensions of 100 gold ducats per year were offered for the assassination of Skanderbeg and the Venetians opened negotiations with the Ottomans to arrange simultaneous attacks on his lands. These talks apparently bore fruit in May 1448 when an Ottoman army led personally by Murad II and Prince Mehemmed laid siege to the Albanian castle of Svetigrad. The Albanian garrison held out until late summer and Skanderbeg harassed the Ottomans as well as defeating the Venetians near Shkoder, but the castle was lost to Murad II. Skanderbeg revenged himself with sieges of Venetian Durazzo and Lezhe, and sent envoys to his Serbian neighbour, George Brankovic, who agreed to go to war against Venice but not against the Turks. Brankovic hoped to obtain parts of the old Lazarevic principality of Zeta.

In August 1448 Skanderbeg also beat the Ottoman Mustafa Pasha in the field at Diber. The fact that the Ottoman threat to Skanderbeg seemed to be receding, the pressure he was applying to Venetian possessions and Skanderbeg's negotiations with Alfonso V of Aragon, who as King Alfonso I of Naples and of Sicily was becoming a rival to the republic in the eastern Mediterranean, forced the Venetians to offer a peace treaty to Skanderbeg.

The treaty signed in October 1448 was generous enough as it ceded territory to Skanderbeg, gave him tax-free buying privileges in Durazzo and paid him handsomely to desist from attacking the republic, but Skanderbeg had other motivations for securing peace with the Venetians. Hunyadi was in southern Serbia with an army and had invited Skanderbeg to join him in an expedition against the Ottomans.[3]

Hunyadi had been refused safe passage across Serbia by Brankovic so when his army traversed Serbian territory he treated it as enemy land and plundered it. Brankovic's reaction was to send envoys to warn Murad II of the Hungarian attack, to explain that the Hungarians' passage through Serbia was by force and perhaps even to offer information on the size of the Hungarian force and its make-up. What was perhaps more significant was that Brankovic was able to prevent many Serbian lords from joining the venture, though some were present on the battlefield of Kosovo, and he prevented Skanderbeg from joining Hunyadi in time for the battle. Skanderbeg did all he could to reach Hunyadi and has been reported as being only 20 miles from Kosovo Polje as the Hungarian army broke apart. Upon his return, Skanderbeg treated Brankovic's lands to an even greater wasting than the Hungarians had. Perhaps he recognised, just as some modern historians have, that if Skanderbeg and Brankovic had been with Hunyadi on the field at Kosovo the battle's outcome might very well have been different.[4]

Hunyadi's army advanced into southern Serbia in October 1448, where at least some troops sent by Skanderbeg joined them as well as the Wallachians of Vladislaus II. Hunyadi's objective was to conquer Macedonia and Southern Serbia, to drive a wedge between Greece and Bulgaria and to effectively split Ottoman Rumelia in two. His army was mainly Transylvanian with a large number, perhaps up to 3,000, of German hand-gunners. There were also war-wagons and plentiful artillery pieces. The heavy cavalry was a mix of mercenaries and the nobles, and there seems to have been a significant amount of light cavalry from Wallachia and Transylvania.

At Kosovo Polje, the site of Serbia's defeat almost sixty years earlier, Hunyadi rested the army and was possibly waiting for Skanderbeg. Then, on 17 October, Hunyadi's forces were surprised by detachments of Murad II's army moving on to the Kosovo plain to their north. Hunyadi had believed that Murad II and the main Ottoman forces were campaigning in Asia Minor.

Hunyadi could now either retreat into Serbia, away from Hungary, and face the possibility of attacks on his marching army, or stand and fight. He chose to fight, for though he had been surprised he had reconnoitred the plain of Kosovo and he felt he had a chance of at least stopping any further reinforcements arriving for the Ottomans if he could take the passes that led towards Ottoman-occupied Albania and Pristina. Detachments of light cavalry were sent to take the passes and, despite reports that they were involved in bloody struggles to achieve their task, they were secured for the Hungarians.

By the night of 17 October a vast Ottoman army had deployed on the southern bank of the River Lab. Hills rose up protecting Murad II's eastern or left flank and his right flank was protected by the River Sitnica. Murad II's camp was positioned on the northern bank of the River Lab. His army probably numbered some 50,000 to 60,000 men. *Sipahis* from both Rumelia and Anatolia were on the field as well as the sultan's guard of Janissaries and his *ghulam* cavalry. The Anatolian levies made up the right wing, with the Rumelians on the left and slightly in advance of the centre and the right. The light horse of each wing rode out ahead of the heavy *sipahi* cavalry lines. The centre of the Ottoman deployment was exclusively infantry and artillery, in three lines. The last line was comprised of Janissaries with the sultan; the second line was artillery, dug in. A defensive ditch separated the artillery line from the first line of infantry made up of *azab* levies.

Hunyadi was obviously attempting to ensure there would be no repeat of Varna at Kosovo. He placed his German and Bohemian hand-gunners behind the war-wagons and field works. He placed the Albanian and Wallachian horsemen, his knights and horse archers out on the flanks. He had placed his camp on a hill and he used this and his supply and war-wagons to create a fortified area. The artillery train was placed among the wagons; the rise gave the cannon a dominating field of fire towards the Ottoman camp. It was a classic 'Hussite' deployment with the wagons anchored to each other by chains and with their driving shafts removed or pulled up to reduce the gaps between each 'little fortress'. Shield bearers would also have been deployed between the wagons and the protective panels for the wheels would have been dropped to make the wall complete. There would have been both hand-gunners and crossbowmen and archers lined up inside the *waggonberg* ready to relieve and to keep the fire rate from within the fortress high. It seems that Hunyadi also kept a unit of the Wallachian horse with him inside the *waggonberg* ready to make a sortie provided that the Ottomans broke before his guns and artillery.

Hunyadi deployed his cavalry in front of his fortified camp and in the flanks in two lines. The centre of the first line had two lines comprised of light horse in the first line and a second line comprised entirely of heavy cavalry. The rest of the light horse was pushed out to the wings.

Hunyadi took personal command of the centre of the second line of cavalry comprised of royal troops, mercenaries and the Transylvanians. The Wallachian knights were also with him under their own banners. Hungarian higher lords and their knights made up the right and left cavalry wings.

The infantry was placed behind fortifications and among the war-wagons. Hunyadi perhaps planned to use the *waggonberg* as a point behind which he could reorganise his cavalry should they undertake any charges against the Ottomans.

It seems that neither side wanted to attack. This made sense for Hunyadi as he was still awaiting Skanderbeg, and perhaps Murad II knew that in order to leave the field the Hungarians had to push him from it – he had certainly set up for a defensive battle. Eventually, skirmishing broke out between the Rumelian cavalry and the Hungarian right. The Hungarian light horse engaged, fired and retired, using the support of their heavy knights to allow them to attack repeatedly and then retreat to regroup. The pressure was, however, mounting and Hunyadi eventually had to release knights and light cavalry from his central body into the fight on his right. Murad II then released his Anatolian cavalry against the Hungarian left and the Wallachian horsemen. The Wallachians fled behind the heavy knights, and the Anatolians, after this initial success, were pushed back when Hunyadi led knights from the centre out to meet them.

At this point the Ottoman *azab* infantry was sent forward to attack a centre that was denuded of much of its heavy cavalry. They initially broke the line but were then met by a hail of fire from the *waggonberg*. The Hungarian infantry counter-attacked and closed the line. The Ottomans had now been stopped on the left and in the centre. Seeing this, Hunyadi pushed more men out to the right where they broke the Rumelians, many of whom fled into the hills, though many also returned to the Ottoman camp to fight another day.

The events of the night of 18 October are unclear. There may have been a Hungarian night attack on the Ottoman line but what seems more likely is that there was a continuing and furious exchange of cannon fire between the two sides. This was unusual perhaps in the period and may have been born of a desire on the part of Hunyadi to push the Ottomans from the field. It was certainly unusual for the Ottomans not to leave the field after one day of battle and then regroup. Murad II had evidently decided that stubborn application was to be the watchword for the night of 18 October and there is some evidence that the Ottomans were imitating Hungarian tactics as Murad II drew up his troops between wagons and covered the gaps between the wagons with shields.

Murad II had certainly lost troopers from his Rumelian left in the previous day's battle but his deployment on the morning of 19 October was entirely similar to that of the day before, excepting that he took the cavalry of Thessaly away from the Rumelians and sent them on a wide march around the Hungarian army. Turakhan, the Beylerbey of Rumelia, led this contingent personally.

Hunyadi may have learnt of the sultan's plan from deserters. He strengthened the left of his army at a cost to his centre and bolstered it further with the cavalry reserve. The right flank remained unchanged. The bulk of the infantry were placed in the centre, backed by most of his mobile artillery.

The Ottomans began the day more decisively than on 18 October. The cavalry of Anatolia came against the reinforced Hungarian left but were held. The Rumelians engaged in skirmishing and their light horsemen almost turned the flank of the Hungarians.

Hunyadi then led his centre against the Ottoman infantry. The *azab* light infantry were driven from the line by artillery and gunfire. The Ottoman artillery and Janissaries were able to halt the advancing Hungarian infantry but when Hunyadi brought the Hungarian cavalry into the fray the Janissary line broke.

To his credit Murad II responded imaginatively and quickly. He ordered his camp commander to reinforce the centre with the camp guards and the army followers. This somewhat motley infusion of men, perhaps surprisingly, was enough to pull the Ottoman line back together and allow the Janissaries to recover their trenches. Hunyadi took what remained of his attackers back to the line in front of the *waggonberg*.

The battle was balanced but there was no obvious place to make a breakthrough for either side until Turakhan Bey arrived with his detached cavalry behind the Hungarian left wing. The Wallachians began surrendering and the Anatolian *sipahis* began to roll up the Hungarian left. Hunyadi ordered a retreat and the Hungarian centre and left showed powerful discipline to be able to disengage and pull away from the Ottomans in good order, although the right wing was annihilated and John Szekely, one of Hunyadi's key lieutenants, was killed.

It was all over, barring the retreat from the field of Hunyadi's remaining troops, by the early hours of the morning. He organised a feint of cavalry troops to distract any Ottoman pursuit and then left the camp with the majority of his forces. He also left a screen of infantry behind to cover the withdrawal. The Ottomans had been badly damaged during their victory; it took them a considerable time to overcome the thinly defended Hungarian camp and Hunyadi and most of his army were able to break away.

Losses in the battle are disputed but it seems likely that, though they lost the battle, the Hungarians fared rather better in a casualty count. Their losses may have been as low as 6,000 men while figures for the Ottomans go as high as 30,000 to 40,000 men. The Rumelians had suffered badly on day one and the *azab* infantry had both been caught by the Hungarian cannon while attacking and hit by Hunyadi's assault on the centre on day two. Murad II's losses explain why there was no effective pursuit of the Hungarians, whose most effective enemies during their flight to Hungary turned out to be the Serbs and not the Turks.

Hunyadi was captured by Brankovic and did not return to Hungary until December. The delay added to his defeat eroded his domestic support. He could not return to the offensive and of his allies, Wallachia would once again accept Ottoman suzerainty, and Albania became the target of Ottoman attentions. Serbia was rewarded for its 'neutrality' by another decade of vassal existence under Murad II and his successor. Brankovic had ordered that all Hungarian soldiers found in Serbia after the battle be taken prisoner. He demanded a huge ransom for Hunyadi as compensation for the damage done by the Hungarians on their way to Kosovo Polje. A payment was promised and Hunyadi was released; it was never paid and the next year there was very deliberate Hungarian plundering of Serbia. Civil war in Bosnia soured relations further as Hunyadi backed the king, Stefan Tomas, and Brankovic lent his support to the Kosaca and Vukcic clans. Hunyadi also confiscated most of Brankovic's lands in Hungary.

With his relationship with Hungary at its nadir and with Skanderbeg also a confirmed enemy, Brankovic had few friends left. He did, however, and ironically given what would occur in 1453, maintain good relations with the Byzantines. His son had married into the Palaiologos dynasty of the Morea and he funded the repair of one of the towers of Constantinople's walls. Of course, Serbia's other friends were the Ottomans but they were beginning to act more and more like puppet masters, and even former possessions such as Pristina were now more or less under Ottoman control with Brankovic having no say in the running of the city or able to draw any commercial value from it.

Since Hunyadi had been effectively neutralised by his loss at Kosovo, Murad II concentrated his attentions on Albania. The peace deal that Skanderbeg had made in order to join Hunyadi in 1448 now looked all the more valuable.

The Ottomans invaded Albania again in 1449 and 1450. In 1449 Skanderbeg may have been forced to pay tribute; this was a tactic he would use again in the next few years whenever he was short of manpower or unable to hold ground against the Ottomans. He bought himself some breathing space in which to reorganise an ongoing resistance that was both impressive and lengthy. In fact, it also seems likely that Skanderbeg never paid the sum of 6,000 ducats that he promised Murad II in 1449 and he renounced his suzerainty the next year. In June 1450 Murad II moved against the fortress city of Kruje with a large army. Skanderbeg undertook a scorched earth policy, left a garrison of only 1,500 men in Kruje and then departed with much of his forces for the surrounding mountains. With a series of hit-and-run raids on the besieging Ottoman forces and its supply caravans, which inflicted heavy losses on the sultan's forces, he kept Kruje secure until the end of the campaigning season and Murad II's retirement from the field.

The Venetians, despite their peace with Skanderbeg, sold supplies to the Ottomans during the first half of the siege. Perhaps they did not want to pay him the monies agreed in the peace treaty of 1448. Skanderbeg attacked Venetian caravans in revenge and this brought the leaders of Durazzo to the negotiating table as intermediaries. It was agreed that, in return for a truce, the Venetian merchants would stop supplying the Ottomans. Kruje's garrison also repelled three major direct assaults on the city's walls. Murad II's troops attempted to cut the water supply of the city but this failed, as did attempts at sapping its walls. Bribery of the garrison also failed and camp sickness carried off more and more of Murad II's troops. He took what remained of the army back to Edirne, where he died a month later.

Murad II had been a most remarkable man. At the outset of his reign he was the sultan of a state that was just emerging from a protracted and damaging civil war during which power had slipped away from the sultan's office and the Porte. European and Asian vassals had also loosened their ties to the sultans during the *Fitnet Devri*. Murad II, through both victories on the field and through a grim determination, had re-established Ottoman authority in the Balkans and in Anatolia by the end of his reign. He also oversaw a modernisation of the Ottoman army with the Janissaries adopting firearms on a large scale during his rule. This made them an even more deadly fighting force but, as we have discussed above, it also drove power back to the sultan, as did the extending of the *devshirme* as more and more men were enslaved and then manumitted as the 'sultan's men'.[5] Murad II's son, Mehemmed II, came to the throne in 1451 at the head of a state and army that had the most extensive and sophisticated artillery in Europe, the largest standing army and an outlook that looked distinctly towards further conquest in Europe.

Back in Albania, Skanderbeg accepted suzerainty under Alfonso of Naples in 1451. He became captain general of the King of Aragon following the Treaty of Gaeta in March and obtained a detachment of 100 Catalan soldiers to garrison Kruje. He was more loyal to this new feudal lord than he had been to Murad II but he still effectively remained an independent ruler. He was also a ruler with few allies. He was largely deserted by the other lords of Albania and Murad II gained a posthumous victory over him as Skanderbeg was reduced to control over Kruje and little else. Albania also suffered poor harvests and famine at this time. Skanderbeg was still, however, able to defeat another Ottoman army sent to Albania by the new sultan in 1452. Then, for a while there was no more war waged on the Albanians by Mehemmed II as Constantinople became the target of the new sultan.

So, Brankovic of Serbia profited from Kosovo, Hunyadi of Hungary lost, as did Skanderbeg of Albania, but what of a man who had stood aside from all the action? For Vlad Dracula, the Christian defeat at Kosovo presented him with an opportunity to claim the throne his father had held until his removal by Hunyadi.

Dracula may not have heard of the demise of his father until the very end of 1447. With his father's death Dracula's hostage status ended but he was offered and accepted a commission in the Ottoman army and it was made clear to him by the Porte that he was considered the rightful Prince of Wallachia. Now perhaps in 1448, among the Christians' distress and disorder, the time was ripe to make his bid. Whether Dracula returned to Wallachia with two precious betrothals from his father: his sword of Toledo steel and his collar with the insignia of the Order of the Dragon on it cannot be known. The story goes that a loyal retainer of Vlad II Dracul, a certain Cazan, carried these items from the dying prince to his offspring in Edirne. According to the legend, Cazan also informed Vlad Dracula in graphic detail of how his father and older brother died. Vlad Dracula apparently swore to kill Vladislaus II in person.

With a small force of horsemen either sponsored or supplied by Murad II or supplied by Mustafa Hasan Pasha of the Danube provinces, Vlad Dracula took the opportunity of Vladislaus II's presence on the battlefield of Kosovo to claim the Crown of Wallachia. He, however, failed to seize Vladislaus II. Vlad Dracula may have assumed that Vladislaus II was dead on the field, but he was very much alive. He escaped capture by Vlad Dracula's men with the assistance of the Prince of Moldavia, Petru III, gathered up troops who were returning piecemeal to Hungary and Wallachia from Kosovo and rode against the usurper. It did not take Vladislaus II long to track down Vlad Dracula and defeat him in battle. And for once a war literally was all over by Christmas.

Vlad Dracula fled first to Edirne but then Vladislaus II began also to show an inclination towards the Turks. This was pure *realpolitik*, with Hunyadi apparently out of the game Vladislaus II was looking to secure his lands against Ottoman reprisals. Vlad Dracula, perhaps sensing that he was in danger if Vladislaus II's overtures were accepted by Murad II, then fled to Moldavia and threw himself on the mercy of its court. Fortunately for him, Moldavia was at this point far from the main field of Ottoman–Christian conflict and was also passing through an interregnum involving the Hungarians and a family attachment to Hunyadi. Petru III 'enjoyed' a brief reign between April and October 1448 and was married to a sister of Hunyadi who is unnamed in the scanty sources available for the period. There were no children but with his Hungarian wife Petru III also got a Hungarian–Croatian advisor, Csupor de Monoszlo. This nobleman, who had formerly commanded troops for Hunyadi, helped Petru III to depose his brother Roman II. Upon Petru III's abrupt death Csupor ascended the throne, retaining it until December 1448. Vlad Dracula was, for now, safe if sidelined from events in Wallachia.

Bogdan II then ascended the Moldavian throne. Vlad Dracula was related to him through his father's marriage to one of his sisters. Furthermore, Bogdan II had sought refuge at Vlad II Dracul's court some years before so now he was simply reciprocating that favour.

Vlad Dracula stayed in Moldavia from December 1449 until October 1451. He became close to the man who would one day be Stephen III 'the Great' of Moldavia. It is likely that Vlad Dracula fought with Stephen and Bogdan II against the Poles at Crasna.

Dracula's stay in Moldavia ended when Bogdan II was murdered by his brother, Peter Aron, in October 1451. He fled with Stephen to Transylvania via the Borgo Pass. This was a dangerous plan as Hunyadi was in control of Transylvania but there were few other options left to the princes.

Vlad Dracula and Stephen headed towards the city of Brasov, by way of Sighisoara. Vlad Dracula had received encouragement from the leaders of Brasov prior to his first attempt on Vladislaus II's throne and he hoped that the *boyars* there would also support him again now.

Hunyadi received word that Vlad Dracula was back in Transylvania and demanded of all the cities that they apprehend him and offer him no succour. Vlad Dracula went into hiding until September 1452, when agents of Vladislaus II discovered him in the vicinity of Brasov. He fled again, this time to Sibiu.

Vladislaus II brought Vlad Dracula in out of the cold through his Turkish policy. Hunyadi had been growing ever more suspicious of the man he had placed on the throne of Wallachia. In January 1451 Vladislaus II had sent a delegation of *boyars* to congratulate the new sultan, Mehemmed II, upon his accession to the throne. This, in Hunyadi's eyes, would have made him little better as a trustworthy ally than Vlad II Dracul had been. Hunyadi then seized the duchies of Fgra and Amla from the Wallachian prince. These were key entrance points into and across Transylvania. There were then open hostilities with Vladislaus II over these territories.

Whether Hunyadi actually valued Dracula or just saw him as a ready-made replacement for Vladislaus II should the need arise is hard to say but he took Dracula into his service and he accompanied him to the opening of the Hungarian diet at Gyor and formally presented him to Ladislaus V. Dracula was present at the king's coronation in Buda and swore allegiance to the 'new' King of Hungary. Ladislaus V, with the consent of the Transylvanian diet, gave Vlad Dracula responsibility for the defence of the Transylvanian frontier. He was following in his father's footsteps, only now the Transylvanian border was about to become a far more dangerous place as the Ottomans were on the march again under their new sultan, who would soon enough gain the epithet *Fetih*, the conqueror.

Mehemmed II had returned to the Ottoman throne following Murad II's death from a stroke in 1451. He was certainly older and a good deal wiser, but equally Murad II had quelled a lot of the elements within the empire and the ruling clique that had caused the younger Mehemmed so many difficulties during his first reign. Mehemmed II also chose to concentrate his efforts and those of the empire on the final reduction of Constantinople. Attempts had been made by the Muslims ever since the seventh century to take Constantinople and Mehemmed II knew that its conquest would secure his prestige in the *Dar al-Islam* and secure allegiances of the tribes in the hinterlands between Ottoman Anatolia, the Mamluk Empire and the tribal confederations of the Kara-Koyunlu and Ak-Koyunlu.

In fact, as vassals of the Turks, the Byzantines had not even been permitted to strengthen the walls of Constantinople and had had to send troops to fight for the Ottomans for decades; perhaps the cruellest example of this obligation came in 1390 when Byzantine contingents had to help in the reduction of Philadelphia, the last isolated Byzantine outpost in Anatolia. Therefore the conquest would be largely symbolic but Mehemmed II knew it would solidify his power over the high military and administrative officials who had served his father for so long and who had caused him such problems during his earlier reign. Centralisation of funds into the Porte was the only way of ensuring the construction of the vast fleet that would be required for the city's conquest. In simple terms too, the Ottoman Empire was going to apply an enormous part of its military muscle to the Byzantine capital's reduction. This naturally required a vast logistics effort, which could only be directed by a sophisticated and centralised bureaucracy based in the sultan's office.

The battle for Constantinople was therefore also a battle between the new sultan and the old guard of advisors and high officials who had served his father. The Grand Wazir Candarli Halil was the leader of the junta that had surrounded Murad II and he looked likely to frustrate the new sultan and his ambitious plan. He certainly had a rich pedigree. His father, Ibrahim Pasha, had also been Murad II's grand wazir and his grandfather, Ali Pasha Candarli, had been Bayezid I's grand wazir. He was renowned for cautious policy decisions but he had also been the architect of the Ottoman victory at Varna. He had a powerbase within the bureaucracy and religious offices of the government but also enjoyed the support of the Janissary corps. Mehemmed II promoted his own men, men such as Zaganoz Pasha and Shibab al-Din Pasha, into high positions but he dare not take on Candarli Halil directly in 1451, or even in 1453 prior to the assault on Constantinople. Mehemmed II moved quickly after his accession and had his younger brother, Kucuk Ahmed, strangled.

This only left Prince Orhan, living in comfortable exile in Constantinople, as an alternative for the old guard to gather around.

Mehemmed II used an argument based on the near disaster of 1444 when the Crusade of Varna had come so close to splitting Ottoman Rumelia in two. He also emphasised that the then despot of the Morea, Constantine, who had taken such liberties during the Crusade, was now the emperor, Constantine XI of Constantinople. The fact that he then called the Ottomans to a religious duty and to the Holy War was perhaps ironic given his later attitude to *Ghaza*, but more of that later. He is given the speech, 'the *Ghaza* is our basic duty as it was in the case of our fathers. Constantinople, situated in the middle of our domains, protects our enemies and incites them against us. The conquest of this city is therefore essential to the future and to the safety of the Ottoman state.'[6]

Constantine XI's dismissiveness towards the new sultan and his threats to release Orhan would also have encouraged Mehemmed II to contemplate a campaign to finally bring Constantinople into the Islamic world.

The problem was the passage across the Bosporus. The Ottomans, provided that Venice and Genoa and other Western maritime powers answered Byzantium's pleas, would have enormous trouble ensuring the safety of any army crossing the strait and would find any assault on the great chain gate that protected the Golden Gate harbour extremely perilous. In terms of navies, the Muslims had been at a disadvantage against their Western foes since the twelfth century[7] with a revolution in Western shipbuilding techniques having taken place in the late eleventh century.[8] I have written elsewhere of how the Western nations might have even kept Palestine and conquered Egypt in the twelfth and thirteenth centuries through a blockade of Egypt's ports but, of course, the blockade weapon was never applied as feuding and defence of profits between emperor and pope, Venice, Pisa and Genoa and the Angevins and just about everybody else precluded it.[9]

Mehemmed II worked hard at resetting the balance of power in the eastern Mediterranean. One of Mehemmed II's first actions was to begin the construction of a massive fortress named Rumelia Hisar at the narrowest point of the Bosporus on the European shore in 1451.

He also began a rapid programme of shipbuilding and recruitment of Christian crews and captains to bring his naval forces, if not to parity, then at least to a level able to compete in the limited waters of the Bosporus with the Western navies. At the outset of the campaign there seem to have been 400 Ottoman ships of all sizes in the Bosporus, including eighteen large warships with seventeen smaller galleons and up to twenty small craft with numerous horse transports.

The sight of the fortress' tower slowly growing as high as the walls of Constantinople seems to have stirred Constantine XI to send pleas for assistance to East and West Europe in February 1452. The response was not promising and Mehemmed II, via Candarli Halil's good offices, was in fact able to renew existing agreements with Venice, Hungary, Serbia and Wallachia. Hunyadi made a demand for Greek territory if he was going to commit troops to the defence of Constantinople and Alfonso V of Naples demanded the island of Lemnos for his naval forces. No agreements were ever made.

Rumeli Hisar was completed by August 1452 and with its impressive ordinance it could threaten any ship passing through to or returning from the Black Sea trade routes. Ordinance was also being produced for the ground assault. Mehemmed II employed the Hungarian cannon maker Orban, who was apparently disgruntled by the lack of funding and materials made available to him by the Byzantines. There were no such problems forthcoming from his new employer.

Constantine XI looked to his own defences as Byzantine diplomacy seemed to have, for once, failed. Catalan mercenaries were hired and silver was stripped from churches to pay them and for repairs to the walls. Then there was a little bit of good news. The Venetians had lost ships to the guns of Rumelia Hisar and so Gabriele Trevisan, the vice-captain of the Gulf, was sent to Constantinople with ships to defend Constantinople and protect Venetian interests. Two transports with troops were also sent. A second Venetian captain, Zaccaria Grioni, brought two warships from Negroponte.

Cardinal Isidore arrived in Constantinople in November 1452. He brought some material support in the form of hand-gunners and archers and he also brought the Pope's requirement that the great schism be healed by Constantine XI's acceptance of the Roman Catholic Church before any further assistance could be expected. He was accompanied by Archbishop Leonard and Genoese troops who had been enlisted at Chios.

Constantine XI soon realised that the provision of more troops was indeed entirely dependent on the acceptance of the union of the churches. A service dedicated to the union was therefore made in Santa Sophia in December 1452 and the heads of the Orthodox Church agreed to the ending of the schism. They could not, however, carry the lower clergy and laypeople with them and widespread rioting followed the service.[10]

Genoa had as much to lose as Venice if Constantinople fell, and arguably more, as Caffa, its great Black Sea port, could be strangled by whoever controlled Constantinople. In January 1453 the Genoese captain Giovanni Giustiniani Longo sailed into the Golden Horn with two large galleys and 700 troops. His men were certainly needed. At the most there were probably 8,500 fighting men defending the walls in 1453. There were up to 35,000 men under arms in the city but most were poorly trained local militia.

The walls of the city were also a problem as, despite Constantine XI's efforts to improve them, they remained, in many places, a relic of Byzantium's past. There were few emplacements for firearms or cannon. The famous floating chain, with its massive buoys, that closed the Golden Horn and ran from a tower below Acropolis Point to the sea wall of Galata was still extant and functional, however.

Constantinople had, of course, been besieged many times before and one advantage it had over almost every other city in Europe was that its walls enclosed a huge number of agricultural enterprises ranging from orchards to animal husbandry. Furthermore, fish could be landed daily from safe harbours and there was abundant water storage in the city. Mehemmed II would have known this and would also therefore have decided on a shock and awe attack; there could be no protracted siege in the hopes that the city could be starved into surrender. To this end the bridges on the approaches to the city were surveyed and repaired to ensure that they could take the load of the massive cannon that was going to produce the required artillery deluge. Forests and even vines were cut down by Ottoman pioneers to ensure a clear field of fire.

In the early spring of 1453 the Ottomans brought their guns up close to Constantinople and took the few remaining Greek-occupied forts surrounding the city. By March troops from Anatolia were crossing at the point protected by Rumelia Hisar.

On 2 April 1453 the floating chain was drawn across the Golden Horn. The official line from the Genoese of the Galata quarter was that they would remain neutral in the coming conflict but many Genoese crossed the Golden Horn to fight with the Byzantines and Venetians. Word then came that Hunyadi had launched a seaborne campaign to outflank the Ottomans. The scheme may even have been proposed but it never came to anything. The Ottoman troops were deployed smoothly around the walls on 6 April but the Ottoman navy suffered a reverse on 9 April and again on 12 April when it attacked the boom-chain of the Golden Horn. Mehemmed II brought large ships from Anatolia into the fray but work had also been started on the construction of a wooden slipway from the Bosporus across the hills behind Galata to access the Golden Horn *behind* the boom.

A night attack on 17 April failed but mangonels were placed near the walls and began their deadly work, and the Ottoman guns including the monster named *Basiliske* were also making breaches in the walls.

On 22 April Ottoman vessels appeared in the Golden Horn, leaving Constantinople invested on all sides. Defending troops had to be shuffled from other places on the walls to defend the part facing Galata. The defenders did, however, manage a naval sortie against the now reduced Ottoman fleet in the Bosporus. Fire-ships were deployed on 28 April under the command of Giacomo Coco, his little fleet comprised of two large transports filled with cotton and wool. He never made it to the Ottoman galleys, however, and his fire-ships were sunk before they could inflict any damage.

A breach was made in the walls at the gate of Saint Romanus on 30 April and a newly devised long-range mortar was added to the Ottoman barrage on 5 May. Its first victim was a Genoese merchant ship. Another night attack was launched on 7 May but it failed; a third nocturnal attack on 12 May was able to penetrate into the Blachernae section of the walls but was then repulsed. The Ottomans concentrated their mining efforts on the Blachernae walls. Serbian miners had been sent to Mehmed II by George Brankovic along with 1,500 cavalry.[11] Much of the ground around the walls had been found to be unsuitable for mining and the Byzantines were able to defeat all the Serbs' best efforts through counter-mines, flooding and even through smoking the miners out. On 23 May several miners and their Ottoman officer were captured underground.

It looked as if a storming of the walls would be required as mining had failed and the breaches in the walls were still insufficient to allow access to the city proper. The Ottomans' engineers therefore constructed a bridge across the Golden Horn to allow a swifter deployment of their forces. Greek fire was used on at the bridge but it remained intact and made the job of defending the walls at every point even more difficult.

On 24 May there was a lunar eclipse and on 26 May Mehemmed II must have wondered if it really was a harbinger of doom as there was news of a European army coming to the relief of Constantinople. He was stretched militarily and was also trying to contain dissent within his camp. He called a council of war. Candarli Halil spoke in favour of a compromise peace and withdrawal but Zaganoz Pasha contended that this relief army was imaginary as there was no unity between the Western nations. Mehemmed II managed to get his proposal that a mass attack should be launched through the council but he must have known that if it was a failure his tenure as sultan might not be too long or too pleasant. It was a huge gamble.

Mehemmed II toured the army's positions on 27 May and a general assault was announced. Fires were lit all over the Ottoman camps, apparently in celebration. It was hoped in Constantinople that these fires were from the burning of stores before a retreat.

Despite lashing rain, the Ottoman infantry started to fill in the defensive ditches around Constantinople in the early hours of 29 May. Then, about three hours before dawn, the Ottoman artillery started up and the *azab* infantry went forward under Mustafa Pasha. The attack was focused on the gate of Saint Romanus. Giustiniani Longo had brought 3,000 troops to the outer walls around the gate and his men inflicted terrible casualties on this first wave of Ottoman troops. This was followed up by a deployment of Ottoman ships attempting to place scaling ladders against the walls but this too was repulsed. A further artillery bombardment ripped through the dawn and then Anatolian troops went at the Saint Romanus Gate. The breaches were still too narrow, however, for them to make ingress and they pulled back to allow the artillery to pound again at the walls. A section came down and the Anatolians forced their way in, only to be driven out again. There was also heavy fighting on the Blachernae walls but no breakthrough.

Mehemmed II only had one more card to play. He brought his palace regiment of Janissaries into the fight. These perhaps 3,000 men were led by the sultan himself as far as the defensive ditches. They then went forward in a highly disciplined movement towards the breach in the wall, where they fought for about an hour before discovering that a small gate had been left open by the defenders after a sortie. About fifty troops ran through the gate and managed to get their banner up on the battlements. It was not a decisive move and it seems likely that the defenders would have been able to eliminate this small foothold had not their commander Giovanni Giustiniani Longo been struck by a musket round at the same time. He was felled by the shot, which would later kill him, and staggered away. The tale, doubtless embellished, goes that Emperor Constantine XI was nearby and called out, 'my brother fight bravely, do not forsake us in our distress, the salvation of the city depends on you. Return to your post. Where are you going?'[12] There was immediate panic brought on by the collapse of Longo and by the sight of the banner.

The Venetians and Genoese made a bolt for their ships in the harbour, but this 'desertion' was probably not what signalled the death knell of the defence of Constantinople; it was rather the discipline and application of the Janissaries and the command and control available to commanders in the elite Ottoman forces that ensured that Mehemmed II and Zaganos Pasha were able to exploit Longo's fall. They poured troops into the breach and into the one tower that they held and the Janissaries then took the inner wall. Then the resistance collapsed as news came that the Catalan mercenaries below the Old Palace had been exterminated to a man.

Orhan tried to escape but was captured and gathered up with other citizens during the sack. He was later recognised and dispatched to the executioner's hands. The emperor Constantine XI possibly died crying out heroically for a Christian among the Turks to take his head, or alternatively he was simply killed in the sack that had begun as soon as the defenders scattered from the walls and would last for the traditional three days. Giovanni Giustiniani Longo was taken by his men on to a galley but died on the journey home to Genoa.

Byzantine notables were brought before the sultan and they handed him exactly what he required: statements that Candarli Halil had been encouraging resistance in the hopes of a negotiated truce. The old wazir was executed forty days after the city's surrender. Zaganoz Pasha, the new wazir, negotiated the surrender of Galata.

Mehemmed II had spent two years preparing his assault on the Byzantine capital. He had proved himself to be a gifted administrator as he meticulously concentrated every available military unit available to him. It also meant that the Ottoman Empire now had a new capital, which had been considered divinely ordained by the Christians and which had always had a fabled legacy for the Muslims, too. It was eventually renamed as Istanbul which, whilst little more than a Turkish corruption of the common Greek term for their capital, *eis tan polin* or 'into the city' with the Turkish for city *bolu* replacing the Greek, aptly summed up the draw that Constantinople had always had on the minds and spirits of the Muslims.

Mehemmed II began consolidating and embellishing his new capital almost immediately. Justinian's cathedral of Hagia Sophia was converted into an imperial mosque, as eventually were numerous other churches and monasteries. The rights of non-Muslim inhabitants were protected to ensure continuity and stability for commercial activities. Having suffered from nearly two centuries of poverty both in terms of expenditure and in terms of population, Istanbul was given a new lease of life by the sultan. Mehemmed II immediately began to repopulate it and properties were offered to the public to entice much needed skilled artisans, craftsmen and traders of all religions and ethnicities to return to the city. Istanbul rapidly grew into a multi-ethnic, multicultural and bustling economic, political and cultural centre for the Ottoman state, whose distant frontiers guaranteed it peace. Its location set at the crossroads of an empire that straddled Asia and Europe guaranteed prosperity.

Its conquest had required the full application of the resources of a centralised economy. Its capture allowed Mehemmed II to monopolise the Ottoman economy. Silver mines, salt and gunpowder all now fell under the sultan's personal economic domain. The Ottomans had proved themselves masters of the complex science of siege warfare, or poliorcetics, and the way they went to war would not be the same again. It was discipline, order and organisation that had won the siege. The fall of Constantinople in 1453 was therefore a death knell for the power of the frontier *beys*.[13] That the sultan was able to judicially murder Candarli Halil so soon after its fall indicates the strength of the sultan's personal power within the state in this period. He was now far more than a warlord who was *primus inter pares*. Mehemmed II effectively created a 'new order' with the establishment of Istanbul. The *Osmanli* simply did not associate themselves with the Turks. Portrait medals produced for Mehemmed II by Constanzo de Ferrera from this period indicate this; they are inscribed in Latin and were based on imperial Roman prototypes.[14]

Mehemmed II continued with Murad II's *devshirme* policy. It has been estimated that 15,000–20,000 Christian boys per year were incorporated into the Janissaries and *kapikulu* during his reign and one fifth of Istanbul's population were *kuls*.[15] Furthermore, many senior Greek officials entered Ottoman service at this time and attained high rank. The incorporation of Christian aristocrats into the Ottoman hierarchy was not uncommon in Ottoman history but the phenomenon gathered pace under Mehemmed II, an example being the conversion of Bosnian lords such as Hersekzade Ahmed Pasha.[16] This drove the Ottoman state even further from its steppe origins and it is evident by Mehemmed II's time that the empire was becoming the instrument of a distinct elite.

Mehemmed II's attitude toward the settlement of Galata shows how removed were the Turks from the core of the state. They were forbidden to settle in the city unless 'they were of high rank'.[17]

Mehemmed II's religious policy was aimed at championing orthodoxy and ensuring that Istanbul became a major centre of the Islamic world. The physical layout of the new city was focused around mosques,[18] and all the major dignitaries of the state were ordered in 1459 to found religious buildings in Istanbul.[19] The proselytising of Orthodoxy was a central element in the Ottoman attempts to bring Eastern Anatolia under control and to prevent the outbreak of 'religious rebellion' against the sultanate. Mehemmed II placed *qadis* in all the towns of the empire and strengthened its bureaucacy. A permanent privy council was formed from his own followers and frontier *beys* and dynastic warriors were effectively 'banished' to the marches. Mehemmed II, in many ways, also made war on the *akinje* and 'Turcoman' element in the empire. The writer Kemelpasazade even alleged that Rum Mehmed, a Greek wazir appointed by Mehemmed II, revenged himself on the borderland cities of Larende and Konya for the destruction of Constantinople.[20]

Later the Turcoman leader, Uzun Hasan, would claim that Mehemmed II 'no longer burnt churches but only mosques', and the claim has a degree of validity about it in this period.[21] In fact, Hasan was perhaps the most potentially dangerous foe that Mehemmed II had to face during his reign; he was certainly far more feared by the sultan than Hunyadi, Skanderbeg or Vlad Dracula because Hasan, like Timur, was the antithesis of the Ottoman centralised state and could attract disenfranchised Turcoman elements. Mehemmed II's campaign against him in 1473 could have ended as disastrously as Bayezid I's 1402 campaign. It did not and this was because the Ottomans were by this juncture technologically far superior to their adversaries and the sultan had ensured that his forces were loyal to him alone.[22]

The question for the other states of the Balkans after the reduction of Constantinople must have been, who next? Skanderbeg paid a secret visit to Naples and to the Vatican in the very same year to discuss its consequences for his lands and for eastern Christendom.

Alfonso V presented a plan for a Crusade to Pope Nicholas V in 1454. Vladislaus II of Wallachia, not surprisingly, swung further in favour of the Ottomans and made further overtures to the sultan, which only increased his Hungarian problems.

Mehemmed II's overriding strategy for the period 1454 to 1459 seems to have been aimed at establishing a solid defence line along the Danube and the Adriatic against Hungary and Venice. This placed Serbia absolutely in the firing line and after two years of campaigning Mehemmed II had all of southern Serbia under control. With this region he also obtained the silver and gold mines of Novo Brdo. Then in 1455 news reached the Hungarian court that Mehemmed II was massing a war fleet on the Danube and mustering men and supplies. In April 1456 Hunyadi convened the Hungarian diet with the explicit purpose of organising the country's defence. With Mehemmed II's troops marching unimpeded through the cowed George Brankovic's Serbia and through Vladislaus II's Wallachia, the next obvious node of defence and therefore target for attack by the Ottomans was Belgrade. The fall of Belgrade would open up the Danube to a Turkish fleet, which hence would be free to attack Buda or even Vienna. Hunyadi declared a general mobilisation and an embassy was sent to Rome to plead for assistance. What was specifically needed from the Pope was a fleet to intercept Ottoman troops moving up from Anatolia. At this juncture King Ladislaus chose to leave for Vienna. Hunyadi found himself back in charge and, despite his loss of standing since 1448, he was able to garner enough support from the nobles to once again obtain effective control of Hungary.

By 1456 Mehemmed II had about 90,000 men in Edirne and a fleet of about sixty ships waiting in the Danube Delta. He also started to produce artillery in small factories in central Serbia, thus saving time and the effort of moving guns from Greece to what was going to be the new theatre of operations, Belgrade.

Hunyadi started to take care of other distractions as well as making Belgrade ready for the Ottoman attack. Croatia had fallen into civil war in 1449 as brothers squabbled over inheritances and turned to the Venetians or the Hungarians to support their claims and their small armies. Hunyadi appointed his son Ladislaus as Ban of Croatia and the threat from Mehemmed II to Belgrade then led to a truce being sealed between the warring parties in March 1456. Hunyadi's other problem was Wallachia. Vladislaus II had raided across southern Transylvania with Ottoman troops. This effectively tied down some of Hunyadi's best troops as they were required to guard against further Wallachian incursions but were desperately needed for the defence of Belgrade.

Hunyadi initially attempted to negotiate with Vladislaus II but the Prince of Wallachia then stirred up a rebellion against Hungary in Fagaras in early April 1456. Hunyadi had also never forgiven Vladislaus II for leaving him in a Serbian prison while securing his own throne back in 1448. There would have been little reluctance on Hunyadi's part when he gave Vlad Dracula instructions to claim the Wallachian throne in June 1456.

Vlad Dracula set out in mid-June through the pass over the Carpathians at Bran with a small force of exiled *boyars* and Hungarian and Romanian mercenaries. By mid-July he had gained the support of the majority of the Wallachian *boyars*. Vlad Dracula chased Vladislaus II down and caught him somewhere near Tirgoviste. Folklore requires us to believe that Vlad Dracula killed his father's murderer in a one-on-one fight on 22 July. Vlad Dracula then returned to his duty at Sibiu, guarding the Transylvanian passes. Hunyadi had obviously realised that effecting a coup in Wallachia and deploying Vlad Dracula in Transylvania would compel Mehemmed II to keep a body of troops on the Danube. Vlad Dracula was both protecting the eastern flank of the Belgrade defensive operation and tying up Ottoman troops that could be deployed to Belgrade.

Vlad Dracula's usurpation was sufficiently successful for Hunyadi to be able to pull most of his crack troops out of Transylvania. He then turned to creating a broad front of resistance to Mehemmed II by appealing to George Brankovic and to Skanderbeg. Skanderbeg was stymied in his attempts to bring an Albanian army to Belgrade by Mehemmed II's deployment of a secondary force against Albania. At least Hunyadi would have had the satisfaction of knowing that the Albanians were tying up forces that Mehemmed II would soon enough need at Belgrade. The Serbs also responded positively to Hunyadi's entreaties – perhaps even Brankovic could see that Serbia was in danger of being wiped off the map if Belgrade, a city in the possession of the Hungarians but essentially Serbian, was lost. The local Serbian population around Belgrade added considerably to the numbers of defenders of the city and a Serbian army of some 9,000 troops attacked the Ottoman main army as it advanced up the pass of Moravia towards Belgrade. There was no way that such a small force was going to stand against the sultan's vast army but their bravery gained time for the defence of the city to be strengthened. Indeed, without the delay the Serbians caused it is possible that Belgrade would have fallen as Hunyadi only arrived at the 'last minute' with the reinforcements that checked the Ottoman push into the city.

Belgrade sits at the joining of the River Sava and River Danube, and in 1456 it was a triple-walled fortress city. Hunyadi had tried to reinforce all the fortresses along the Danube but he realised that the Ottoman hammer must fall most heavily upon Belgrade simply because it was the strategic lynchpin of the line. He then sent more than 5,000 Hungarian, Czech and Polish mercenaries to the city. Hunyadi had lavished what money he had on Belgrade's defences as far back as 1442 and his choice of commander in 1456 was an excellent, if perhaps obvious one. When Michael Szilagyi called on the populace to help him defend their city they flocked to help both as militia but also in labouring to raise the defences yet higher and stronger. Hunyadi then moved on to the recruiting of the field army he knew he would require to break any Ottoman siege. With the initial defence of Belgrade taken care of Hunyadi set about raising this force and gaining allies. Three hundred years before Frederick the Great tutored his generals that 'the art of defending fortified places consists in putting off the moment of their reduction'. Hunyadi had clearly recognised that fortification could never be the total solution to the problem of winning the war, and that offensive action would be required both to relieve Belgrade and to defeat the enemy.

Hungary's nobility failed Hunyadi at this point, with many refusing to participate in the field army. Many cited the king's absence as reason to withhold their help but senior lords with estates in southern Hungary did rally to the cause and among the minor nobility Hunyadi still remained the 'White Knight' and a hero. He managed to pull together a field army of about 15,000 men, of which about half were either mercenaries or Transylvanian troopers. This hardly seemed adequate, however, and the papal legate wrote to the Pope expressing the apparent hopelessness of the situation:

> This kingdom is on the eve of a terrible disaster, for neither with its own resources nor yet with the aid of the empire can it bring together forces sufficient to cope with the Turk. Our only hope is that God will listen to the prayers of your holiness and move the hearts of the princes to send their fleets. So pressing is the peril that the delay of a day or even of an hour may bring about such a defeat as shall make all Christendom weep for evermore.[23]

But then there was the people's army, a popular mass movement mobilised by the preaching of priests and monks throughout Hungary, Serbia and the Holy Roman Empire. The lead in this Crusade was taken by the 70-year-old Inquisitor, John of Capistrano, who preached, 'God wills it that we chase the Turks out of Europe and for whosoever follows me, I will obtain plenary indulgence for him and his family!'

Capistrano's Crusaders were armed, in the main, only with slings and clubs, though there were those among the minor nobility who brought spears, horses and armour to Hunyadi's camp at Seghedin. By the end of the siege there may have been up to 30,000 men with Hunyadi.

Early in June Hunyadi took his field army down the River Danube and then crossed it. From the river's southern bank he started a fighting retreat, skirmishing with the Ottoman formations making their way up to the city. On 2 July John of Capistrano brought Crusader reinforcements to Belgrade in five large transport ships. He then tried to sail down the Danube with three more ships of Crusaders to join Hunyadi in the field but he was struck by a storm and he returned to Belgrade with his men on foot.

By 4 July Hunyadi was in danger of being cut off from the city if he remained south of it, such were the number of Ottoman troops now at the walls of Belgrade. The arrival of the Ottoman fleet below the city sealed his decision and he took the field army up to the north-east of Belgrade at the fortress of Zemun. The Ottomans started an artillery barrage of heavy siege guns on 4 July. John of Capistrano left the city to join Hunyadi in the field.

Hunyadi commandeered every boat and ship, including those of the Hungarian Danube fleet, he could lay hands on and gathered them together at Slankamen. He then took this assortment of about 200 vessels down the Danube to challenge the Ottomans before Belgrade's walls. He coordinated his attack with Szilagyi in Belgrade and set the date for the assault as 14 July. Szilagyi had about forty ships moored at the city docks and crewed by Serbian irregulars.

Hunyadi's fleet was flanked by 15,000–20,000 Transylvanian militia and Crusaders under John of Capistrano's command marching down the southern bank of the river. Hunyadi's flagship was a well-built galleon. The Ottoman fleet left its blockade of the city and sallied forward to meet the Hungarians. The battle lasted five hours with the flanking infantry attacking any Ottoman vessel that was forced to the riverbank and with Hunyadi's men at arms pouring fire into the Ottoman galleys. Then the Belgrade boats joined the fray and turned the battle. The Ottomans lost about three-quarters of their fleet and had to burn many of the immobilised ships to prevent them being captured by the victorious Christians. The destruction of the Ottoman fleet and its blockade allowed fresh equipment and men to be shuttled into Belgrade every night.

Mehemmed II kept up the pressure despite this setback and his artillery had by now destroyed the city's outer walls. The Hungarian artillery, outgunned as it was, could, however, claim a success when a lucky shot killed the Beylerbey of Rumelia.

Morale was fragile in the Ottoman camp and it seemed as if the defenders were getting stronger whilst their own troops were weakening. Therefore Mehemmed II decided to risk a general assault on 21 July. He had superior numbers and his troops were able to breach the outer walls and reach the inner fortress before its drawbridge could be secured. A Hungarian counter-attack led by Hunyadi and his body-guard attacked the Janissaries from behind but the Ottomans managed to burn the drawbridge, which allowed them to continue attacking the inner walls whilst remaining protected from sallies from within the fortress. The Hungarian field troops then, however, effected a crossing from the north side of the River Sava and deployed troops in small boats to take on the Ottoman troops within Belgrade's outer defences. By the evening the Ottomans had been pushed out of the city.

Hunyadi followed up this success with an attack on the Ottoman siege works the next day. Troops from Belgrade joined with the Crusaders of John of Capistrano from across the River Sava and smashed into the Ottoman lines. The fighting was disorganised as the Hungarian and Serbian troops broke on the Ottoman trenches and Ottoman cavalry launched counter-attacks on the knots of men struggling to reach the Ottoman artillery to destroy it. Seeing that the Crusaders were bogged down, Hunyadi threw in the rest of the Hungarian forces. His veterans and mercenaries finished the Ottoman resistance and captured the main artillery positions. The lighter pieces were immediately turned around and trained on the Ottomans' positions. A full assault with artillery support was then launched on the Ottoman camp. The Janissaries put up a stubborn defence against the successive Crusader attacks but their commander was killed and even Mehemmed II was injured in the battle. The sultan then tried to counter-attack to regain his own guns from Hunyadi's men but his troops would not go forward again after a third attempt failed.

At nightfall the Ottoman army withdrew from its camp and retreated. The Hungarians found vast quantities of treasure and materiel in the camp. Mehemmed II may have lost as many as 24,000 troops before the walls of Belgrade. The wounded sultan retreated to Sofia, turned on several of his generals and had them summarily executed.

In Rome, Eugenius IV called the relief of Belgrade 'the happiest event of my life'. It was soon to be followed by tragedy as within days John Hunyadi, now over 60 years of age and in poor health brought on by years of war and crushing responsibility, contracted the plague that was sweeping the camps and died at Zenum in Serbia. John of Capistrano also succumbed to the disease that had been flaring up in the Danube plain all through the summer, and which had probably arrived with Ottoman transports and been carried from Anatolia.

Hunyadi's son, Laszlo, took official command of Belgrade during the winter of 1456–57 and Hunyadi was not the only major magnate to die in 1456. In December George Brankovic died and the usual Serbian succession problems re-emerged. In the anarchy that erupted, Mehemmed II even laid claim to the Serbian throne, with his right based on his Serbian stepmother, but in fact he had other problems beyond Serbia. Skanderbeg, doubtless inspired by Hunyadi's victory, had brought his troops out of the mountains and had begun attacking the Ottoman garrisons stationed in Albania. Mehemmed II had to dispatch a number of expeditions to push him back into the mountains.

Mehemmed II also had problems and unfinished business in Greece. The Byzantine despots in Morea, the brothers Demetrios Palaiologos of Mystras and Thomas Palaiologos of Patras, went to war against each other and Thomas tried to draw the Western powers into the conflict. Mehemmed II arrived in Greece in 1458 and annexed the northern regions. By early 1459 Athens was taken, and a year later Thomas was forced to flee Patras. With the fall of the Morea in 1460, the Byzantine Empire finally ceased to exist. All of Greece, with the exception of a few Venetian-controlled ports, was now under direct Ottoman authority.

Mehemmed II was able to return to the Serbian question in 1458. The state was swiftly made extinct. Mehemmed II moved north and invaded Serbia one final time, making good on his claim to the Serbian throne. What lands that remained of the old vassal state of Serbia were occupied outright by Mehemmed II's forces. It was an easy victory and there was very little the Hungarians could do given the power vacuum that followed Hunyadi's death.

The year 1456 had seen the appearance of Halley's Comet. Comets were seen in both the medieval West and medieval Islam as harbingers of plagues, wars or other disasters. Hunyadi and John of Capistrano's deaths and the dismembering of Serbia would all have confirmed the link between calamity and the comet's appearance. However, on the only extant coin of Vlad Dracula's reign, a comet is depicted on the reverse side with the Wallachian eagle on the obverse side. Perhaps Vlad Dracula saw the comet as a portent of better things to come for him; certainly 1456 had seen his fortunes turn around and he was formally elected by the high *boyar* council in August of that year and confirmed by the metropolitan in the cathedral of Tirgoviste with the title of 'Prince Vlad, son of Vlad the Great, sovereign and ruler of Ungro–Wallachia and of the duchies of Amia and Fgra'. He went immediately into a small flurry of diplomatic correspondence, and this is not surprising given the events at Belgrade and George Brankovic's death. Vlad Dracula would have had major concerns over the flank of his lands and required information on both the condition of Transylvania and of the Hungarian front. The mayors of the important towns of Transylvania and Hunyadi's son, Laszlo, all received communications from the new *voivode* but the bulk of Vlad Dracula's letters at this time seem to have been to Moldavia, and to disgruntled *boyars*. He was aiming for the removal of Peter III Aron and the restoration of the Moldavian royal line through his ally and cousin, Stephen, who was currently taking refuge at Vlad Dracula's court.

Vlad Dracula may have simply been venting his spleen because of his hatred for Peter III Aron but there was also a pro-Hungarian aspect to his planning for a coup in Moldavia. Moldavia had traditionally maintained a policy of vassalage toward Poland to preserve its independence from Hungary. Its location in the extreme north-east, beyond both the Danube and Wallachia, had spared it any involvement with the Ottomans until 1420, when Mehemmed I raided Moldavia after suppressing the Bedreddin rebellion. During the 1430s and 1440s the principality was wracked by civil wars, of which Sultan Murad II took advantage. By 1455 Peter III Aron had accepted Ottoman suzerainty and agreed to pay tribute. Replacing him with Stephen, the kinsman of Vlad Dracula, a vassal of the Hungarian king, would pull Moldavia into the circuit of Hungary and away from Poland, and also perhaps give the Ottomans another foe to be concerned about.

In 1457, at the head of 6,000 Wallachian troops, Stephen took on Peter III Aron at Doljesti. He defeated him and gained a second victory over him at the Battle of Orbic, after which he was crowned as Moldavia's prince. It looked like Vlad Dracula's first success.

With Hungary weakened despite the success at Belgrade, Vlad Dracula was cautious in his initial relations with the Ottomans. He gave a courteous reception at his palace in Tirgoviste to Mehemmed II's first embassy. The Ottoman emissaries demanded a yearly tribute of 2,000 gold ducats and the same right of free passage for the sultan's army through Wallachia that Vladislaus II had always given. Thus safe Ottoman access for raiding the rich towns of Transylvania was the price of Mehemmed II's recognition of Vlad Dracula's reign. He had to assent and did so readily. He did, however, perhaps wisely, decline to travel to Istanbul to make his obeisance to the sultan. He would certainly have remembered what happened to his father in 1442.

Vlad Dracula's act of tribute to Mehemmed II may have offered him a degree of security from the Ottomans but these were turbulent times and it is notable that he placed his base in the north of Wallachia. It was where he might expect increased loyalty among the populace as his family's origins were there, and where he could obtain some protection, as Skanderbeg did, from any pursuing Ottoman forces by retreating into the mountains. He also never let his base stray too far from his Transylvanian possessions. Castle Dracula, or more correctly Poenari Castle, was the key fortress and was located just to the north of Curtea De Arges, which also needed to lie easily within Vlad Dracula's reach as the ecclesiastical capital also held extensive political power and influence over the populace. Indeed, traditional tales describe how the church would communicate with the castle's keepers each night through light signals. The security of the church was tied very much to that of the *Voivode* Dracula.

Poenari had a history going back to the Basarab princes in the fourteenth century but by 1456 it was in ruins having suffered attacks by both Tatars and Turks. Vlad II Dracula obviously realised the potential as a bolthole for a castle perched high on a steep precipice of rock, and worked hard at making it impregnable. Even today it requires nearly 1,500 stairs for any tourist to stand atop its walls. Its renovation very clearly violated his vassalage to both the Ottomans and the Hungarians and their prohibitions on defensive works, and was built to a very high standard of engineering for the time. The five towers gave the defenders the potential for setting up crossfire on any attackers and the central cylindrical tower has stone reinforced with brick to withstand siege artillery. The castle is, in fact, small and the garrison could have been no larger than 100 men, but then these would have been Vlad Dracula's most loyal men as this was his last station of defence. The presence of a secret tunnel is perhaps pure folklore but fits well with the idea of this castle being Vlad Dracula's last resort and haven.

Vlad Dracula also needed, in order to create revenue, to be able to project power into the plains surrounding the Danube. To this end he founded the fortress of Bucharest in June 1458, building on and linking several villages in the area around the River Dimbovia. He also fortified the nearby monastery of Snagov and a line of minor forts along the plain and river.

Vlad Dracula may have needed these defence points against the Ottomans but he also needed them, potentially, against internal enemies. It must be remembered that the violent political landscape of Wallachia had seen no fewer than twelve princes sitting on the throne from 1418, including Vlad Dracula's own father. The *boyar* class could take away just as easily what they gave and the lack of the principle of primogeniture made Radu a potential candidate for the throne as well as any illegitimate son of Vlad II Dracul and indeed any grandson of Mircea. Vlad Dracula summed up the situation very succinctly in a short speech recorded by the *meistersinger* Michael Beheim:

> He (Dracula) asked the assembled noblemen:
> 'How many Princes have you known?'
> The latter answered each as much as he knew best.
> One believed that there had been thirty, another twenty.
> Even the youngest thought there had been seven.
> After having answered this question
> Dracula said: 'Tell me how do you explain the fact that you have had so many Princes in your land? The guilt is entirely due to your shameful intrigues.'[24]

The *boyar* class would also have inclined towards continued peace with the Ottomans and antagonism to the Hungarians, who were of course, at present, Vlad Dracula's sponsors.

Vlad Dracula therefore went to war against the *boyar* class because he could not be sure they would not depose him in order to please Mehemmed II, because they had a 'ready-made' candidate in Radu who remained under the care of the Ottomans, because there were certainly still partisans of Vladislaus II among the *boyar* class, and also because the general rule for extinguishing political conspiracies is to make a pre-emptive strike.

The other rule that tyrants tend to follow when dealing with conspiracies, either real or imagined, is to eradicate all opponents in one fell swoop and to ensure that retribution is extended to all of their kith and kin.

There was a massive purge of *boyar* families in the first two years of Vlad Dracula's reign and only those men who had returned to Wallachia with him in 1456 were safe. The purge was bloody but there is some evidence that if Vlad Dracula had not struck first then he would have been deposed. The *boyar* Albu the Great had organised an unsuccessful revolt just a few months after Dracula had seized power, but he still maintained a private army and continued to agitate for Vlad Dracula's removal. Vlad Dracula's men ambushed him and then impaled him along with his entire family. Only Albu's brother survived and fled to Brasov, which was rapidly becoming home to many more dissidents as Vlad Dracula continued his purge.

Vlad Dracula struck hard in the spring of 1457 during the Easter celebrations that required the *boyars* to attend Vlad Dracula's palace at Tirgoviste. Some 200 of the *boyars* attended along with their families. Leading citizens of the capital were also invited to the feast. Just as the guests finished their meals in the main banqueting hall of the palace, the old *boyars* and their wives were taken by Vlad Dracula's men and impaled beyond the city walls.

The *boyars'* offspring were manacled and chained to each other and then marched for two days up the River Arges to the ruins of Poenari Castle. Their slave labour was then applied to Vlad Dracula's rebuilding of the castle. They fired bricks and carried them up the precipitous slopes to build high towers and keeps.

The mass murder at Tirgoviste was probably the origin of Vlad Dracula's epithet 'the Impaler' and it decimated the old *boyar* class. Those who were not murdered fled to Transylvania or even to Ottoman-controlled lands. Vlad Dracula replaced much of the old aristocracy by offering confiscated lands to new men, many of whom were of very low birth and owed their fortune entirely to Vlad Dracula. Vlad Dracula also placed another government body above the council of *boyars*: the *arma*. The *arma* was in theory created to carry out the decisions of the *boyar* council but was in fact almost exclusively dedicated to the administering and carrying out of the executive decisions of the prince. The *arma* was constituted in the main of well-paid mercenaries with complete loyalty to Vlad Dracula. Another innovation was Vlad Dracula's creation of the *viteji*. This had an air of a meritocracy about it as it was a military officer class drawn from free peasant soldiers who performed well and bravely on the battlefield. They were also the nucleus of the peasant armies that Vlad Dracula was to rely on throughout his reigns to fight against foreign invasions. Finally, there were the men of Vlad Dracula's standing army, or bodyguard, the *sluji*.[25]

In some ways and in miniature Vlad Dracula was emulating Mehemmed II's far larger achievement of centralisation in the Ottoman Empire. Vlad Dracula's attempts at becoming an autocrat with as much power in his little state as the sultan had in the empire also led him to be a generous patron of the Romanian Orthodox Church. He granted tax immunities and other privileges to monasteries and built new and extended old church buildings, and in return he expected submission to his will and support from the pulpit. He allied himself in particular with the monastery of Snagov, one of the many candidates for the location of his body. Certainly his treasure was kept safe by the monastery during the Ottoman invasion of Wallachia in 1462. The Roman Catholic Church was extending its base throughout Transylvania and Wallachia in the early period of Vlad Dracula's reign and, while there is evidence of him directly attacking monasteries and even of impaling Catholic priests, he appears, more commonly, to have used intimidation in order to replace Western abbots with Romanian appointees.

In 1459 Vlad Dracula refused to pay tribute to Mehemmed II. The payment required from the sultan's vassal was carefully calculated as both a monetary sum and in terms of grain and animals to be sent to Istanbul; Wallachia was generally viewed by the Ottomans as a vast granary. There was also, of course, the *devshirme* to be fulfilled, too.[26] Vlad Dracula's decision to stop payment to the Ottomans at first sight seems odd and he would pay for it in 1462. It is hard to fully explain his motivation for challenging Mehemmed II in 1459 but he may have been encouraged by changes taking place in Hungarian politics. If so, then he was sorely misguided.

November 1456 had seen the return of the king, Ladislaus V, to the 'front line'. Count Ulrich of Celje, a long-standing political enemy of the Hunyadi clan, brought the young king to Belgrade, which was under the command of Ladislaus Hunyadi. Celje was a supporter of the Habsburg factions, a partisan of Elizabeth of Luxembourg and of Ladislaus V in the Hungarian civil war of the early 1440s and a bitter opponent of Hunyadi over the settlement that the Hungarians had forced upon Croatia in 1447, even going as far as to lead an invasion of Hungary in 1450 with Habsburg support.

Ladislaus Hunyadi's concern would have been that Ladislaus V would become the Celje clan's mouthpiece to do both their bidding and that of Frederick III. Hunyadi granted Ulrich safe conduct into Belgrade but then the drawbridge leading to the fortress was suddenly closed, and the king and Count Celje were cut off from their bodyguard. Then, during an argument, the count was murdered by Hunyadi's men. Ladislaus V found himself a virtual prisoner of the Hunyadi clan and was undoubtedly pressured into taking an oath not to retaliate against Ladislaus Hunyadi. The young king bided his time and was finally released from Belgrade. In March 1457 he struck, arresting and executing Ladislaus Hunyadi and seizing his younger brother, Matthias Corvinus. Michael Szilagyi immediately rebelled against the king.

Then, in November 1457, Ladislaus V died without an heir. Michael Szilagyi brought 14,000 men to the capital and this was enough to convince a council of nobles to elect Matthias Corvinus Hunyadi as king.

At the time Matthias was still imprisoned in Prague and he was only recognised by a handful of Hungarian magnates and Croatian lords. Frederick III used the resistance to Matthias to his advantage to ensure his own, or his son's, accession to the throne should Corvinus die without an heir and he kept the official Crown of Hungary, that of Saint Stephen, which had come into his possession with the child Ladislaus V back in 1440. In fact, Matthias was not officially crowned until March 1464 but he was in de facto in control of the majority of Hungary from 1458 onwards. It may have been the fact that a Hunyadi was once again in control of Hungary's destiny that encouraged Vlad Dracula to thumb his nose at Mehemmed II.

The problem was that Matthias spent the early years of his reign as a juvenile monarch attempting to free himself of the guardianship of his uncle, Michael Szilagyi, and later showed far more interest in Central European affairs than in the Balkans. He did nothing to prevent the extinction of Serbia and seemed to view Belgrade and the Danube–Sava junction as the natural defence line against the Ottomans.

The power struggle in Hungary also directly affected Vlad Dracula as both the king and his guardian cast about for allies. Matthias looked to the German elements within his state for support and this included the rich Saxon merchant towns of Transylvania and along the Wallachian border, whilst Szilagyi looked to garner support from vassal lords. Vlad Dracula plumped for Szilagyi, and this is not surprising as he must have built a relationship with Hunyadi's brother-in-law that would have been far stronger than any that he might have had with the young king during the years he spent with John Hunyadi.

Vlad Dracula had also been involved with Szilagyi during the earlier competition with the Habsburgs for the Hungarian Crown that had broken into the open with the killing of Celje in Belgrade. In 1457 Vlad Dracula had become Szilagyi's agent in Transylvania for punishing any of the German cities that opted for the Habsburgs and Ladislaus V. In fact, up to this point, Vlad Dracula had shown a great deal of interest in maintaining good relations with the Saxon cities. Indeed, many of them had supported his insurrection against Vladislaus II. The citizens of Brasov, in particular, were generous to his cause and he wrote to them in September 1456 and described them as 'honest men, brothers, friends, and sincere neighbours'. This flattery was followed by something more concrete: a commercial treaty promising defence against the Ottomans and the right to unimpeded trade across Transylvania and Wallachia. The Saxons had generally enjoyed strong trade rights in the region ever since the days of Mircea but Vlad Dracula seems to have gone further in his favouring of them than even his grandfather, and this was despite the fact that the Saxons were already taking away business from Wallachian merchants as they changed their trade routes in response to Mehemmed II's increasing encroachments into the Balkans.

In the summer of 1457 all this changed. The Germans of Bistri in north-eastern Transylvania revolted against Szilagyi, probably because he was squeezing them for revenue. Szilagyi called on Vlad Dracula to bring the region to heel. Bistri was well fortified, possibly a reason why the citizens thought they could resist Szilagyi's demands, but Vlad Dracula's troops soon penetrated the defences and began looting and burning. Many of the 'ringleaders' of the revolt fled to Brasov and Sibiu. Vlad Dracula was rewarded by Szilagyi with a castle dominating the Borgo Pass.

Vlad Dracula had stirred up a hornets' nest in Transylvania. The German cities came together and the royal captain general of Transylvania, Count Oswald Rozgony, threw his support behind their league. Vlad Dracula singled out Brasov in particular as being disloyal and treacherous, and given how the warm sentiments of 1456 had dissipated so quickly this is perhaps not surprising.

Brasov responded in 1458 to his threats with a campaign of subversion in Wallachia against Vlad Dracula. There was a whispering campaign that spread the rumour that the prince had, in fact, undertaken vassalage to Mehemmed II despite his protestations to the contrary. Perhaps this was another reason why Vlad Dracula had taken the very dangerous step of withholding tribute from the Ottomans. The burghers of Brasov also materially supported the Dnesti. It will be remembered that Dan II, the legitimate son of Vlad II Dracul's uncle, had contested the throne with Vlad Dracula's father. Now Dan III, the brother of Vladislaus II, established himself in Brasov, where he claimed the throne of Wallachia after being 'elected' by a group of Dnesti *boyars* and other lords who had fled Vlad Dracula's purges of 1457.

Then the city of Sibiu found another candidate for the Wallachian throne, from within Vlad Dracula's own bloodline. His half-brother, known as Vlad the Monk, was given money to raise forces and soon attracted other groups of *boyars* to his cause. Vlad the Monk possibly attracted the support of Sibiu because he promised to extend the trade rights of the city and other towns allied with it even further than Vlad Dracula had promised in 1456.

As Transylvania exploded into revolt, a third candidate emerged from the Dnesti clan. A son of Dan II, Vlad II Dracul's mortal enemy, Basarab Laiot made a raft of promises to the Romanian *boyars* and the German merchants.

Vlad Dracula's first move was one of economic warfare. He withdrew all protection of trade for the German cities and encouraged the merchants of Wallachia and those of the Italian republics with favourable tariffs. He added onerous stipulations to any trade undertaken by Saxon merchants, requiring them, for example, to unpack their wagons for inspection by Wallachian officers and merchants at Tirgoviste. The Saxons were then compelled to sell to Wallachian merchants at prices far below what could be achieved further along the Balkans trade routes. This move worked to Vlad Dracula's advantage in the propaganda war that was now being fought inside Wallachia as the, admittedly small, Wallachian trader and artisan class backed him as he opened up trade with the renascent Istanbul that Mehemmed II was doing so much to bring back to its former glory.

The Saxon merchants did as much as they could to avoid Vlad Dracula's customs officers and it did not take long for him to start a campaign of terror to bring the merchant cities to heel. Between 1458 and 1460 Vlad Dracula undertook the bloody deeds that made him infamous and which would be propagated across Europe by the 'new' media of woodcut pamphlet printing. The 1485 work of Bartholomeus Gothan, *About an Evil Tyrant Named Dracole Wyda*, the 1488 history of Vlad the Impaler by Marcus Ayrer, detailing his atrocities, and the 1500 pamphlet with a woodcut of Matthias Hupfuff depicting Vlad

Dracula eating amid hundreds of impaled victims, were all produced in German and are all products of this bloody period. The *Nurnberg Chronicle* of 1488 carries the following catalogue of atrocities; its author used a compressed timeline in order to increase the horror of Vlad Dracula's deeds:

> Both women and men, young and old perished. Some he brought home with him to Wallachia and impaled them all there. He declared a peace and during the same he had many merchants and waggoneers from Wurtzland impaled. He also had a large family extinguished and impaled, from the smallest to the largest, young and old. Ambassadors numbering fifty five were sent from the Kingdom of Hungary and Saxony and Transylvania into Wallachia. Dracula kept them waiting for five weeks and had stakes made for their impalement ... Meanwhile he went into Wurtzland and destroyed the grain and had all the crops burned and he had the populace led into captivity out of the city called Kronstatt. Then Dracula rested near Saint Jacob's Chapel. He had the outskirts burned. Also, when the day came, early in the morning, he had women and men, young and old, impaled around the hill by the chapel and sat down among them and ate his breakfast with enjoyment.[27]

Sibiu and Brasov were singled out for special attention by Vlad Dracula. In simple terms they were the most Saxon districts of Transylvania, and they fell within the duchies of Fgra and Amla, which were technically possessions of the Prince of Wallachia in Transylvania. Sibiu was ordered to give up its support of Vlad the Monk and Brasov was told that Dan III was also to be treated as an enemy of the state. Neither city responded to the ultimatums.

Vlad Dracula's brutality and poor judgement as the ruler of a state obscure his qualities as a soldier and field commander, and the opening of his 'Saxon campaign' shows him at his best in this regard. He took a small cavalry force quickly across the mountains in the spring of 1458, he passed the Turnu Ro or 'Red Tower', the colour of which Romanian legend ascribes to the blood of so many Turks who have bled upon it in their futile attempts to take it, and reached the valley of the River Hirtibaciu. This was a skilled and deliberate targeting of the lands of the Saxons who directly supported Vlad the Monk. He brought fire and death to the villages and then, like a lightning storm, he moved on to the lands around Brasov. It was reported that he obliterated the village of Bod and retained only a few of the population for impaling later as a demonstration in Tirgoviste; everyone else was killed on sight. Talme was also burnt to the ground and the population was slaughtered.

Any Saxon merchants found trying to break the blockade on their trade were subject to impaling and other horrific tortures. The scene of Vlad Dracula boiling alive 600 Saxon merchants of Birsei was recounted in pamphlets throughout the German-speaking world and beyond in the late fifteenth century.

Michael Szilagyi joined Vlad Dracula's campaign but failed to take Sibiu in October 1458. He stayed in Transylvania, however, and quartered his troops at Sighisoara. Vlad Dracula's appalling war of attrition seemed to have borne fruit when Szilagyi brought the main Saxon towns to the negotiating table and an accord was reached in November 1458 between Vlad Dracula and Brasov. The elders of Brasov agreed to surrender Dan III and his supporters to Vlad Dracula and agreed to pay Szilagyi 10,000 florins for war damages in return for the restoration of Brasov's traditional commercial privileges. The treaty fell apart rapidly as Szilagyi was captured and imprisoned by Matthias Corvinus and Brasov reneged on its promises. The king then went one step further and threw his support behind Dan III.

Vlad Dracula's response was bloody and quick in coming. In the opening months of 1459 he raided in the valley of the River Prahova, destroying villages in the environs of Brasov. He burned crops and killed every living thing in his path. His raiding was malevolent but also obviously aimed at eroding the will of Brasov for harbouring Dan III. He smashed through the suburbs of Brasov and created the very public tableau described by the *Nurnberg Chronicle* of a prince eating a hearty breakfast among a forest of impaled bodies and the sound of limbs being hacked off of those who remained alive. Though whether we should believe the extra details the *meistersinger* Beheim tells us of Vlad Dracula 'dipping his bread in the blood of the victims' is debatable.

In fact, the whole venture was pointless. Dan III and his supporters were not in Brasov and Vlad Dracula's actions only hardened the citizens of Transylvania's resolve to see him removed from power.

In April 1460 Dan III invaded Wallachia but was quickly defeated and captured. Vlad Dracula had a grave dug for his enemy whilst Dan III waited beside it and even had to listen to his own funeral service before Vlad Dracula beheaded him. He then killed all his captured followers by impalement.

Vlad Dracula then plundered Brasov and refused to make peace with the Saxons until Vlad the Monk was in custody. The summer of 1460 saw further raids into Transylvania by Vlad Dracula in search of Vlad the Monk, who was known to be hiding in the district of Amla. He burned the town of Amla and impaled its citizens, after forcing a priest to lead them in a perverse procession to the site of their murder. The burning and killing continued through half of Amla district and the city of Amla itself witnessed the massacre of all of its citizens, who were assembled along with prisoners from other villages. The victims were suspended on hooks and pitchforks and hacked to death.

The *meistersinger* Beheim claims that 30,000 Germans were killed in the genocide. His numbers may be spurious and when writing of exterminations it is not uncommon for historians to throw doubt on the numbers provided by the chroniclers of the past. There has certainly been a trend among modern historians for making far more conservatively sized mounds of dead than the original sources had portrayed. In some respects this is commendable. Historians have a duty to create hypotheses about the past: it is, after all, a social science that we are engaged in, and the question of magnitude is always a question we are likely to ask and be asked. But, even if we can 'prove' such suppositions as 'each household should be multiplied by five to calculate the population affected' or that 'the square hectarage of the remains of a city could not possibly have supported as many people as the contemporary historians claimed were slaughtered there', I would suggest that this is still not as useful, historically, as gauging the psychological impact of having nearly all your neighbours killed and next year's crops destroyed. Whether the number killed was 70,000 or 7,000 does not matter; the question of magnitude of terror depends on the numbers left *alive*, and the sources on the massacres in Transylvania make it very clear that this number was a fraction of those who died.[28] Amla, as a city, never rose again.

Matthias Corvinus had generally stood aside from the war in Transylvania but he was approached by the German cities to broker a peace deal in the autumn of 1460. The first provisions required a somewhat brutal swap of dissidents between Vlad Dracula and the Saxon cities. All commercial privileges were also returned to their 1456 conditions by the new treaty.

Two final aspects of the treaty of 1460 are odd in that they required the Saxon townships to pay Vlad Dracula sufficient annual funds to maintain a 4,000-strong mercenary army, ostensibly to be used against the Ottomans, but also required Vlad Dracula to pay compensation for the destruction of property that he had caused. The peace between Vlad Dracula and the Saxons was very fragile indeed and the Saxons may only have committed to the payment for Vlad Dracula's mercenaries as a response to the Crusade called by Pius II in 1459, of which more below. With the accord guaranteed by the Hungarian king, Vlad Dracula could now return to the repression of Wallachians and to preparing for his part in Pius II's venture.

In fact, given Vlad Dracula's policies inside Wallachia, it is at first glance surprising that Dan III was unable in 1460 to rouse the Wallachian–Romanian population to support him. Perhaps the fact that Vlad Dracula had cast off the Ottoman yoke that fell heaviest on the peasants of Wallachia and had imposed a justice which was certainly brutal and arbitrary but also more evenly applied to all members of Romanian society than anything than had gone before, at least in living memory, allowed him to keep a grip on the populace. Certainly any prince who gave any recognition or protection to the peasantry of Wallachia was a novelty. Romanian peasants had joined with the repressed Hungarian peasantry against the nobility in 1437 and had undertaken many other rebellions that grew out of the desperation of their situation.

Vlad Dracula's atrocities in Wallachia were also selective and seldom directly involved the peasantry. His targeting of gypsies and of the beggars and vagabonds of the Romanian lands, and a tale of his immolation of a huge number of beggars whilst they dined as his guests in Tirgoviste and his boiling alive of a gypsy leader who was then force-fed to his clan were explained away by Vlad Dracula as a service to others in Wallachian society:

> These men live off the sweat of others, so they are useless to humanity. It is a form of thievery. In fact, the masked robber in the forest demands your purse, but if you are quicker with your hand and more vigorous than he you can escape from him. However, these vagabonds take your belongings gradually by begging – but they still take it. They are worse than robbers. May such men be eradicated from my land![29]

Vlad Dracula was perhaps just clearing up his domestic agenda in time. The peace accord that Matthew Corvinus had brokered in Transylvania would at least open the door to Hungarian and Saxon support if the Ottomans attempted to conquer Wallachia, and it looked increasingly likely that they would. As discussed above, Mehemmed II was mopping up Serbia and the Morea in the late 1450s, and a crossing of the Danube and thereby control of the river and the access to the Black Sea that this would give were the next logical strategic goals for any conquest of the whole of the Balkans. Belgrade would also have to be taken but that nut, of course, had proved too tough to crack in 1456. The new campaigns would centre on the Danube plain of Wallachia and also draw Moldavia, a state little involved in the long conflict up to now, into war with the Ottomans as Mehemmed II worked towards securing the Danube Delta.

Pope Pius II saw how Mehemmed II was now directly threatening the Catholic populations of Transylvania and Hungary and in June 1459 he summoned a congress of the Christian princes at Mantua. He tried to inject some enthusiasm for the Crusade he planned to proclaim by issuing a bull instituting a new religious order of knights. They were to bear the name of Our Lady of Bethlehem and to have their head-quarters in the Island of Lemnos. The order, however, never seems to have been formed and certainly never undertook any recorded activity. Crusading, it would seem, was either in its senescence or in its death bed. The Pope waited patiently for the arrival of the princes' delegates until September, but even then attendance was scant. This was not entirely surprising. England was enduring the Wars of the Roses, while France was not in the giving vein as the Pope had preferred Ferrante, the bastard son of the recently demised Alfonso V of Aragon, for the throne of Naples to a pretender put up by the House of Anjou. Gregory of Heimburg, representing Frederick III, had been excommunicated in 1458 over ecclesiastical politics and this was only a symptom of how the German Empire was beginning to reject ultramontane papal policies in this period.[30] Gregory was openly disrespectful to Pius II during the congress and his grudgingly given promise to raise 32,000 footmen and 10,000 cavalry was never honoured.

Poland was distracted from Balkan events as it was embroiled in a long war with the Teutonic Knights and at this juncture Moldavia was a vassal state of the Polish king and followed his line. Albania had secured a three-year truce with Mehemmed II and was not ready to break it. Almost in desperation, Pius II sent a monk, Fra Ludovico da Bologna, to the Muslim states to the east of the Ottomans in Anatolia to try to forge a two-front union against Mehemmed II.

The venture looked to be dead; even the transfer of the head of Saint Andrew to Rome and the Pope travelling in person to Ancona to lead the Crusade could not seem to resuscitate it. The Pope was certainly clutching at straws when he wrote to Mehemmed II to attempt to convert him to Catholicism. Perhaps he listened too much to the emissaries of Uzun Hasan of the Ak-Koyunlu who, as we have seen, accused Mehemmed II of burning mosques or perhaps he had heard the rumours that Mehemmed II no longer stood up as every Ottoman was expected to do whenever the martial music of *Ghazism* was played in Istanbul. Either way, the Pope was misled by Mehemmed II's apparent rejection of Islam. As we have seen above, Mehemmed II was, in fact, rejecting the tribal element in his empire as he centralised his state. Not standing for *Ghazism* was designed to mark him out as above all others and mosques in this period, just as they are today, could very easily become the focus of self-legitimising militant Islamic leadership amongst the grassroots. Such a thing was anathema to Mehemmed II's project just as it is to virtually all Middle East polities today.

Vlad Dracula responded to the Pope's call. Perhaps he felt he had no choice given that Mehemmed II now appeared to be planning an endless campaign of conquest, perhaps he hoped to secure funding or perhaps we should be generous enough to suggest that the prince had been called back to the vows he had inherited from his father as a member of the Order of the Dragon.[31] He may also, more pragmatically, have been following the lead of his ally, Michael Szilagyi, who also opted for resistance. Unfortunately Szilagyi was captured by the Ottomans whilst reconnoitring in Bulgaria, after the fall of Smederevo. He was taken to Istanbul and tortured for information on Hungary's military disposition and preparations. He was sawn in half, presumably for not divulging any secrets.[32]

Vlad Dracula wrote in surprisingly friendly terms to Brasov in September 1460. Perhaps he realised that with his commitment to the Crusade he would need every Catholic ally he could muster and there was also, of course, the question of the funds to maintain 4,000 mercenaries:

> An embassy from Turkey had now come to us. Bear in mind that I have previously spoken to you about brotherhood and peace ... the time and the hour have now come, where the Turks wish to place upon our shoulders ... unbearable difficulties and ... compel us not to live peacefully with you ... They are seeking ways to loot your country passing through ours. In addition, they force us ... to work against your Catholic faith. Our wish is to commit no evil against you, not to abandon you, as I have sworn. I trust that I shall remain your brother and faithful friend. This is why I have retained the Turkish envoys here, so that I have time to send you the news.[33]

Various chronicles record that the Ottoman envoys had their turbans nailed to their heads by Vlad Dracula. Whether this was tit-for-tat for Szilagyi's killing or a direct provocation of the sultan is hard to know but the non-payment of tribute, the frequent incursions of Ottoman *razzia* parties into Wallachia looking for plunder and children for the slave market and Vlad Dracula's impaling of these raiders and reprisals against Ottoman possessions on the River Danube, and his refusal to attend the sultan in Istanbul all made for a tense stand-off during 1460 and 1461. During this time the Ottomans chipped away at the River Danube's defences and took the fortress of Giurgiu. A full deployment of Ottoman might was delayed by distractions in Anatolia with Karaman and Uzun Hasan, which would not be fully resolved by Mehemmed II until 1473.

A duplicitous exchange of letters followed between the sultan and his vassal Vlad Dracula as both were playing for time. Vlad Dracula gave Mehemmed II what the Irish call 'the poor mouth' as he told of how the Wallachian treasury had been emptied by the Saxon wars to such an extent that paying the tribute that was due would break the state, make it untaxable in the future and make it easy for the Hungarians to take the country under their control. He offered payment in kind of children and horses.

This, and the offer of settling a Danube border between Vlad Dracula's lands and the empire's, was enough to bring an offer from the sultan of an emissary, Hamza Pasha, the *bey* of Nicopolis, to visit Vlad Dracula's capital to negotiate. However, at this point Mehemmed II appears to have discovered a secret and seditious correspondence between Vlad Dracula and Matthias Corvinus and contrived to trap his vassal.

Hamza Pasha moved the planned meeting to Giurgiu and sent a certain Thomas Catavolinos, a Greek in Hamza Pasha's service, to escort Vlad Dracula from Tirgoviste to the meeting. He was to arrange an ambush close to Giurgiu. Vlad Dracula seems to have been one step ahead of both Catavolinos and Hamza Pasha and was followed at a prudent distance by a troop of his bodyguard's cavalry. As the trap was sprung it was the Ottomans who were ambushed. Vlad Dracula then rode on to Giurgiu, where he disguised himself as an Ottoman Turk and demanded in fluent Turkish that the guards admit him. His men gained admittance by mixing in with the Ottoman soldiers and set about killing, burning and looting. War had essentially been declared and over the winter of 1461 Vlad Dracula did his utmost to let the Ottomans know it.

The River Danube was frozen and Vlad Dracula's men crossed and re-crossed it as they raided throughout Ottoman Bulgaria. Once again Vlad Dracula's soldierly skills have to be admired as he raided and moved across the length of the River Danube at phenomenal speed, surprising and attacking the Ottomans at every point from Serbia right through to the delta. He broke his forces into small raiding parties that could move quickly and live off the land as he attempted the capture or destruction of what would be key jumping off points for any Ottoman invasion of Wallachia and Transylvania.

Vlad Dracula confirmed his body count to Matthias Corvinus in a letter in February 1462. He boasted particularly of the multitude of enemy killed:

> I have killed men and women, old and young, who lived at Oblucitza and Novoselo, where the Danube flows into the sea, up to Rahova, which is located near Chilia, from the lower Danube up to such places as Samovit and Ghighen. We killed 23,884 Turks and Bulgars without counting those whom we burned in homes or whose heads were not cut by our soldiers ... Thus Your Highness must know that I have broken the peace with him. (Mehemmed II).[34]

As a postscript, Vlad Dracula sent the king two large bags of the heads, noses and ears he and his men had cut off their enemies.

The 1,000 Ottoman troops who had been captured with Hamza Pasha and Thomas Catavolinos were impaled outside Tirgoviste after a forced march from Giurgiu. Taller stakes were reserved for Catavolinos and Hamza Pasha, almost certainly not as a sign of respect.

A response had to be expected and Vlad Dracula must have hoped that his despoiling of each river port along the River Danube's length would be sufficient to stop the Ottomans at least during the summer. It was not and whilst Mehemmed II was engaged in reducing Corinth he was still able to send the grand wazir, Mahmud, with an army of 18,000 men to capture Brila, a port on the Wallachian side of the Danube. After taking the port he then struck north into Wallachia on a giant raiding mission. Vlad Dracula caught up with the Turks' rearguard as they were trying to re-cross at Brila and were loaded with booty and captives. It was recorded, though it seems very doubtful, that Vlad Dracula killed 10,000 of the Ottoman army.

Whatever the scale of victory really achieved at Brila it was enough to bring Mehemmed II into the field in May 1462. Vlad Dracula had accounted for the fact that the Ottomans were now an impressive naval or, in this case, riverine power. He had destroyed Danube ports and fortified the key positions along the Wallachian river border; however Mehemmed II still deployed the fleet on the Danube as he needed it to support the invasion across the river he had planned to launch from Bulgaria.

Vlad Dracula's problem was that, despite his depopulation and destruction of the more obvious crossing points, he still could not be absolutely sure of where the sultan would cross or even if he would cross in force at one point or disperse his forces. Given the imbalance between the troops and resources available to each commander this severely stretched the Wallachians.

The army that Mehemmed II was bringing was certainly impressively large. He had conquered Trebizond and made a peace accord with the Karamanids that allowed him to release Anatolian levies for the Wallachian campaign. He set out in May 1462 from Istanbul.

The army he brought with him was sufficient not just to make reprisal attacks on Vlad Dracula but to reduce Wallachia completely and turn it into a province. There were at least 60,000 regular troops and 30,000 auxiliaries, including Bulgarians and Serbians and Anatolian *akinje* freebooters. There were also 120 cannon.

Vlad Dracula was still casting about for allies and support as this vast army lumbered towards his domains. Things looked hopeful for a while as the Venetian ambassador to the Hungarian court pleaded the Wallachian prince's cause to both the Pope and the republic's senate. The ambassador was obviously also agitating with Matthew Corvinus, for he wrote to the senate that the Hungarian king had promised to lead his army into Transylvania to support the Wallachians. Perhaps the ambassador had got caught up in the frenzy of adoration for the feats of Vlad Dracula in 1460–61 that had swept across Europe, and not surprisingly, had reached the Pope, whose planned grand Crusade now seemed to have been taken up by Wallachia alone.

The problem was that, despite protestations to the contrary, there was no way that Matthias Corvinus was going to commit the Hungarian army to Transylvania at a time when he was still at loggerheads with Frederick III over the Crown of Hungary. He was more than happy to take the Pope's crusading money and to use the presence of the small Hungarian garrison of Chilia as justification for this – in 1448, Petru II had handed over Chilia to Hunyadi, in effect giving Hungary control of the strategic area on the Danube, with access to the Black Sea – but no more help was to be given to Vlad Dracula. The enthusiasm for Vlad Dracula's endeavours in Western Europe also turned out to be a chimera as no great or small power responded and, as we will see, Stephen of Moldavia even joined the Ottomans.

In desperation, Vlad Dracula attempted to seal a marriage into the Hungarian royal house to secure more support but this came to nothing despite the prince's willingness to convert to Catholicism.

Vlad Dracula executed a mass levy of the Wallachian citizenry. This may have produced a fairly motley assortment of peasants of military age and some younger men and boys but the same had applied to the Hussite armies that had inflicted so many defeats on the chivalry of Europe and in the woodlands and wetlands of Wallachia such a force was capable of inflicting enormous harm on even well-disciplined and skilled soldiers such as the Janissaries. Furthermore, the *viteji* had all come from this rank of society so they knew how to whip the peasants into action, how to organise them and how best to use them on the battlefield. The townsmen handled the few firearms available and the war-wagons, bombards and cannon, of which there were also only a few.

This 'raking' of the countryside and towns added to Vlad Dracula's core forces gave him about 30,000 men, or more correctly men, women and children. Of these, about 20,000 were definitely infantry with about 10,000 cavalry. The cavalry was composed of the 'new *boyars*' and officers who had come through the ranks. They were generally well armed with leather, possibly lamellar, armour and mail and plate for the *boyars*. Vlad Dracula also had his standing bodyguard of the *sluji* and gypsies who could act both as a core around which the army could rally and also as a flying corps of cavalry for raids and reconnaissance. The old Wallachian families of *boyars* abandoned Vlad Dracula and fled to the Carpathians to await the outcome.

Vlad Dracula's scouts roved up and down the length of the Danube watching for the Ottomans. Finally the Ottomans were sighted at Vidin. The Ottomans had advanced in two parts. Sultan Mehemmed II took the bulk of their army up the river by ship, probably with the goal of entering the River Olt and attacking Vlad Dracula's capital, whilst a force designated to protect the flank of the fleet and to force a crossing marched from Philipopolis in Bulgaria. The Ottomans tried to send an advance party over to the northern bank. They were raked with fire and arrows by the Wallachians, who emerged from the forest and retreated quickly. Then, in the first week of June 1462, a major landing was attempted at Turnu, which had been burned in 1461 but which was still useable once the Ottoman engineers had got to work. The Ottoman artillery had slowed the progress of the army already, and would become even more of a drag on its march once it entered the appalling roads and swampy lands of Wallachia proper, but at Turnu it was indispensable. Numerous cannon were deployed to cover the night crossing and the Ottomans even took light field artillery over with their first wave. The fighting was hard and bitter on the riverbank and the Ottomans dug trenches to defend their beachhead against furious Wallachian cavalry counter-attacks. Only when all the infantry, including the Janissaries, had been ferried across the river in seventy commandeered barges did the Ottomans dare to advance from the thin strip of bank that they held. During the securement of the beachhead 300 Janissaries were killed and the rest of the Ottomans were nearly thrown back into the river. The firepower of Vlad Dracula's war-wagons and the added height that the Wallachians would have gained from the war-wagons' firing platforms would have made their fire more accurate and, of course, the protection of the wagons would have made it even harder for the Janissaries, advancing through the forest, to make their fire count. A barrage involving 120 cannon was required to clear the field of the Wallachians. Mehemmed II personally rewarded the advance parties that had held on so tenaciously. He gave them 30,000 ducats to divide among themselves. It had doubtless been a close-run thing.

The sultan had brought his replacement *voivode* with him to the campaign. Vlad Dracula's brother, Radu, rode at the head of 4,000 horsemen of his own. The Ottomans moved slowly northwards towards Tirgoviste from Turnu via the monastery of Glavacioc. Bucharest and the monastery of Snagov were both briefly threatened but the Ottomans, as we will see below, were suffering severe logistics problems – especially in terms of water – and were not capable of besieging either place. They held all their resources back for Tirgoviste.

Now that the Ottomans were over the river, Vlad Dracula changed his tactics. He realised that pitched battles and even limited engagement were not options. He moved to a guerrilla war that aimed to give the Ottomans nothing for all their endeavours. Grain stores and crops were burned, wells were poisoned and all livestock and peasants were evacuated from regions as the army withdrew. Fighting through the dense Vlasia forest with the constant risk of ambush was hard enough for the Turks but Vlad Dracula also dammed small rivers and diverted their waters to create marshes to literally bog down the Ottoman army, and peasants dug huge traps and covered them with timber and leaves.

The summer added to the miseries of the Ottomans during the days and Vlad Dracula made the nights terrible. Each day saw a daily hunt for water but even the Anatolian *azabs* and African troops could not find clean potable water and they suffered just as much as the European levies from thirst and heat exhaustion. Each night saw the Ottoman troopers exhausted by the day's marching and short of food, having to break out their entrenching tools and surround their camps with earthworks. Any Turks beyond the 'safety' of the earthworks were taken and killed by the Wallachians, who knew their forests well. Only a few horsemen were needed for such raids and their psychological impact was as important as the physical damage they inflicted. Any captives were impaled to add to the horror of the Turks, who were losing comrades night by night. Whether the stories of Vlad Dracula releasing hardened criminals (it is a little difficult to believe that he actually *had* any hardened criminals in his prisons given his penchant for impaling and harsh justice) and individuals infected with tuberculosis and plague to mingle with the invaders and kill them either actively or 'passively' should be believed is a different question but there was certainly also 'camp sickness' for the Turks to contend with.[35]

The Lord Impaler, or the Kaziglu Bey, was wearing his enemy down but Mehemmed II still continued to close on his prey and by June he had besieged Vlad Dracula in the mountains above Tirgoviste. If a general rule of engaging with any enemy is to empathise with him and understand him, then Vlad Dracula would have held an advantage as he had lived among the Ottomans for so long. He perhaps understood better than any other Christian enemy of the Turks, with the obvious exception of Skanderbeg, how he could make them realise that the costs of victory over him would become close to pyrrhic very quickly. The famous night attack was an attempt by Vlad Dracula to find the straw that would break the camel's back – the killing of the sultan himself. Vlad Dracula tortured the Ottoman troops and officers he had captured in previous raids until they told him the exact location of Mehemmed II's camp. The best cavalry, perhaps as many as 7,000–10,000 troopers, he could find among his forces were then gathered together for the daring raid.

The attack took place on the night of 17 June 1462 and lasted some three hours, though it has been suggested that there was further skirmishing that extended into the next day and which accounts for the high reported casualties for both the Wallachians and the Ottomans. It seems possible that Ottoman prisoners were taken on the raid in order to help the Wallachians pass by and then kill the camp's sentries. Then, when the Wallachians were at the trench line surrounding

Mehemmed II's camp, their cavalry crashed in swinging torches and swords and loosing arrows. At one point it seemed that Vlad Dracula had found his prey when a particularly fine tent was torn down but it contained a prize that could only be a consolation – two wazirs, who were immediately done to death.

It was Mehemmed II's Janissaries who saved him. They massed around the sultan's tent and brought such a barrage of arrows and fire upon the raiders that no Wallachian would challenge them. The raiders went instead for booty and easier pickings and victims. Vlad Dracula was everywhere encouraging the killing and also trying to draw men into the key fight within the battle, for the sultan's head. He was failed ultimately by his second-in-command; the *boyar* Gale did not execute his assigned part of the plan with an attack from the other side of the camp's perimeter.

The Janissaries were then rallied by Mihalolu Ali Bey and advanced to push Vlad Dracula and his cavalry from the camp. They captured 2,000 Wallachian troopers during their advance through the camp and it is possible that they managed to wound Vlad Dracula. The Janissary of Ostrovitza tells us of the confusion and terror of the night:

> Although the Romanian Prince had a small army, we always advanced with great caution and fear and spent nights sleeping in ditches. But even in this manner we were not safe; for during one night the Romanians struck at us. They massacred horses, camels, and several thousand Turks. When the Turks had retreated in the face of the enemy, we (the Janissaries) repelled the enemy and killed them. But the sultan had incurred great losses.[36]

The Turks may have lost up to 15,000 men; Vlad Dracula's losses, given his limited resources, were also damaging, however, with about 5,000 lost. He would not gamble on another pitched battle with Mehemmed II and only a few days later the Ottomans were able to reach Tirgoviste. It presented a formidable task for the besieger as Vlad Dracula had expended great expense and no amount of slave labour to strengthen its walls and gates. A detachment of Ottoman cavalry was sent out to the north of the city to cut any routes of ingress for supplies and returned with yet another tale of terror for a campaign that had already begun to look more and more like a *danse macabre*.

A forest of impaled bodies had been discovered stretching more than 2 miles long in a huge crescent that was half a mile wide at its centre. Some 20,000 Ottoman captives, decomposing rapidly in the summer heat, made up Vlad Dracula's carefully cultivated arboretum. The higher stakes of Catavolinos and Hamza Pasha rose above their companions but not above the stench. This was the last straw for the Ottomans. The same night an extra palisade was thrown up around the sultan's camp and the next morning the army withdrew from Tirgoviste.

The Turkish fleet, which had been pretty much neutralised during the campaign by Vlad Dracula's destruction of the ports of the Danube, re-entered the fray only to evacuate the army across the river. Plague then struck at the Ottomans and by 22 June the army was in full retreat from Wallachia. Vlad Dracula scored one more victory over the Ottomans at Buzu on 26 June when he defeated Evrenos Pasha.

Stephen of Moldavia used the Ottoman retreat and Vlad Dracula's near exhaustion to attack the fortress of Chilia. Mehemmed II gave him men for the task, probably in order to vent his spleen against Vlad Dracula. Stephen's 'betrayal' of his cousin and erstwhile fellow fugitive would probably have received a nod of understanding if not approval from Vlad Dracula. Stephen would have been worried for his own flank and the protection of Moldavia's Black Sea trade routes if the fortress and the city of Akkerman fell completely to the Turks. There were also Hungarian troops garrisoned at Chilia and there was certainly no love lost between Stephen and Matthias Corvinus, but border security would have been uppermost in the Moldavian king's mind. Ultimately the assault was unsuccessful and Stephen received a leg wound that he would carry for the rest of his life. The Hungarians came out as winners as their garrison along with the Wallachians put both the Moldavians and Ottomans to shame and Matthias was also able to claim a share of the Pope's crusading funds.

On 29 June the Ottomans burnt Brila and left Wallachia. They reached Adrianople in the second week of July.

Mehemmed II was no stranger to adversity. His first reign had been a disaster, the attempt on Constantinople had, at times, looked to be a gigantic failure and his army had withered before the walls of Belgrade. The Wallachian campaign must still, however, have rankled. He seemed to have gained nothing in the war but did still have one last cast of the die. He left Radu, Vlad Dracula's handsome brother, with a small contingent of Ottoman troopers and his own detachment of Wallachian *boyar* cavalry up in the Brgan region of Wallachia. Dissident *boyars* had been visiting his camp all through June to make obeisance and to suggest that Vlad Dracula could be removed by a rebellion and replaced with his brother. We suggested earlier how well Vlad Dracula understood his enemy. It would be remiss not to extend the same compliment to Mehemmed II. It seems that the sultan knew very well indeed just how Wallachian politics worked.

A ceremonial sword of the Order of the Dragon now held in the Neue Burg, Vienna. Both Vlad Dracula and his father were inducted into this Catholic order of Christian leaders, who swore to combat heretics and the Ottomans. This was despite both Vlad Dracula and his father being Orthodox Christians. (Author's collection)

This statue on the Charles Bridge in Prague records one of the most unpleasant aspects of Ottoman rule in Eastern Europe: slavery, and in particular the *devshirme*, or harvest of young Christian boys, for service in the elite Janissary corps. Vlad Dracula rebelled against the Ottomans in 1459 after refusing to honour agreements allowing for the forced deportation of 500 Wallachian boys. (Author's collection)

The famous night attack in which Vlad Dracula and his Wallachian cavalry came close to killing the Sultan Mehemmed II took place in June 1462 as a last-ditch attempt by the Impaler to save his throne. It is depicted here in *The Battle with Torches* by the Romanian painter Theodor Aman.

Curtea De Arges was the seat of the Patriarch of the Romanian Orthodox Church. Vlad Dracula granted tax immunities and other privileges to monasteries and built new and extended old church buildings. In return he expected submission to his will and support from the pulpit. (Author's collection)

Vlad Dracula used peasants as infantry in his army in an attempt to make up for his lack of regular troops. These conscripts often used their agricultural tools as weapons but this was not a disadvantage in battle. The Hussites had defeated Crusading armies with just such weapons. A peasant depicted here in the stained glass of Chartres Cathedral shows how the length and weight of a flail made it an ideal weapon for close quarters fighting, especially for men deployed in war-waggons. (Author's collection)

The tomb of Vlad Dracula's grandfather, Mircea I, is in the beautiful Cozia Monastery. Mircea was regarded by the Ottomans as the most courageous and shrewd among all the Christian princes of his generation. (Author's collection)

The Byzantine-style icons of Cozia Monastery are indicative of Wallachia's deeply rooted adherence to the Orthodox Faith. Vlad Dracula's political conversion to Catholicism in 1475 to gain Hungarian support was certainly one factor that precipitated his fall from power in 1476. (Author's collection)

Pope Eugenius IV was one of the architects of the disastrous 1444 Crusade of Varna in which Vlad Dracula's father participated. The Pope had hoped to 'to snatch the Catholic flock from the yoke of miserable servitude'. (Author's collection)

The 1444 Crusade of Varna from a Polish chronicle of 1564. The King of Hungary and Poland, Vladislaus III, was killed by Murad II's Janissaries as he led a foolhardy charge against the Ottomans after Jonas Hunyadi had come close to winning the battle. The king's death led to the rout of the Christian army. (Library of Congress)

A recreation of a Hussite war-waggon. Vlad Dracula also deployed such waggons against the Ottomans. The protection they provided for his infantry and hand-gunners was invaluable as he was consistently outnumbered by his foes. (Author's collection)

Vlad Dracula was portrayed in the 1979 Romanian film *Vlad Tepes* as a patriot fighting for his country and saving Europe from the Ottoman invaders. This description bears very little resemblance to the historical truth. (Doru Nastase)

George Skanderbeg, along with Jonas Hunyadi and Stephen the Great, was given the title of *Athletae Christi* by the Pope for his long resistance to the Ottomans. He became a legend in Western and Eastern Europe and his statue now stands in the centre of Tirana, in Skanderbeg Square. (Author's collection)

The helmet of Skanderbeg. When Ottoman troops discovered his tomb they took small fragments of his bones and made them into amulets in the hope that these charms might instil in them the same martial valour their enemy had displayed. (Author's collection)

Castle Dracula, or more correctly Poenari Castle, owed much of its strength to the precipitous heights on which it was perched. It was also renovated and strengthened by slave labourers, many of whom were the sons and daughters of *boyars* whom Vlad Dracula had massacred in 1457. (Author's collection)

John of Capistrano's preaching that 'God wills it that we chase the Turks out of Europe' among the peasants of Hungary and Serbia brought an army of rag-tag Crusaders to the defence of Belgrade in 1456. The Ottomans were defeated but both Capistrano and Jonas Hunyadi died of plague after the city was saved. (Author's collection)

Istanbul from a map of 1550. During their conquest of the city the Ottomans overcame the great chain gate that protected the Golden Gate harbour by means of a wooden slipway from the Bosporus. They brought their ships overland across the hills beyond Galata and into the Golden Horn *behind* the boom. (Library of Congress)

940   De Græcia   Liber IIII.   941

Constantinopolitanæ urbis effigies, quam hodie sub Turcæ inhabitatione habet.

The famous walls and towers of Byzantium were no match for the artillery of Mehemmed II. The angular walls could not deflect the impact of cannonballs fired from the Ottomans' giant *Basiliske* cannon and there were few emplacements for firearms or cannon to return fire. (Library of Congress)

One of the fine Ottoman tents abandoned by the sultan's army before the last and ultimately unsuccessful siege of Vienna in 1683. The Ottomans were eventually defeated in the Balkans not by dashing knights or by princes such as Vlad Dracula but by professional soldiers through a war of attrition. (Author's collection)

Nikolae Ceausescu used the iconography of a re-invented Vlad Dracula to celebrate his own 'strongman' status. In 1976, the 500th anniversary of Vlad Dracula's death was used to bolster ideas of self-sacrifice and the superiority of the state over the individual. It is perhaps appropriate that Ceausescu suffered a similar fate to that of Vlad Dracula, as he was executed by his own people.

Vlad Dracula was in many ways the protégé of Michael Szilagyi. Szilagyi was one of the heroes of the siege of Belgrade in 1456 but in 1457 he was responsible for unleashing Vlad Dracula on a reign of terror among the German cities of Transylvania. Szilagyi was later captured by the Ottomans and tortured. He was sawn in half as he refused to divulge the Hungarians' defence plans to Mehemmed II. (Library of Congress)

Vlad Dracula fortified the monastery of Snagov in 1458 against any Ottoman raids into the Danube plain, but in Wallachia's violent political landscape a prince also needed such secure places in case of internal revolt. No fewer than twelve princes sat on the throne from 1418 to 1458. (Author's collection)

Vlad Dracula's cousin, Stephen the Great of Moldavia, inflicted a crushing defeat on the Ottomans at Vaslui in January 1475. He also mimicked Vlad Dracula's scorched earth tactics and successfully entreated Matthias Corvinus, the Hungarian king, to release his cousin from arrest and to reseat him on the throne of Wallachia in 1476. (Author's collection)

Stephen the Great of Moldavia was entirely more pious than his cousin Vlad Dracula. His 'celebrations' after his impressive victory over the Ottomans at Vaslui included the building of a magnificent monastery at Voronet with a vast mural depicting Judgement Day and fasting for forty days to show his devotion to God, to whom he said the victory should truly be attributed. (Author's collection)

Vlad Dracula added the Chindia Tower to the Wallachian capital and royal court of Tirgoviste. In the seventeenth century, the royal court was burnt to the ground by the Ottomans and the capital was moved to Bucharest. (Author's collection)

Sighisoara was the headquarters of Vlad Dracula's father, Vlad II Dracul, during his time as governor of Transylvania. It was an ideal fortress as its thick defensive walls could withstand the field artillery of the Ottomans and it was located in the centre of the border with Wallachia, a state that Vlad II Dracul coveted. (Author's collection)

The Selimiye Mosque graces the Ottomans' first European capital of Edirne. It was built in 1568 as the Ottoman Empire was facing up to a series of problems including a tough new opponent in the shape of the Habsburg Empire, financial crises and army and civil revolts. Despite ongoing reverses, the Ottomans still held Wallachia as a subject state until 1878, more than 400 years after Vlad Dracula's death. (Author's collection)

Vlad Dracula's greatest enemy, the Sultan Mehemmed II, conquered Constantinople in 1453. Churches such as the Hagia Sophia were converted into mosques but Mehemmed II in fact pursued a tolerant attitude towards the religion of his subjects. The sultan was, in fact, as interested in conquering Muslim foes as he was in the sub-jugation of Christian states. Even at his death in 1481 he was planning to wrest Egypt and Syria from the Mamluk Sultanate. (Author's collection)

4

THE FALL:

DRACULA'S LOSS OF WALLACHIA

I suppose one ought to pity any thing so hunted as is the Count. That is just it: this Thing is not human – not even beast. It is enough to dry up the springs of pity in one's heart.[1]

Vlad Dracula received letters of thanks from the Genoese colonists from Caffa on the Black Sea as his defiance on the Danube had tied up 300 Ottoman ships that were to have been sent against them by Mehemmed II. Vlad Dracula might have hoped for more from the East as back in May 1462 he had sent to the khan of the Golden Horde suggesting a joint attack on the Ottomans. As was usual in all of these proposed European–Asian joint ventures against a common enemy this came to nothing.[2]

The sultan's army had gone but in fact the war was turning against Vlad Dracula. It has been suggested in a recent work on strategy that the term 'a duel' is a 'bad metaphor'[3] for the complexity of approach that warring sides need to undertake if they are to be successful in any contest. The basic problem with what Vlad Dracula had undertaken was that it was acted out as just that: a duel with Mehemmed II. The struggle exhausted Wallachia physically and it was bleeding to death. Crops had been burnt, waters had been poisoned, land remained untilled and the flower of its soldiery had been sacrificed in the long contest of attrition, in the pitched battles on the banks of the River Danube and during the night attack. But there was more to this in Vlad Dracula's lack of any definitive and successful strategy to take on Mehemmed II. Wallachia was also corroded from within by the actions that Vlad Dracula had undertaken during his solidification of power. He was essentially bereft of internal allies and his near-genocidal war with the Saxons virtually guaranteed that Transylvania would not show any great loyalty when push came to shove. If strategy really is 'the central political art. It is about getting more out of a situation than the starting balance of power would suggest. It is the art of creating power',[4] then Vlad Dracula was an abject failure as a prince.

The concept of *princeps* and why some monarchs endured and others did not, and why some dragged their states into destruction and others became their country's saviours, is certainly beyond the scope of this volume. A close reading of Machiavelli might reveal some gems but one thing is certain, the key action of any successful prince in the medieval age and beyond into the modern age was to balance the forces within the state. Shakespeare's Richard II, and perhaps even the real Richard, only realised once they had lost power that 'to monarchise, be fear'd, and kill with looks'[5] might infuse a monarch with vain conceit but that the most important task any monarch could undertake was the bridging of factions within his realm and to be a touchstone of unity. The creation of factions that Richard II achieved with his sponsoring of the Order of the White Hart, which was not as inclusive or capable of bridging aristocratic rivalries as the Order of the Garter or the Order of the Dragon, was entirely the opposite of what a prince should aim to do. Vlad Dracula made the same mistake when he attacked the *boyar* system rather than subverting it to his needs as a shrewd prince might. Certainly he created a group of men similar to Richard's men of the order with his *sluji* and *viteji* but the *boyars* of Wallachia were a class who had lands in Hungary, connections in Transylvania and blood ties in Moldavia; they *were* Wallachia.

This is not to suggest that monarchs were not dependent on exclusive bodies of followers. The Norman kings of England had their household as the core of all the armies they ever gathered together to make war on their neighbours. Indeed, the *familia regis* of Edward I could expand from 'a little company of peacetime guards' into 'the dimensions of a small army',[6] but this *expansion* was really the point. The military household was made up of men whose extended family, feudal relationships and 'clientage' extended outwards into every part of the nobility of the kingdom. Vlad Dracula destroyed any hope of such an arrangement because he essentially ripped the heart out of his state with his violent destruction of the *boyars*. Gibbon was not far wrong when he labelled two of the greatest emperors Augustus and Diocletian as 'crafty' as they never sought to destroy any institutions of the state but rather sought either to usurp it themselves or to effectively cancel out or neutralise all of the powers of those same institutions.[7] Vlad Dracula was a fine general and tactician but a poor war leader and strategist. He was also a brute who could attract little loyalty once fear was removed from the equation, and a very poor prince. His need for the *sluji*, like Richard II's need of the Men of Cheshire, was related to his degrading of the office of monarch.

The Crusader kings of Jerusalem were, in practical terms, no more than the *primus inter pares* among a group of almost equally powerful Crusader states, but the princes of Antioch, Edessa and Tripoli still recognised the superiority in title of the king. The reasons were partly because he sat upon the holiest throne in Christendom and held most lands that could be disseminated as fiefs to maintain a large 'base' of vassals. But this would not have been enough to maintain power over the other Palestinian magnates if it had not been that the first five kings of Jerusalem were 'tough, active and responsible'.[8] Vlad Dracula stripped away any veneer of holiness or any reverence his people and the higher lords of his lands might have felt for him by his direct involvement in acts of horror and in what might best be described as 'rough justice'.

The monarch was the last repository for justice in the medieval world. To him was given the rights of pardon and punishment, and using them in a balanced manner inspired loyalty among all the people by the simple hope of clemency and fairness. The continual application of punitive measures could do nothing more than drive those awaiting the prince's 'justice' into rebellion and make everyone else feel as if they were just waiting for the axe to fall on them. A skilled monarch such as Baldwin II of Jerusalem used his reputation as an avatar of justice to gain consent from subjects and magnates for an extension of the benevolent powers of the Crown. This was even to the extent of giving the Crown powers undreamt of before in feudal society, as he did with the introduction of the *etablissement* giving the king powers of retribution against acts of *lèse-majesté*.[9] Vlad Dracula could not achieve anything like this simply because he lacked statecraft and because he involved himself, and the Crown, in acts of bloody revenge that commonly present him as nothing more than a rage-fuelled tyrant.

With an exhausted state and with former followers peeling away from his cause, Dracula escaped to the mountains of Transylvania at the end of 1462. After the trial of strength with Mehemmed II it was a whimpering end to his first reign. Radu III was recognised as Prince of Wallachia by most of the *boyars* and Matthias Corvinus gave his recognition soon after.

Radu III could claim that with him at the helm Wallachia would remain free of Turkish occupation and of the *devshirme*, though these liberties were in fact in no small part due to the sheer bloodiness of Vlad Dracula and the people of Wallachia's resistance to Mehemmed II's invasion. Radu III could, however, play on the fact that he was the only acceptable candidate of the House of Dracul to the Ottomans, and any continuance of the reign of Vlad Dracula could bring nothing more than repeated invasions and the desolation of the country. Radu III had also made a political marriage with one Maria Despina, a member of the clan of Florescu, uncompromising enemies of Vlad Dracula, who had been in exile since 1456.

Radu III 'the Handsome' pursued his brother along the River Arges' valley and up to his bolthole, the castle of Arges. Cannons supplied by the Ottomans were set up to bring down the walls. Folklore has Vlad Dracula's mistress throwing herself from the top of the castle as she learned of Vlad Dracula's rapidly collapsing fortunes, but the truth of her demise or otherwise is in fact not known; Wallachian medieval gender history is virtually an undeveloped discipline. The stretch of river below the castle is, however, known to this day as Riul Doamnei, or the 'Princess River'.

Vlad Dracula made a dramatic escape across the slopes above the castle and rode on to Brasov, apparently on a horse that had been shod backward to confuse any pursuers. He and a small party of diehard mercenaries waited there for King Matthias Corvinus at Konigstein, a Hungarian fortress built by John Hunyadi. The news was that Matthias would arrive soon with detachments of the Hungarian army to watch for developments in the war between the two brothers. In fact, the king took until November to travel from Buda to Brasov. It is possible that the king's tardy progress was entirely deliberate and allowed him to see which faction was going to win Wallachia, even though he wrote reassuringly to Pope Pius II that he was riding to the aid of his vassal Vlad Dracula. There was even talk, once again, of a marriage union between the houses.

Vlad Dracula finally met the king in the town hall of Brasov but he was already a political inconvenience as Radu III had been wooing the German towns of Transylvania with commercial concessions and compensation for his brother's acts. Brasov and Bran recognised Radu III's reign and Sibiu soon followed. These little economic powerhouses were vital to the filling of Matthias' treasury and he followed their lead and gave official recognition to Prince Radu III of Wallachia in November.

Matthias also signed a truce with Mehemmed II and killed dead the Crusade that he had already garnered funds for from the curia. The money would come in handy as Matthias had seen opportunities in the difficulties that Frederick III was currently experiencing with his subjects over taxation to challenge him both for the Habsburg estates and for the imperial Crown.

So what to do with Vlad Dracula? The king graciously granted him a body of soldiers under the leadership of Jan Jiskra, whom we last met during his attempt to thwart John Hunyadi's *Longum Bellum*. Jiskra was now, in fact, employed by Matthias despite his previous allegiance to the now dead Ladislaus V. Vlad Dracula's gypsies and Hungarian mercenaries and the men of Jan Jiskra were to act as an advance guard to a Hungarian army that would follow Vlad Dracula into Wallachia to retake the throne. At Konigstein the party stopped while their war wagons were lowered down from the fortress, sitting high up on the mountain ridge, to the valley floor below. By 6 December the last of the war-wagons were down and Vlad Dracula's men waited for him in the Valley of the Saxons. Then Jiskra struck, seizing Vlad Dracula whilst he was still in Konigstein and arresting him in the king's name. It seems likely that the entire undertaking had been a set-up from the very beginning, contrived to isolate Vlad Dracula but also to ensure he would fall safely into the arms and gaol of the king and not of any of the German towns that might choose to obtain vengeance on their one-time tormentor.

To counter any backlash from Vlad Dracula's admirers in Western Europe, which of course included the Pope and the Venetian senate, both enthusiastic donors to the Crusade funds of 1459, a batch of letters was hastily produced around Christmastime 1462 which seemed to implicate Vlad Dracula in a plot with Mehemmed II and Stephen of Moldavia to capture the King of Hungary. The Saxon cities added their condemnations of Vlad Dracula but even with all this 'evidence' there was no denunciation from the Papacy and a noticeable amount of doubt over the veracity of the letters from the Venetians. Matthias' speedy conclusion to the Crusade and his peace with Mehemmed II also occasioned comment even at the Polish court. It may have been because of the general disapproval of the king's arrest of the Crusader of the Danube that Vlad Dracula soon found himself only under house arrest rather than the close confinement he had suffered. He was housed at the king's summer palace at Visegrad overlooking the River Danube, where he performed a double function for the Hungarian Crown. It was useful to have a rival claimant to Radu III's Wallachian Crown among the king's court and it was useful to have the man the Ottomans most feared among his entourage when the emissaries of the Porte came to visit and to clarify the provisions of the treaty. Dracula was offered entrance into the Hungarian royal family provided that he renounced his Greek Orthodox faith and became a Roman Catholic. He also obtained the rank of captain in the Hungarian army. It was a comfortable captivity and Vlad Dracula was even invited to the ceremonies of inauguration of Matthias, who had, at last, been able to secure the Crown of Saint Stephen from Frederick III under promise of 80,000 ducats – which had almost certainly been partly raised from Pius II's crusading donations to the Hungarian king – in the summer of 1464.

There was a papal coronation in 1464 too as Pius II died whilst hopelessly awaiting the departure of his crusading army for the East from Ancona. A Venetian, Pope Paul II, was elected. A newly aggressive Venice, and a new policy for the republic in the Balkans, was to be expected but when Venice had tried to drive the Ottomans out of the Peloponnese from 1463 to 1464 its army, despite the presence of hand-gunners and heavy cavalry, had been given a very bloody nose by the Ottomans. In fact, this was to be the last major Venetian land offensive in the East. The navy and her garrisons in the Balkans were to be the republic's defence but, as we will see, these were soon breached by the sheer audacity of Mehemmed II, whose vision of conquest was boundless. Venice bound itself into treaties with Hungary and Skanderbeg in Albania in 1463 but this had done little to protect Bosnia and Hercegovina in the same year. After Mehemmed II had forced Skanderbeg to sign a new truce he had turned north and overrun both Bosnia and Hercegovina. Bosnia was conquered outright but Hercegovina, with Hungarian assistance, staved off complete occupation. It would continue as a border state until 1481.

Hungary was looking more and more exposed by Mehemmed II's chipping away of the smaller surrounding states and this was another reason for Matthias' quick recognition of Radu III as Prince of Wallachia in 1462. A *voivode* who would at least show some deference to the Hungarian Crown was preferable to one who was completely in the grip of Istanbul or one who was provoking Mehemmed II as Vlad Dracula had been. The king's Wallachian policy was, however, thrown into a degree of doubt in January 1465 by the capture of Chilia by Stephen in Moldavia. Chilia was a key strategic outpost and, even though it was garrisoned by Wallachians until Stephen took it, the Hungarians essentially considered it to be their possession. There was only irritation at Stephen's act from Matthias at this point and no response.

At this juncture it might seem that no one was fighting the Turks. Pope Pius II's Crusade had died or withered away and even the presence of a famous and feted leader, Skanderbeg, at its head could not bring it back to life. In fact, though, Skanderbeg had been fighting an almost interminable war against the Ottomans since the accession of Mehemmed II and had also embroiled himself in the ongoing conflict between the House of Aragon and the Angevins of southern Italy.

Back in 1453 Skanderbeg had tested the mettle of the new sultan by raiding and he also took some territories and a castle around Berat from the Ottomans. Alfonso V responded to this initial success by sending troops from Naples to join with Skanderbeg and the Albanian lords. Skanderbeg then tried to hold together a complex group of allies, two of which, Venice and Aragon, were at each other's throat in almost every other theatre in the eastern Mediterranean. Skanderbeg even came close to war with his own 'ally' Venice as it withheld funds in protest over his closeness to Aragon. Into this mix Skanderbeg also added an increasingly strong relationship with the papacy.

With this complex web of support behind him and with the promise of a Crusade from the West, Skanderbeg went to war as the captain–general of the armed forces of Aragon in June 1454. Unfortunately he overreached himself with an attempt to reduce the fortress of Berat. Skanderbeg's army of Albanians and Aragonese troops besieged the fortress town for several months and the garrison commander was reduced to calling for terms of surrender. However, instead of pressing the siege at this vital moment Skanderbeg took half his forces from the fortress. He left behind a detachment of cavalry and Aragonese troops to conclude the business but the Ottomans were already en route with a relieving force and they caught the besieging force in a surprise attack. The cavalry was decimated, and Skanderbeg's problems were doubled by the fact that they were Arianiti cavalry – his main supporters among the lords of Albania. In one engagement the political power of the Arianiti was destroyed. The destruction among the Aragonese troops was just as severe.

The debacle at Berat reduced Skanderbeg's prestige and there were defections from the higher lords to the Ottomans in the second half of the 1450s with castles also being sold to the Ottomans, even by Skanderbeg's own nephews.

Then, in the summer of 1457, Mehemmed II committed 70,000 men to complete the reduction of Albania. Isak Bey and Hamza Kastrioti led the invasion and the fact that Mehemmed II had chosen two commanders who were highly knowledgeable about Albania and drawn from its aristocracy seemed to pay dividends as for several months there was no response from Skanderbeg and they ravaged the countryside.

Then, in September, as the Ottomans were encamped in a field known as White Water between Lezhe and Kruje, Skanderbeg appeared suddenly and attacked the camp. The surprise was complete and the damage wrought on the Ottoman army was enough to force its retreat from Albania and to secure a five-year peace treaty from Mehemmed II. Hamza Kastrioti went to a Neapolitan prison.

This victory was enough to secure an increase in donations from the papacy and Skanderbeg was appointed as captain-general of the Holy See in December 1457. The Pope also pressured Ragusa and Venice to release Crusade funds to Skanderbeg and furnished him with a small number of galleys. This was a useful supplement as Skanderbeg's chief patron up to now had been Alfonso V and he died in June 1458.

In 1459 Skanderbeg captured the fortress of Sati from the Ottomans but he gave it over to Venice as he quickly recognised that the son of Alfonso V, Ferdinand I, was unlikely to prove as able as his father or as supportive, as he quickly became mired in southern Italian affairs. Soon enough this proved true and it was Skanderbeg who had to go to the aid of the Aragonese in 1461. He reaffirmed his armistice with the Ottomans in April 1461 and then landed in Apulia with 1,000 cavalry and 2,000 foot to challenge the Angevin petty Prince of Taranto. His victory was swift enough for Ferdinand I to be secure on his throne before the end of 1461 and Skanderbeg returned home with his Albanians.

In short order he defeated three Ottoman armies that were sent into Albania by a sultan who must have been beginning to wonder what he had to do to end Skanderbeg's career of resistance. The third army was defeated near Skopje, and the city subsequently hosted the peace talks that concluded with a ten-year treaty between Mehemmed II and Skanderbeg in April 1463.

As discussed above, by 1463 Venice had entered into a war with the Ottomans over the Peloponnese. The failure of this venture and Venice's move to a defensive style of war against Mehemmed II made Skanderbeg invaluable to the republic. He secured funding, galleys and a guarantee of Albanian independence in any territorial negotiations between Venice and the Ottomans.

The Crusade of 1463, as we have also seen, was largely a damp squib with only Vlad Dracula among the lords of the interior responding, but Skanderbeg also went to war in November 1463 and he attacked the Ottoman troops garrisoned at Ohrid. In April of the next year, at the Battle of Vaikal, Skanderbeg defeated an army under the command of the Albanian commander Ballaban Badera. However, in an engagement following the battle several Albanian noblemen including relatives and close friends of Skanderbeg were ambushed and captured. They were sent to Istanbul, where Mehemmed II proved that Vlad Dracula did not have the monopoly on mindless cruelty. The twenty-one captives were subjected to a fifteen-day trial of slow skinning before being hacked to pieces and fed to dogs. Skanderbeg had offered prisoner exchanges and the payment of a ransom to no end.

Skanderbeg kept fighting, and indeed kept winning, against the Ottomans but in this now protracted war of attrition, without allies, it was probable that the very fabric of Albania would be destroyed, as Wallachia's had been, if Skanderbeg kept resisting. At the end of 1464 he defeated Ballaban Pasha at the second Battle of the White Field as the Pasha tried to envelop the smaller Albanian force between his own and Jakup Bey's army. The war became more brutal now with the mass execution of all Ottoman prisoners in an act of revenge for the Istanbul atrocities. Jakup Bey's army was then defeated a few days later near Tirana.

The year 1466 saw the sultan himself in Albania leading an army of some 30,000 men to the siege of Kruje, the fortress that had turned his father back out of Albania in 1450. The garrison was relatively small but the fortress was built to modern designs and hard to strike at with artillery due to the precipitous nature of the surrounding ground. After several months there was still no progress and Mehemmed II resorted to destruction of the surrounding countryside and to constructing the new castle of Elbasan. He kept his army in Albania using Elbasan as a central base and, while he returned to Istanbul, it continued to press the siege of Kruje.

The winter of 1466 was spent trying to raise funds in Italy from first the papacy and then the Aragonese in Naples. Upon his return to Albania, Skanderbeg began to organise troops to break the siege of Kruje. On 23 April 1467 Skanderbeg broke the second siege of Kruje and went on to attack Elbasan. He failed to take it at the first attempt and settled down to besiege it. However, the lack of heavy artillery ensured that there could be no progress.

Once again Skanderbeg had defeated Mehemmed II's forces and the sultan returned in person in the summer of 1467 to break the siege of Elbasan. Skanderbeg eluded capture and fled to the coast with his field army but Mehemmed II meted out the punishment he could not inflict on his chief tormentor on the country. Crops were burned, villagers were enslaved and Kruje was besieged again – and yet again unsuccessfully.

Skanderbeg, who showed a grasp of the situation far beyond any that Vlad Dracula had demonstrated, could see how the toll of the war on the peasants and towns was inevitably going to erode loyalty to his cause.[10] He therefore called a 'war council' in January 1468 in the hopes of creating another united league among the Albanian lords. It is appropriate that this meeting took place in Lezhe, the city where the first league of lords was formed under Skanderbeg's leadership back in 1444, and it is perhaps fitting that it was also in Lezhe where Skanderbeg died during his attempts to reform the union of 1444. He died of malaria on 17 January 1468.

Skanderbeg's death, in fact, led to some respite for Albania as several lords took vassalage under the Ottomans and Mehemmed II let the threat of arms achieve for him what actual war had failed to achieve whilst Skanderbeg was alive. During this period there was a mass migration of Albanians to Italy.[11]

Skanderbeg had led the Albanian resistance for twenty-five years with minimal support from any the neighbouring Christian states or from his admirers in Western Europe. It is said that when the Ottomans finally conquered Lezhe their troops searched for the tomb of Skanderbeg, not to desecrate it but to take small fragments of his bones from the grave to wear as amulets that they hoped would bring them the same martial valour as he had displayed always.[12] He was given the title of *Athleta Christi*, or Champion of Christ, by the papacy.[13] John Hunyadi had also been honoured by the title and it would later be bestowed on Stephen III of Moldavia, who would also earn the epithet of 'the Great' for his successes against the Ottomans.

Stephen's greatness as a defender of Europe against the Turks still, however, lay in the future. In 1467 he was engaged instead in a war with Matthias Corvinus, who had finally responded to Stephen's capture of Chilia. Perhaps the Hungarian king should have waited a little longer again as he was defeated by Stephen at the Battle of Baia-Mare in December. Matthias was wounded in the fight and was lucky to leave the battlefield alive.

The King of Hungary then left the affairs of Wallachia alone for some time as he concentrated on his pet project of forming the mercenaries both he and his father had often relied on into the nucleus of what would become his Black Army. He also worked hard on improving the Hungarian fleet and enhancing its firepower. This new model army was created largely from Bohemian Hussites, German knights and Polish and Serbian mercenaries. Matthias' vision was to use this force that was loyal only to him to tame the aristocracy and to overcome the usual problems facing any prince who wanted to win the throne of the Holy Roman Emperor – that it was an elected office and that it required the granting of favours to the princes of the Imperial Diet to achieve election. It seems likely that Matthias intended to use his Black Army to bring Germany or at least south Germany and Austria under his direct control without recourse to the Imperial Diet system. He eventually failed in this venture but the 30,000 troops he had massed by the time of his death in 1490 were certainly a powerful force that would campaign in winter and did achieve several victories over the Ottomans, three of which were during the competition for Bosnia that took place between Matthias and Mehemmed II in 1463–64.

The Black Army was expensive to build and expensive to pay and there were further distractions for Matthias when his extraordinary taxes caused a rebellion in Transylvania in 1467. The Black Army was employed to put down the insurrection and in 1468 it was employed by the king in his war on George of Podebrady for the Crown of Bohemia. Matthias conquered Moravia, Silesia and Lausitz, but he then got bogged down in Bohemia. He managed to get himself elected as king on the strength of the Catholic Estates in May 1469, but the Hussite lords would not submit. All of this was an obvious distraction from Balkan affairs.

Wallachian and Moldavian affairs were heating up. Radu III mobilised in 1470, ostensibly to gain revenge for the taking of Chilia away from his control by Stephen of Moldavia, and to expunge the stain on his vassal lord Matthias' honour that its loss had caused. Ironically he turned not to the King of Hungary for support in this venture but to the Ottoman sultan. This is perhaps not surprising as, given the Ottoman subjugation of Serbia, Montenegro and Bosnia and 'pacification' of Albania, Radu III's little state was virtually surrounded on all sides and his every move was almost certainly being watched by Mehemmed II. And, of course, Matthias was distracted by his imperial ambitions.

Moldavia had, up to now, been outside the orbit of the Ottoman Empire but, given the above events, the theatre of which lay to the west of Stephen's kingdom, and the changing priorities of the Polish Crown, which had traditionally been the vassal lord of the kings of Moldavia, Stephen, just like Radu III, may have been concerned about isolation of his country. If Radu III went over to the Ottomans fully then Moldavia's entire western flank was open to invasion. It seemed unlikely that the Poles would intervene – memories of 1444 and the death of Vladislaus III on the battlefield at Varna tempered any desire to become entangled in Balkan affairs. Furthermore, in 1463 at the Battle of the Vistula Lagoon the Teutonic Knights' fleet was defeated by ships from Danzig and Elbing under the sponsorship of the Polish Crown. The Teutonic Order then submitted to vassalage under the King of Poland in 1466. Following this the Poles seem to have identified their destiny to be in an eastern and northern empire, and not to their south.

Stephen therefore had to look to his own resources and following Radu III's initial attacks on his lands in 1470, which clearly had Ottoman backing, he decided on a policy of removing Radu III of the Dracul and replacing him with a Dnesti who was currently taking refuge at Stephen's court, Basarab III Laiot. And so the Janus-faced character of Wallachian throne games continued. There was some low-level skirmishing and raids and counter-raids over the next few years but then Stephen took the offensive in earnest in autumn 1473. He brought Radu III to battle on the River Vodnu just west of Bucharest. Radu III, never a bold general, was made more confident by the support of an Ottoman contingent in his ranks but he was soon witnessing the defeat of these troops and his own. He fled the field and took refuge in Bucharest. The city was captured by Stephen on 24 November 1473 and Radu III fled again. This was enough for the Moldavians to proclaim Basarab III Laiot the new Prince of Wallachia. It seems that Radu III fled in some haste as his treasure, all his clothes (he was apparently quite a dandy), his standards, and worst of all, his wife, Maria Despina, and his daughter were left behind. Stephen would later take the daughter, Maria Voichi, as his wife.

Radu III was not finished yet, however, and Ottoman money and troops kept him in the game. Radu III took his headquarters to Giurgiu but both Hungarian favour and Ottoman interest in his fate was waning. He lost another battle against Stephen and Basarab III Laiot made it clear to the Turks that he had no intention of changing the arrangements of Radu III vis-à-vis Ottoman influence in Wallachia and its flow of tribute to Istanbul. This was certainly not what Stephen had envisaged, but then Wallachian politics were always difficult to control for hopeful puppet masters.

Radu III was already yesterday's man by the time he died in January 1475 probably of tertiary syphilis. Basarab III Laiot was fast proving to be Mehemmed II's man and so, almost inevitably, Matthias Corvinus began to turn to Vlad Dracula to be his man in Wallachia. Henri of Navarre famously said that '*Paris vaut bien une messe*', and Vlad Dracula decided quickly enough that conversion to Catholicism, the price of the Hungarian king's support for him in Wallachia, was an easy enough decision to make in order to regain the throne, especially as the alternative was continuing house arrest and an ignoble exile.

With this conversion Vlad Dracula could also fulfil the marriage proposals that had been made back in 1462. The Hungarian king selected a lady from the outer circles of his family and the proposed nuptials had a particular resonance as the lady in question was Ilona Szilagy, the daughter of Vlad Dracula's greatest ally during his first ascent to the Wallachian throne and during his 'wilderness years', Michael Szilagy. Ilona was Matthias' cousin and Vlad Dracul was therefore entitled to add the blackbird of the Hunyadi clan to his insignia along with the dragon of Sigismund's noble order.

Vlad Dracula remained in the twin cities of Buda and Pest, but moved out of his confinement and into his own house. He had two sons with Ilona and his eldest, but illegitimate, son Mihnea also lived with him and at the Hungarian court. He was being re-assimilated into the society of princes and the Hungarians worked hard both to suppress and to denigrate the German pamphlets produced in Saxony that listed Vlad Dracula's war crimes in Transylvania. There was fierce backtracking on the statements that the king had made about Vlad Dracula back in 1462 too, and the charges that the Saxon cities had attempted to bring against Vlad Dracula were quietly quashed by the king's lawyers. There was an enthusiastic response to his re-emergence in the political scene from Italy as Ferrara, Milan, Venice and the papal legate wrote of their happiness at his release.

Mehemmed II had been distracted by worrying developments on his Anatolian front in the early 1470s. The sultan had sent emissaries to the Mamluk Empire of Egypt and Syria in April 1473 suggesting a union of forces in the war against Uzun Hasan and the Ak-Koyunlu confederation. Ibn Iyas records that the mission came, 'bearing copious gifts and letters, so that friendship should be established between the Ottoman and Mamluk Sultans, on account of Uzun Hasan'. Uzun Hasan's intercepted letters to the Pope and the Doge of Venice proposing that they should assault the Ottoman and Mamluk sultans by sea while Hasan attacked them by land were produced for the Cairo court's inspection. The Mamluk sultan was convinced enough to proclaim his neutrality and to allow the Ottoman army to pass by the Mamluk northern outpost of Malatya on its way to engage Uzun Hasan's vast army. Sultan Qaitbay sent ambassadors on camels to the distant fortress to give further reassurance of Mamluk non-aggression. With his southern flank therefore secure, Mehemmed II turned north-east to meet Uzun Hasan's army. They met in battle on 11 August 1473.

As noted earlier, it was the discipline and the firepower of the Ottomans that defeated Uzun Hasan and the head of Hasan's son, Prince Zeynel, was sent to Sultan Qaitbay's court as a gift.[14]

With this successful campaign essentially concluded and his armies reaching into the lands of the Golden Horde and simultaneously threatening the Genoese colonies of the Black Sea, Mehemmed II turned again to Europe and to Moldavia. He ended the siege against the Albanian–Venetian possession of Shkoder and assembled the troops this freed up in Sofia in September 1474. This was probably unwise as the siege in Albania had been hard going and the march from Sofia to the Moldavian border would take at least a month given the terrain and the fact that it was coming to the end of the year and winter was close. Mehemmed II's plans were already perhaps over-ambitious but the sultan always drove himself hard and inflicted the same kind of discipline on all his subordinates. In fact Suleiman Pasha, the leader of the army, was given longer-term plans that even envisaged a spring encampment in Poland for his army, after the defeat of Moldavia, before it moved on to link up with the sultan's army to then dismember Hungary.

Suleiman Pasha had at least been given an impressive army to carry out this not insignificant task. He had about 120,000 men with a core of Janissaries and *azab* infantry, as well as about 30,000 *sipahis* and light Tatar cavalry. There were certainly also Bulgars and Serbian cavalry, too. Bulgarian peasants were also conscripted to clear forests and shovel snow, and to build small bridges over the marshes of Moldavia – perhaps Mehemmed II had remembered the terrain of Wallachia and how it had slowed his guns' passage through the country.

Suleiman Bey's army crossed the frozen Danube into Wallachia between Vidin and Nicopolis. In Wallachia, whilst the Ottomans rested, they were met by Basarab III Laiot and 17,000 Wallachian troopers. Basarab III Laiot had now apparently chosen a side.

Pope Sixtus IV had responded to the obvious threat of a renewed assault on Europe by Mehemmed II with a call to Crusade primarily aimed at calling Matthias Corvinus to his duty as a Christian king but also at the rulers of Poland, Moldavia and Bohemia. Stephen of Moldavia was said to have responded, 'We are ready to resume the struggle for the defence of Christendom with all the power and heart which Almighty God had chosen to invest in us.' He did not fail to match his lofty words but the response from the rest of Christendom had been miserly. Matthias Corvinus sent 1,800 troops. The King of Poland, Stephen's liege lord, sent only 2,000 men. Stephen managed to recruit some 5,000 Szekely mercenaries or fortune-hunters. His own army of Moldavians boasted only twenty cannon and about 15,000 troops. Stephen had a *viteji* of well-armed heavy cavalry, just as Vlad Dracula had, and like the Wallachian he also had a conscripted peasant army of around 30,000 men, drawn from citizens over the age of 14.

Mehemmed II had planned his land invasion of Moldavia to be supported by an attack from the Black Sea against Chilia. This never seems to have got any further than planning. However, Stephen still faced overwhelming superiority in numbers from his enemy. He therefore followed a similar plan to that of Vlad Dracula in 1463 and, minus the more horrific passages, of Vlad Dracula's retreat through Wallachia. As Suleiman Pasha pushed into Moldavia in December 1474 he found nothing but burning fields and poisoned waters. There was no one to blame or punish because the population and their livestock had been evacuated to the mountains in the north of the country. There were also ambushes and hit-and-run raids to contend with for an army that was already being exhausted by the march.

Stephen concentrated his forces around Vaslui and gained time to do so by a masterly plan that acted like a folding bag. Progressive blocks were placed upon the Ottomans' path by divisions of the Moldavian army, which would then fade away as the Ottomans moved into battle formations. Then, when the Ottomans returned to columns for marching, the ambushes would begin again. Eventually all the Moldavian divisions reached Vaslui and the defensive position that Stephen had had plenty of time to prepare. He had also ensured that Vaslui and the villages around it were not 'scorched' and would appear inviting to Ottoman scouts and foragers.

The news soon enough reached Suleiman Pasha that the Moldavian army was at Vaslui and that they were sitting among villages stocked with the year's grain. The Ottomans headed for the Moldavian army knowing that they had to go through it to reach the capital of Suceva, where they hoped to garrison and gain some protection from the winter. They had to cross the River Barlad in order to reach Vaslui and Stephen's positioning of his army and his harassment of the Ottomans funnelled them to a narrow crossing over the river that would require extensive engineering if they were to bring their heavy guns over it. This was the Inalt 'High' Bridge, the same spot where his father had defeated the Poles in 1450 and where Stephen had fought at the side of Vlad Dracula. If the Ottomans made it across the bridge without incident and entered the valley beyond, they would find that it was surrounded on all three sides by steep, densely forested hills. The ground in the valley was also marshy and the massed ranks of cavalry and infantry would find both movement forward and marshalling into some semblance of order difficult. It was a perfect defensive position.

A thick, freezing fog was recorded on the morning of the battle. On 10 January 1475 Suleiman Pasha tried to force his way over the bridge, across which Stephen had thrown several palisades, and every cannon he had on the field was aimed at the structure. The Moldavian cavalry along with peasant archers and the king sat back in the forests out of view. Only the mercenaries – men at arms and cavalry – and Szekely cavalry and infantry seem to have been out in the field as a screen to protect the artillery.

Then Stephen sent a military band out into the field, or at least that is what has come down to us in the chronicles. Apparently the sound of the band's drums and bugles made Suleiman Pasha, who was doubtless peering through the fog, think that the whole Moldavian army had taken the field and was waiting in the valley ahead.

Suleiman ordered the advance but when his troops reached the bridge the Moldavian artillery opened up. Arrows then began to fall among the Ottoman advance guard and hand-gunners added to the deadly crossfire that came at the Ottomans from three sides. The *azab* infantry got across the bridge along with elements of the *akinji* cavalry. They chased at shadows as the infantry line ahead of them faded into the fog and retreated, and they were struck by rapid attacks from the Moldavian light cavalry.

Suleiman Pasha then tried to send his *sipahi* cavalry across the bridge but it collapsed under their weight before all of them were across. Those who got into the valley and the Ottoman troops who had managed to survive the attacks from the artillery and the archers managed to link up, a tribute to the discipline of the Ottomans and to their junior officers as the commander was still on the further bank of the river and unable to control the van of his army.

The Ottoman van confronted the mercenaries and Szekely troopers but only once they had crossed the marshy plain. The Ottoman infantry, almost certainly nearly exhausted by this point, reached the Moldavian line but their charge was repelled. The Moldavians retreated further up the valley and once again the Ottomans managed to carry out a highly skilled manoeuvre as the *sipahi* cavalry now engaged the Szekely troops in the centre and the Janissaries and *azab* infantry moved out to try to flank the Moldavian line. The Szekely troops were pushed back and forced to retreat again under the pressure of the *sipahis'* repeated charges. Suleiman Pasha would not have known how the battle was going for him but he tried to pour more men across the river to join the fray.

In fact, it was too late for his men in the valley as Stephen with the Hungarians and Poles, the *boyar* cavalry and his *viteji* came down from every side of the valley followed by the peasant infantry. Many of the concealed Moldavian troops were now behind the Ottomans, who had advanced a good distance up the valley, and who could now hear bugles calling Moldavian troops to the battlefield from positions far behind them. The Ottoman van was completely surrounded and beyond any help from its commander.

The Ottoman troops in the valley were already broken and running for safety and from the battlefield before Suleiman Pasha called the general retreat of the whole army. The Wallachians immediately deserted their newly acquired allies and fled the field following Basarab III Laiot. Suleiman Pasha managed to regain some degree of control over his army and it is to his credit that it did not disintegrate completely over a four-day retreat through a bitter winter and across lands already denuded of shelter and sustenance, during which he was pursued and harried by the Moldavian light cavalry and the Poles. He reached what he thought would be the sanctuary of Wallachia but Basarab III Laiot's treachery went beyond simple desertion and on 20 January he ordered attacks on Turkish stragglers and managed to secure an Ottoman standard to prove his 'loyalty' to the Hungarians and to Stephen.

The casualties among the Ottomans were immense. Forty-five thousand men died on the field or in the retreat. Four Pashas had been killed and 100 standards were taken. Stephen showed that he also had a capacity for barbarity, though perhaps not as honed as that of Vlad Dracula, as he impaled all his prisoners except those of the highest rank and burned the bodies.

The battle and its spectacular result gave Stephen a position of enormous prestige from which to beseech the Polish court for more men and treasure to pursue the war with the Ottomans. He sent four Ottoman commanders and thirty-six enemy standards along with booty from the Ottoman camp to King Casimir. The Pope and Matthias Corvinus also received gifts of prisoners and standards. Apparently Stephen not only refused to celebrate his victory but went on to fast for forty days to show his devotion to God, to whom he said the victory should truly be attributed. It may have been God's victory but Matthias certainly tried very hard to claim it as his own; 'the arrogant Matthias writes to the Pope, the Emperor and other kings and Princes, telling them that he has defeated a large Turkish army with his own forces under the *Voivode* of Wallachia.'[15] The Pope was far more gracious and, as noted above, Stephen joined an exclusive club that included John Hunyadi and Skanderbeg when he was made an *Athleta Christi*. King Casimir did nothing for his vassal and suffered a whispering campaign at his own court accusing him of miserliness and indolence.

Stephen's great victory also made for a smaller triumph for Vlad Dracula. Stephen wrote to Matthias in June 1475 requesting the king's support for replacing Basarab III Laiot, who had proved to be a highly unreliable ally, with Vlad Dracula. Stephen wrote warmly of his wish to end the feud with his cousin, whom he flattered by reporting to the king that he had only heard good things said of Vlad Dracula.

The victory of Stephen in January 1476 ensured that his words now carried more weight than when he had been the enemy of Hungary. Matthias made Vlad Dracula his lieutenant for the campaign he planned for Bosnia in January 1476 but he proceeded cautiously on the matter of placing Vlad Dracula back on the Wallachian throne.

Vlad Dracula was able to return to Transylvania after the idea of the Bosnian campaign was shelved for the first half of 1475, and he was even able to impose a payment of 200 florins from the mayor of Sibiu for the upkeep of his new headquarters at Arghi. He was not, however, allowed during this time to take residence or even control castles in the Brasov region; his crimes were too well remembered there.

In October 1475 Vlad Dracula travelled to Merghindel to meet with Matthias as the king planned his Bosnian operation. A winter campaign was planned.

Matthias took an army of about 5,000 men into Bosnia at the turn of the year. He had managed to get the venture labelled as a Crusade and had obtained papal funding. Vlad Dracula and the Serbian ex-despot, Gregorevi, acted as his lieutenants. The Hungarian army scored an initial success with its capture of the city of Sabac in February 1476, and this was enough for Matthias to declare victory and return home, leaving Vlad Dracula and Gregorevi as joint commanders with the task of taking Srebrenica. The objective was as much economic as strategic as the area around the city was rich in silver mines.

Vlad Dracula soon enough reverted to form. His first tactic was a stroke of genius with Hungarians disguised as Turks managing to enter Srebrenica during a monthly market. The Hungarians caused such chaos inside the city that when Vlad Dracula appeared with more troops at the gates and walls there was no defence worth the name put up by the garrison. If the citizens and Ottoman troops had known their fate they would certainly have fought harder. The city was burnt to the ground and Srebrenica witnessed an atrocity that was as appalling in its ferocity as the genocide of 1995, even if it lacked the scale of that particular outrage. Every Ottoman was impaled and the city was burned to the ground. Everything of value was plundered. The looting and killing then rolled on to Kuslat and Zwornik.

The papal legate, Gabriele Rangoni, seems not to have been at all appalled by Vlad Dracula's acts: 'He tore the limbs off the Turkish prisoners and placed their parts on stakes ... and displayed the private parts of his victims so that when the Turks see these, they will run away in fear!'[16]

The war with the Turks, with its grinding length and its lack of Christian successes, added to the tenacity and martial skills of the Ottomans, had made men of blood such as Vlad Dracula acceptable even to the Curia. Vlad Dracula was not, however, likely to make himself acceptable as a *voivode* to anyone within much closer vicinity of his viciousness. But that was what he now aimed at; a second ascension to the Wallachian throne.

DEATH AND RESURRECTION:

DRACULA'S RETURN TO POWER, MURDER AND IMMORTALISATION

And then find this great Un-Dead, and cut off his head and burn his heart or drive a stake through it, so that the world may rest from him.[1]

Moldavian affairs dominated the first half of 1476 for Mehemmed II and as the summer approached Moldavia also began to fill Matthias Corvinus' thoughts too. For Vlad Dracula the invasion of Moldavia by Mehemmed II looked like a godsend; it was the vehicle that brought him back to the throne of Wallachia.

Vaslui had been a huge shock for the sultan and he planned an elaborate revenge involving the newly submitted Tatars of the Golden Horde and an invasion of Moldavia from Basarab III Laiot's Wallachia. Mehemmed II brought 150,000 Ottoman troops alone into the fray and to these were added 10,000 Wallachians and 30,000 Tatars under their khan, Mengli Giray. The Tatars came into Moldavia from their lands to the north-east of Stephen's lands. They began pillaging but were then chased from the country and decimated by columns of Moldavian cavalry. The khan lost a son and two brothers, and returned from the venture with only one horse.[2] He refused to challenge Stephen again.

Mehemmed II then committed his Ottomans to the war in June 1476. He led them in person and it was evident that Stephen and his small army could not stand against such a vast army. Once again a scorched earth policy was instituted along with the evacuation of the Moldavian populace to the mountains. Mehemmed II took Akkerman, which gave him control of the Danube Delta, and he linked up with what was left of the Tatars' forces in Bessarabia. Stephen had a field army of fewer than 20,000 men, which was certainly not enough to retake Akkerman.

Instead, in July 1476, Stephen chose to make a stand in a densely wooded area in which the Ottoman weight of numbers would make less difference and arranged his troops for a defensive battle. As the Ottomans advanced the Moldavians set fire to the foliage and this, added to a withering hand gun fusillade, forced the Janissary advance guard to falter and forced them to crawl forward in order to make any ground. Mehemmed II turned the battle with a headlong charge of his close bodyguard, which overtook the Janissaries of the vanguard and carried them with it into the Moldavian line. This did not break immediately but only after some truly brutal close quarters fighting that took a huge toll on both sides. What was left of the Moldavians fled the field. The viciousness of the battle and the stubborn resistance of the hugely outnumbered Moldavians are attested to by the name the battlefield acquired from the white of the bones that covered it and could be found in the soil for years afterwards. It became known as the White Valley, or Valea Alba.

Stephen had lost a pitched battle and retired to Poland to lick his wounds and to build another army. What Mehemmed II had won is hard to gauge. He had at least vented his spleen and restored the prestige that Ottoman arms had lost at Vaslui but he was still locked out of the major centres of Moldavia. Suceava, Neamt and Hotin all resisted the sieges that were set and the army was still the victim of hit-and-run raids by Moldavian troops and irregulars. Stephen had also done a good job of removing any comfort or food for the invaders and as the army began to starve there was an outbreak of camp sickness, which was possibly cholera or plague.

The Ottoman threat was then fading and Stephen had certainly done enough to prevent Mehemmed II from achieving anything beyond the capture of Akkerman. The Ottoman campaign in Moldavia, even if it was fading quickly into a retreat, and particularly the support it enjoyed from Basarab III Laiot was enough, however, to convince Matthias Corvinus of the need for intervention. Vlad Dracula was chosen as his agent.

Vlad Dracula had been agitating for a chance to retake the Wallachian throne right from his return to Transylvania in March 1476. The success of the Bosnian 'Crusade' and the support of the Hungarian Diet and the Governor of Transylvania no doubt influenced Matthias in his decision to support Vlad Dracula's claim, but it was the backing of Stephen of Moldavia that really fixed the king's favour on him. Vlad Dracula joined the king at Turda in Transylvania in the summer of 1476 to plan a campaign aimed at pushing the Ottomans from Moldavia and unseating Basarab III Laiot.

The army that was assembled in southern Transylvania in the autumn of 1476 was about 25,000 strong and included Hungarians, Transylvanians, Wallachians and Serbs. The command fell to Stephen Bathory, a loyal retainer of the king, but both Vlad Dracula and Vuk Brankovic acted as army leaders and probably made most of the decisions on tactics and the running of the campaign. It had been planned that this not insignificant but certainly not large force would link up with the Moldavians before tackling the Ottomans and Wallachians. Valea Alba changed these plans completely. The army, instead, made a rapid march towards the River Siret, to meet up with the remaining forces of the Moldavian field army. They found Stephen at the Ooituz Pass. Fortunately for the allied forces, the Ottomans had been so damaged by pestilence and famine that they were able to defeat Mehemmed II, who was probably on the point of withdrawing from Moldavia anyway, on the banks of the River Siret in early August 1476.

The campaign then moved into its second, and for Vlad Dracula key, phase: war on Basarab III Laiot. The army went into quarters in Brasov until Stephen and his 15,000 Moldavians were ready to make their attack on Wallachia from the north-east. In November both armies moved into Wallachia with Bathory's army attacking from the west to make a pincer with Stephen's forces. Basarab III Laiot scraped together a few *boyars* and their men but had to turn to Mehemmed II in order to form any kind of army to challenge Vlad Dracula or Stephen. Mehemmed II was generous and gave his vassal the support of 18,000 Ottoman troops. With this force Basarab III Laiot met Vlad Dracula's army near the town of Rucr in the valley of the River Prahova. The battle was bloody and as hard fought as that of Valea Alba. At least 10,000 men were lost by each side but Vlad Dracula and Bathory held the field at the end of the day and despite their losses they were able to continue their advance into Wallachia. Stephen was also enjoying success and had cleared north-east Wallachia of Ottoman troops by 8 November. Tirgoviste fell easily to Vlad Dracula and Stephen then arrived at Vlad Dracula's old capital with his troops.

Vlad Dracula followed the line of the Dimbovia River all the way to Bucharest, which also capitulated to the allies without making any real resistance on 16 November. Basarab III Laiot was in full flight from Stephen and Bathory's armies and had lost his capital; he had nowhere to go except to the Turks. Vlad Dracula was by this time the *Voivode* of Wallachia once more, even if he had not been crowned yet. Perhaps Stephen could sense, however, that Vlad Dracula's grip on power was tenuous, the crimes of his previous reign were not forgotten and the Wallachian *boyars*' loyalty to any prince was always a fragile thing. He supplied his cousin with 200 knights to act as a close bodyguard to supplement the few men of his *sluji* who had survived the 'wilderness years'.

On 26 November Dracula was crowned once more as *Voivode* of Wallachia. It was to be a short reign but news of it was welcomed by Venice and Pope Sixtus IV. With Matthias apparently reoriented to war against the Turks and Stephen the *Athleta Christi* and Vlad the feared Impaler in the van it looked for the first time since the death of John Hunyadi as if Eastern Europe would unite and resist Mehemmed II's ambitions. The word 'Crusade' was even whispered in courts and in the Curia.

It was a false dawn. Vlad Dracula would be dead by December and Stephen the Great would toil on against the Ottomans for the next nine years with scant support from the Hungarian king, who involved himself in wars in Bohemia and Austria and rarely deployed even a fraction of the Black Army in the defence of Christendom against the Turks.

Basarab III Laiot returned to challenge Vlad Dracula with Janissaries to back his venture. It seems that Vlad Dracula was killed in an engagement among the marshes and forest near Bucharest. Whether he was killed by the Ottomans or was the victim of his own men is hard to say. Certainly his head was claimed by the Janissaries. It was taken to Istanbul where it was displayed on a stake for all to see, presumably until it rotted.[3]

The skirmish in which Vlad Dracula was killed may have been an ambush but whether there was treachery involved and the trap was laid by Wallachian *boyars* or whether it was a chance encounter between two sides that were fighting a bloody tit-for-tat war in the forests of Wallachia we will never know. He certainly had a small bodyguard of Moldavian knights with him and one recording of his death states that it was these men who killed their lord accidentally. In this version of the story Vlad Dracula's men had survived the ambush and were putting the Turks to flight when he rushed alone to higher ground to survey the battle better. He was mistaken for an Ottoman and one of his guards struck him with a lance. Vlad Dracula then killed five of his own men in either rage or fear and he was pierced numerous times by the arrows of his own *sluji* and of the Moldavians.

The fog of war may then explain Vlad Dracula's demise but the above scenario does not seem likely given that he fought and rode with these same men every day. They would have recognised him even in the heat of battle.

Another version of the death of Vlad Dracula has him being attacked by Basarab III Laiot backed by 4,000 Ottoman regulars. In this account Vlad Dracula has a total of 2,000 men with him, including all his Moldavian bodyguards, but he never gets the chance to meet Basarab III Laiot in battle as a Turkish assassin enters the Impaler's camp and quietly kills him.

Dracula was killed with great cunning, because the Turks wished to avenge the enmity which he had borne against them for so long and also the great damages inflicted upon them. They hired a Turk (to act) as one of his servants with the mission of killing him while he served him. The Turk was apparently instructed to attack Dracula from the back. He was then to cut off his head and bring it back on horseback to the sultan.[4]

This scenario seems even more unlikely than Vlad Dracula being killed by his own guard and we need to apply an historian's version of Occam's razor to the multiple stories of the death of the *voivode*. Given the type of warfare that Vlad Dracula was engaged in of raids and counter-raids and the simple fact that he was outnumbered in every engagement it seems most likely that he was killed in a very straightforward way during a skirmish. That his head was taken post-mortem by his killer is hardly surprising or unusual. He is also certainly not alone in dying a less than glorious death after a much more outlandish and 'glory-filled' career. Cesare Borgia was killed in an almost meaningless fight with a party of knights in Navarre and was left, stripped naked, in a ditch and Richard Coeur De Lion, the man who had bested Saladin at Acre, Arsuf and Jaffa, died of an infected arrow wound inflicted during a siege of a small and unimportant French castle.

Sordid anticlimactic and unromantic or un-chivalric endings to the lives of warriors are to be expected. There is no need to look for the hand of conspiracy in Vlad Dracula's death, or to over-complicate how it occurred. What is more important, and the application of our version of Occam's razor helps us to distinguish this key question from all the hypothesising on how Vlad Dracula died, is *why* he was killed and why his third reign was so brief. Then it becomes obvious that this third reign was doomed from the outset. His failure to extinguish the threat of Basarab III Laiot and the degree of support the Ottomans were willing to give Basarab was Vlad Dracula's chief undoing. However, there were other factors that made Vlad Dracula's reign a 'third time unlucky'. He had, as we have seen, eroded all sense of loyalty (admittedly a fairly rare commodity in Wallachian politics at the best of times but Mircea I the Old did manage to cultivate it) among the nobility in his first and second reigns and he had failed to find any effective replacement for, or counterbalance to, these men. Another touchstone of loyalty and unity in the Wallachian political system, the Orthodox Church, had also been alienated by Vlad Dracula's conversion to Catholicism. He had lost the bourgeois of the Saxon towns back in the early 1460s. His last possible outlet of support, if he really wanted to cut cards with the Devil, the Ottoman Porte, was also closed to him. The atrocities of 1462 and the forest of impaled Ottoman troops outside Tirgoviste would never be forgotten. There could be no deals between Mehemmed II and 'Kaziglu Bey'.

The Lord Impaler's mangled and headless body was apparently found by two monks from the monastery of Snagov. The traditional story says that they then interred the body in the chapel of Snagov in a crypt facing the altar of the principal chapel in the last days of December 1476. Vlad Dracula had, of course, been a generous patron of the monastery. One month later Stephen of Moldavia heard rumours of the death of his cousin and some weeks later ten men, the only knights to have survived service in Vlad Dracula's bodyguard, confirmed the death of their master to him. Stephen wrote to Matthias Corvinus and the news spread over Eastern and Western Europe, but there was no great lamentation.

Basarab III Laiot took Bucharest and sat once more on the throne of Wallachia. His fifth and final reign was ended by Stephen of Moldavia in 1477. Stephen placed a Dnesti, Basarab IV Tepelus, on the throne but Wallachia's revolving door monarchies continued and it was only the strength of Stephen the Great's sword arm that kept the Ottomans from crossing the Danube and taking Wallachia and Transylvania into Mehemmed II's empire.

Vlad Dracula's chief antagonist, Mehemmed II, would live for another five years past the Impaler's death. During these last years of his life he did not relent from his warlike ways. Caffa had fallen to his armies in 1475 and, as we have seen, the Khan of Golden Horde was forced into vassalage at this time. The Moldavian wars took up the years 1475–77 and he returned to Albanian and Venetian affairs in 1477 with massive assaults on the Venetian-held coastal cities and the mountainous interior of the country. There was no Skanderbeg to halt the conqueror's progress this time and even Montenegro, which had achieved independence from Brankovic's Serbia in 1451 and which had managed to retain that independence, though under conditions of tribute and vassalage to the Ottomans in the 1470s, also disappeared under the rising Ottoman tide in 1479.

Mehemmed II's ambition was seemingly limitless. By 1480 it was obvious that his attentions were turning to the Mamluk Empire, his great rival in the Middle East. In June 1480 he attempted to take Rhodes from the Knights of Saint John, whom he had accused of piracy against Muslim merchant shipping. What is very obvious, though, is that Rhodes lies opposite Alexandria and that its seizure was part of a larger strategy to first secure the sea passage from Constantinople to Egypt before making war on Egypt in 1481. The campaign failed against Rhodes' impressive citadel and the dogged resistance of the knights. The island fortress held out and 3,500 Ottoman troops were killed during the initial repulse of their assaults. The retreat from the island cost another 5,000 or so troops.

Then, in 1480, Mehemmed II launched an audacious attack from Albania. Gedik Ahmad Pasha landed in Southern Italy and captured Otranto.[5] There was a brutal sack of the city and the massacre of 800 of the citizens who refused to convert to Islam – they are still remembered as martyrs in Italy to this day. The Pasha then raided inland and struck Brindisi. The Duke of Naples drove them back to Otranto, and the majority of the army then sailed back to Albania but a small garrison was left behind. Rumours abounded in Italy that Mehemmed II himself was coming to Italy to raid Rome and capture the Pope. Indeed, the Pope himself was considering fleeing to Avignon. In May 1481, a joint Neapolitan–Hungarian force besieged the remaining Ottomans in Otranto.

Meanwhile the sultan, having set the Italian operation in motion, was far away from Otranto as it came to its disappointing conclusion. In April 1481 he was at Konya gathering all his Asian levies together. Later Ottoman chroniclers write that he 'was preparing to attack in person the Mamluk sultan, who was at loggerheads with the lords of Aleppo and Damascus'. To his contemporaries it was impossible to know where Mehemmed *Fetih* wished to go or what he wished to conquer next. Not even his generals knew; Mehemmed II was dying and even whilst doing so he still wished to campaign. He died at Maltepe, near Istanbul, on 3 May 1481. It is possible that he was poisoned by his doctor on the instructions of his son, Bayezid.

The news of the sultan's death caused an outpouring of elation in Europe, church bells were rung and the jubilant cry all over Venice was '*la grande aquila é morta!*' (the great eagle is dead).

Almost no one in his own lands mourned Mehemmed II. His conquests and his wresting of more than twenty different states from his enemies during his reign had required harsh levels of taxation and customs fees, and thirty years of almost continuous campaigning for his army. He had consistently debased the silver coinage of the empire so that it was reduced by more than 30 per cent over the thirty years of his reign. He broke fundamental property laws, distributing *waqf* lands and endowments[6] as *timars*, and set himself against the *ulema*, the religious establishment, by denying them the traditional gifts of the sultan and spending the money instead on artillery. His last military venture, the Otranto campaign, ended when news of his death and the succession crisis that followed it reached the garrison, which quietly capitulated.

What Mehemmed II had left the Ottomans, though, was a very dangerous legacy for all their neighbours. The Mamluks of the thirteenth century had seen themselves as the champions of Islam, almost divinely ordained to defeat the Mongol invasions and Crusaders. Their greatest sultans, al-Zahir Baybars and Qalawun, had given them the leadership and military capability to do it. In the same way Mehemmed II had left the Ottomans a great and growing imperial consciousness, especially through his conquest of Constantinople. Through his centralisation of the Ottoman State and regularisation of its army, his reordering of its financing, his expanding of the Janissary corps and his investment in a powerful fleet, in artillery both for the field and for sieges and in handguns, he had also given them the means to realise an imperial ambition.[7]

Mehemmed II was a cruel and harsh man but also a cultured[8] and intelligent leader. His cruelty and the terror he was capable of turning on both his own people and those of other lands was also entirely a political instrument.[9] He was not rage driven like Vlad Dracula, whose use of terror was, at times, entirely nihilistic. Of course there was no way that warfare in the Balkans was ever going to become the gentlemanly engagement that it had evolved to become between the *condottieri* of Italian chivalry. There could be no leisurely show of a charge and counter-charge with a few blows laid upon the opponent, after which the 'defeated' commander conceded the field. The war in the Balkans was a war of survival for dynasties and of religion, ethnicity and thereby of identity for the men engaged.[10] It was a zero sum game for states such as Wallachia, Serbia and Moldavia caught between the Ottomans and Hungarians. It was a natural home for the more brutal elements of war that so easily slip out and cry havoc from von Clausewitz's 'politics by other means'.

What Vlad Dracula, Hunyadi, Skanderbeg and Stephen of Moldavia, as well as the Ottoman sultans, were involved in was what von Clausewitz referred to as 'a gradual exhaustion of the physical powers and of the will by the long continuance of exertion'[11] through a war of attrition. The idea that the purpose of a defensive war is to stop your enemy doing what he is doing by making it untenable or too expensive in terms of men, expenditure or moral energy (simply so horrific that it intimidates or repels the invader from wanting to continue the contest) was applied by geniuses of war such as Frederick the Great and was certainly applied in modern conflicts such as the Great War when von Falkenhayn aimed simply to 'bleed France white' at Verdun, and in 1945 at Nagasaki and Hiroshima.

What holds true for Mehemmed II's 'terror' and even to the application of Weapons of Mass Destruction is that the ends always remained in sight. Vlad Dracula, as we have suggested, was a brilliant tactician and field officer but he had no grasp for the actions of a prince or of a general. He engaged in a war in which the ends of that war were consumed by the means taken to achieve them. In such a 'total war' it is impossible to muzzle the dogs of war once they have been allowed to slip the leash completely. All constraints slip away and the war becomes as damaging to one's own state and people as it does to the enemy. The only thing that Vlad Dracula's war of terror offered was war without end, which is by definition both pointless and without reason.[12]

Vlad Dracula therefore deserves his place as the exemplar of the medieval tyrant 'in blood stepped so far' for his crimes on the battlefield, in domestic politics and for the sheer barbarity of his punishments.

For his army he reserved the right to examine the wounds of his men. Certainly there were rewards for those who suffered wounds on the chest, arms and thighs but those who showed evidence of wounds on the back of their body were summarily executed by impalement on the grounds of cowardice. Discipline in German armies in the same period was recorded as being harsh. Executioners and their gallows accompanied the army, in which robbery bought the loss of a hand and deceit would see a man being clubbed and made to run through a lane formed by the army's war-wagons. This was rough justice; Vlad Dracula's acts had nothing to do with justice.

For his people he brought mass slaughter. Estimates range from 40,000 to 100,000 people over his six-year rule. He may at least have shown the virtue of being fairly indiscriminate in much of his killing in that he murdered Moldavians, Wallachians and Transylvanians as well Bulgarians and Hungarians and was not that fussy about creed or religion either. Despite being a member of the Order of the Dragon he was as happy to kill Catholics as he was Muslims, Orthodox Christians or Jews – though, of course, especial attention was reserved for the Catholic Saxon Germans during his essentially economic war with them and for the gypsies who undoubtedly irritated the prince through the simple difficulty of taxing their itinerant lifestyle.

He was also not usually class-conscious (one reason why the Communist regime of Romania attempted his rehabilitation) and decimated the *boyars* but also reserved not just killing but elaborate tortures for the peasantry, too. Making an example of traitors and those of power in the state is common in order to deter others or the followers of important agitators. Heads being placed on city gates are an all too common image of the ancient, medieval and early modern world. But why it was necessary to impale peasants, beggars and those other generally powerless individuals of the Middle Ages – women and children – is impossible to answer unless we accept the fact that Vlad Dracula simply enjoyed murder and inflicting misery. The refinements of his impaling stakes, which were not 'overly sharp' to ensure the tearing rather than puncture of tissue, and the coating of them with oil to ensure the victim slid down enough to be pierced from anus to mouth after being pulled on to the stake by two powerful horses attached to his or her legs, show an interest in the mechanics of torture that no monarch should display.

The litany of other assorted punishments, including the cutting off of noses and ears and blindings, were again not uncommon in the late Middle Ages and early modern period. Elizabeth I of England used the cutting off of ears as a deterrent for vagrancy among the disbanded armies of her father and brother, and blindings were common in the higher politics of Byzantium. However harsh these punishments and retributions were though, these were thought-out policies and acts. Vlad Dracula's were not. The papal legate Modrussa recounted Vlad Dracula's cruelties to Pope Pius II and succinctly captured their purely sadistic and gratuitous nature:

> He killed some of them by breaking them under the wheels of carts; others, stripped of their clothes, were skinned alive up to their entrails; others placed on stakes, or roasted on red-hot coals placed under them; others punctured with stakes piercing their head, their navel, breast, and, what is even unworthy of relating, their buttocks and the middle of their entrails, and, emerging from their mouths; in order that no form of cruelty be missing, he stuck stakes in both breasts of mothers and thrust their babies onto them; he killed others in other ferocious ways, torturing them with varied instruments such as the atrocious cruelties of the most frightful tyrants could devise.[13]

Vlad Dracula's horrific acts were, of course, what in fact, in the end, immortalised him. Largely this was thanks to the pen of Bram Stoker but, as we have seen, macabre tales of his murders published by

German pamphleteers were already in circulation throughout Europe before his death and German Catholic monks who fled the burning of their monasteries and churches also bore witness to the crimes of the Impaler. These tales reached the ears of the *meistersinger* Michael Beheim and when his words were published they were prefaced by gory woodcut prints showing Vlad Dracula eating breakfast whilst in his forest of impaled bodies. The legend of Vlad Tepes, the Impaler, had begun to take hold and the historical Vlad Dracula faded away, which was entirely appropriate given that he stood among some of the greatest men of the medieval age. Murad II, John Hunyadi, Mehemmed II, Skanderbeg and Stephen of Moldavia all towered above him in the stuff of greatness.

The printing press of Gutenberg was what really spread the legend of Vlad Dracula across Europe and also brought it to a growing literate public eager to read more than just political statements and religious works. The *meistersinger* Michael Beheim's work *Story of a Bloodthirsty Madman Called Dracula of Wallachia* was particularly popular at the court of Frederick III and in the streets of Germany. It certainly carries some dramatic scenes, such as this one where a lay-brother, Hans the Porter, responds to Vlad Dracula's demands to know what will become of him upon his death. Hans the Porter replies bravely:

You are a wicked, shrewd, merciless killer, an oppressor, always eager for more crime, a spiller of blood, a tyrant, and a torturer of poor people! What are the crimes that justify the killing of the pregnant women you have impaled? What have their little children done, some of them three years old, others barely born, whose lives you have snuffed out? You have impaled those who never did any harm to you. Now you bathe in the blood of the innocent babes who do not even know the meaning of evil! You wicked, sly, implacable killer! How dare you accuse those whose delicate and pure blood you have mercilessly spilled. I am amazed at your murderous hatred! What impels you to seek revenge upon them? Give me an immediate answer to these charges.

Vlad Dracula's answer borders on paranoia:

> I will reply willingly and make my answer known to you now. When a farmer wishes to clear the land he must not only cut the weeds that have grown but also the roots that lie deep underneath the soil. For should he omit cutting the roots, after one year he has to start anew, in order that the obnoxious plant not grow again. In the same manner, the babes in arm who are here will someday grow up into powerful enemies, should I allow them to grow into manhood. I wish to destroy and uproot them. Should I do otherwise, the young heirs will otherwise easily avenge their fathers on this earth.

Vlad Dracula was apparently so outraged by the brother's answers that he impaled Hans himself, and even went so far as to impale the unfortunate donkey of the brother.[14]

As we have seen, these pamphlets were common fare right through to the end of the fifteenth century, with the presses of Bartholomeus Gothan printing *The Life of Vlad Tepes* in 1484. Gothan was somewhat itinerant and he moved from Magdeburg to Lubeck in 1484, and then to Sweden in 1486. His movements and the workings of his press in these cities would have disseminated his work, *About an Evil Tyrant Named Dracole Wyda MCCCCLVI Years after the Birth of Our Lord Jesus Christ, This Dracole Wyda Carried out Many Terrible and Wondrous Deeds in Wallachia and Hungary*. The fact that it was written in Low German would also have aided its rapid transmission across much of northern Europe.

Ambrosius Huber of Nuremberg was possibly the first publisher to add woodcut pictures to his text, *Vlad the Impaler*. The idea was taken up and Matthias Hupfuff's 1500 pamphlet carries the now famous scene of Vlad Dracula eating amid hundreds of victims dangling from the spikes on which they had been impaled. Hupfuff published his work in Strasbourg and the tale of Vlad Tepes therefore spread west of the German lands.

A link to Vlad Dracula, however tenuous, through Stephen Bathory, whom he had fought with during the war of 1476, became significant much later during the process of 'vampirisation' of Vlad Dracula. Stephen Bathory was the governor of Transylvania from 1479 until his death and a bizarre episode in the later Bathory family's history helped with Vlad Dracula's transformation into Bram Stoker's eponymous character. Stephen's great niece was the Countess Elizabeth Bathory, who had more than 600 girls killed in order to bathe in their blood in an attempt to keep her looks. The Gothic writers of the eighteenth century leapt upon such tales and Transylvania became the land of monsters for the movement.

Vlad Dracula was also brought back to life by Balkan nationalist movements in the nineteenth century. He was treated more generously by fiction writers and poets than he had been or has been by historians and this is not entirely surprising as the tracts that were written about him as a national hero who had so valiantly resisted the Turk were based largely on the Romanian oral traditions relating to his life. Romania was a country with a very low level of literacy and no written language until the sixteenth century,[15] and as is not uncommon in such societies the 'history' of events and men was passed down the generations through story telling. The middle of the nineteenth century saw the effects of the 1848 revolutions in Western Europe also spreading to the East. Wallachians, Moldavians and Transylvanians all looked to shrug off Turkish and Russian domination and interference in their affairs. Emerging nations need what Socrates would have called a 'foundation myth'. These renascent nations had been under the Turkish yoke for so long that they had to look back a very long way to see independent heroes and princes. Vlad Dracula was a very promising candidate according to the oral tradition.

The Dracula Castle Epic was an example of the type of romance produced in the seventeenth century. Though written in 'Church' Slavonic as history, it used a large amount of oral Romanian tradition to fill in the blanks for the early history of Vlad Dracula's reign and particularly his building of the castle of Poenari.

The evolution of the Romanian language and its acceptance among the literati as an acceptable language for writing literature in saw the production of a long epic poem by Ion Budai-Deleanu in the late eighteenth century, which then saw publication in the 'revolutionary era' in 1875, under the title of *Tiganiada*, or the Gypsy Epic. It pursued a theme of Vlad Dracula leading an army of gypsy slaves in a campaign against the Ottomans. The poem also introduced the old Romanian tales of *strigoi*, or vampires, and other evil spirits among Vlad Dracula's enemies.

The literature of the second half of the nineteenth century, following the formation of the Romanian state, or more correctly the United Principalities of Moldavia and Wallachia or The Romanian United Principalities, commonly looked back to Vlad Dracula as an archetypal warrior for independence and nationhood. Again, there was very little historical analysis here and, as if to prove Jean Cocteau's pronouncement that 'History is truth that becomes an illusion. Mythology is an illusion that becomes reality',[16] it was poets who created the great general who was offered to the people as a rallying point and hero. The poet Dimitrie Bolintineanu, in his 'Battles of the Romanians', extolled Vlad Dracula's military exploits. And the 'Third Letter', an 1881 ballad from the pen of the poet Mihai Eminescu, called on the Impaler to come once again and save his country, though by this time it was as likely to be a war of liberation from the Russians as from the Turks that was required.

Not all the poets were charmed by the fantasy of Vlad Dracula as the fearless Crusader for the Wallachian people. In 1874 Vasile Alecsandri wrote 'Vlad Tepes and the Oak Tree', a piece that showed Vlad Dracula as a harsh overlord of his people and which concentrates on the mass impalement of the *boyars* at Tirgoviste. The bravest challenge to the idea that Vlad Dracula should be lauded as an icon of Romanian national identity and freedom, however, came from an historian. Ion Bogdan, in a treatise of 1896 named simply *Vlad Tepes*, presented him as a bloodthirsty tyrant whose cruelty could only be accounted for in terms of a mental disorder. Bogdan did not attempt to explain the atrocities of Vlad Dracula away as so many historians both in the past and in our time have tried to do. This was commendable because if history is truly to offer 'modern man' anything at all then accepting that any atrocity or even misguided governance can be framed as being tolerable by the standards of its time just will not do. If we condone the sins of the fathers we run the risk of excusing them in ourselves and this, as was seen in Srebrenica in 1995 when a distorted view of history was brought to bear on contemporary affairs, is a truly dangerous action. Furthermore, of course, it is simply dismissive of the humans of the past to suggest that we are any more civilised or less capable of accepting barbarism now than our forefathers were. The horror at Vlad Dracula's deeds that can be seen in accounts from both the Christian camps and in Ottoman writings make this very clear.

Bogdan's Vlad Dracula was a man with a diseased mind who killed and tortured for sadistic pleasure, and he really got to the heart of Vlad Dracula when he succinctly described the empty nature of his reigns. Vlad Dracula was a prince who had waged 'a battle that he then lost through his flight'.[17]

6

AFTERMATH, HISTORY
AND MYTH:
THE LEGACIES OF
DRACULA AND HIS RIVALS

… lest the Turk should think that they were preparing to bring in foreign troops, and so hasten the war which was always really at loading point.[1]

Mehemmed II spent the early years of his reign fighting against the frontier and tribal elements in the Ottoman Empire. His successors' struggles were with the men of the *kapikulu* and with 'harem politics'.

Mehemmed II's immediate successor Bayezid II's initial problem was that his accession was disputed by a younger brother, Cem, who had gathered support from the Turcoman tribes still used as auxiliary forces in Anatolia by the Ottomans, and had then called for a share of the empire. Cem's forces were defeated quickly but he was not captured and remained a thorn in his brother's side for years to come. He fled to the Mamluk Sultanate in August 1481. Cem remained in Egypt for several months but when he came to the Mamluk sultan with plans for an invasion of the Ottoman Empire in March 1482 there was no support forthcoming. He was allowed to leave the sultanate but received no material support and was defeated by his brother a second time in August of the same year. This time he fled to the West, where he ended up being housed in the Vatican and being used by the Papacy and the Venetians as a check on his brother's European ambitions right up until his death in 1495.[2]

The problem for Bayezid II and the sultans who followed him was not, however, so much that of errant brothers; it was rather that the Janissaries and *kapikulu*, like so many Praetorian guards before and since, had become king-makers. Indeed, Bayezid II owed his position to the Janissaries. When Mehemmed II had died the grand wazir had tried to install Cem but the Janissaries murdered the minister and placed their favoured candidate on the throne. The fact that Bayezid II owed this debt to his own slave-soldiers began an insidious process of the limiting and eventual paralysis of the office of sultan.

Bayezid II did, however, achieve some important military objectives during his reign. By 1485 the Ottomans had captured all Moldavia's Black Sea coastal territories, and Stephen the Great was forced into renewed vassal status. Strategically this was important as it linked Ottoman territories to those of their vassals, the Crimean Tatars, and it cut off the European Christian states from direct access to the lucrative trade of the Black Sea. There were successes against Venice too with sea raids only 30km from the Mother Republic itself and the taking of Venetian possessions in the Peloponnese.

In 1504, on his deathbed Stephen the Great of Moldavia advised his son to make his submission to the Ottomans. The hero of Vaslui, like Skanderbeg, clearly recognised the damage to his people that continued resistance would inflict. Stephen also felt that his struggle was becoming hopeless in the absence of Christian unity.[3] So, it looked like business as usual for the expansion and success of the Ottoman Empire but added to the Praetorian dilemma was the fact that, just as Vlad Dracula had fought for the small patch of land called Wallachia, the Ottomans were fighting over a small patch of the globe. Outside of the eastern Mediterranean and western Asia hugely significant events were occurring. In 1497 Vasco da Gama rounded the Cape of Good Hope and the age of blue ocean politics had begun. This is not to suggest that the Western Europeans had some grand strategy for defeating the Ottomans via global trade route domination, but just as tactics will take a commander only so far, far-reaching strategies require bold decisions, an ability to look beyond the immediate theatre and the insight to grasp opportunities.[4]

By 1510 the Portuguese were threatening Ottoman Indian Ocean trade and with Sultan Selim I's conquest of the Mamluk Sultanate in 1517 the Ottomans 'inherited' a war with the Portuguese in both the Red Sea, where Jeddah was threatened, and along the Persian Gulf. The Ottoman admiral, Piri Reis, tried to draw his masters' attentions to the risk to the entire empire from the Europeans sailing in the Indian Ocean and he produced an analysis of Portuguese activity in a prologue to his *Kitab-i-Barhriyye*, a seafaring manual. Though Suleiman I showed some interest, the opportunity to stop the Europeans at this early juncture was lost when the arms and ships built up for a campaign in the Indian Ocean were used instead in the Mediterranean in 1531.

A 'second front' in the Europeans' war with the Ottomans was therefore effectively opened, however coincidentally just as Selim I was destroying one rival, the Mamluks, and severely chastening another, as he did with his crushing defeat of the armies of the rising Safavid Empire of Persia in 1514 at the Battle of Chaldiran. The problem with these victories was that the acquiring of the Mamluk Empire also embroiled the Ottomans in conflicts as far away as the Upper Nile and Sudan. Furthermore, even though Shah Ismail's army was defeated at Chaldiran, his followers, the Qizilbash, were not only to be found inside the borders of his Persian state. Many disaffected elements in Ottoman Anatolia were also drawn to his cause including provincial *sipahis* who had been dispossessed of their *timars* and had seen them being granted instead to members of the *kapikulu* and Janissaries. Even as early as 1511 an 'army of the dispossessed'[5] under the founder of the quasi-religious movement, Sahkulu Qizilbas, had caused havoc in Anatolia as they marched through it burning villages and towns and roasting a provincial governor alive on a spit.

Just as Eastern Europe had been wracked by the Hussite Revolution and Central Europe would be scourged by the Thirty Years War (1618–48), the Ottoman Empire was now experiencing an immense challenge from the Shia division of the Muslim faith. Selim I's response to the Qizilbash and to Shah Ismail indicates just how much heretical belief was seen as a threat to the very fabric of the empire:

You have subjected the upright community of Muhammad ... to
your devious will [and] undermined the firm foundation of the faith;
you have unfurled the banner of oppression in the cause of aggression [and] no longer uphold the commandments and prohibitions of
the Divine Law; you have incited your abominable Shia faction to
unsanctified sexual union and the shedding of innocent blood.[6]

It is probable that the ideological challenge of Shah Ismail's Shia
state and the need to prove to the community of the faithful that the
Ottomans still held the mantle of *Ghazism* was part of the reason for
the Ottomans' explosive return to the European theatre under Selim I's
son, Sultan Suleiman I, the Magnificent.

Suleiman I's initial achievements were certainly impressive. He
accomplished what Mehemmed II had failed to do, the reduction of
Belgrade in 1521. His taking of the city, the besieging of Rhodes in the
following year and his subsequent assaults on Hungary showed perfect
diplomatic timing as, despite the best efforts of the papacy from 1518
onwards to try to bring peace between the Holy Roman Empire and
France, there was none to be had. The Curia also tried to bring Venice,
Poland and Hungary together into a Crusade or Holy League against
the Ottomans but there was no union to be found among the major
European powers. Venice was prepared to kowtow in order to retain
Cyprus under payment of tribute to the Porte, Hungary had abandoned
what was left of its Balkan ambitions and allies with a peace treaty in
1513 and Poland had also signed agreements with the Ottomans.

In fact, the Ottomans at this juncture appeared to have more trouble with Muslims than they did with Christian foes as once again in
1519 Anatolia burned with rebellion. This time the leader was the son
of a self-proclaimed Messiah and the revolt, backed by Shah Ismail,
was only put down with extreme difficulty and the prosecution of a
campaign of extermination followed by the public dismembering of
its leader, Sah Veli.

Suleiman I proceeded to the second siege of Rhodes, and this time
it was successful. This victory would, however, seem insignificant in
1526 when compared to the Battle of Mohacs, where the chivalry of

Hungary and Bohemia was destroyed in only two hours by superior Ottoman firepower and discipline. Hungary simply ceased to exist once it had passed through the turmoil of Ottoman plundering, civil war among petty lords and the dismemberment of its northern provinces by the Habsburgs. Suleiman I did not, in fact, need to even occupy the country as old animosities between the peasants and aristocracy that had simmered away since 1514, when peasant uprisings had been ruthlessly crushed, erupted once more in the shape of Ivan the Black, a fanatic self-proclaimed Serbian prophet, whose peasant army was only one of the violent forces that ripped Hungary apart.

The problem for Suleiman I was that victory at Mohacs brought him face to face with the Habsburg Charles V, and whilst the new Holy Roman Emperor burned with the fury of a zealot equal to that of any *Ghazi* fighting for the faith,[7] he was also a supreme politician and was certainly no believer in the old ways of warfare. He had defeated and captured Francis I, the avatar of chivalry,[8] at Pavia in 1525 and would defeat him in Italy as a whole through a war of attrition that employed full-time professional troops and mercenaries. This would also be the key to his frustration of the ambitions of Suleiman I on his eastern front. In 1527 Croatia accepted Austrian–Habsburg rule – in truth there was very little choice available to the Croatians – and the troops of the Croatian lords were assimilated into the Habsburgs' *Militargrenze*, or military frontier. The *Militargrenze* at this point meant nothing more than a collection of strongholds and minor forts manned by paid-for border troops, the core of which was the standing army that the Habsburgs had formed after their humiliation at Domazlice in 1431. This 'defence system' overlooked the main Ottoman invasion routes into Central Europe and signified a change in the European approach to the Ottoman war; away from the dashing Crusade and expeditions led by royalty[9] and into one of frustration and a wearing down of the enemy's ability to maintain an army in the field at a protracted distance from secured territory. The troops of the *Militargrenze* also continued the fight against the Ottomans for entire campaigning seasons and beyond with raids and probing patrols.

It was the competence of the Austrians and the obstinacy of their defence of Vienna in 1529 that caused Suleiman I's apparently unstoppable successes to come to an abrupt end beneath the 6ft-thick walls of a city defended by Archduke Ferdinand and a small garrison of only 16,000 professional soldiers. The Ottoman bombardment failed to erode either the walls or the morale of these troops and mining failed when the troops and citizens of the city undertook large-scale sorties to clear the Turks from the walls and beyond. During the retreat from the city the Ottomans also lost a number of Danube forts as Archduke Ferdinand undertook a counter-attack that lasted into 1530.

The year 1532 saw another Ottoman attempt on Vienna, which had become the sixteenth-century equivalent of Belgrade in the fifteenth. This time the sultan's armies did not even reach the city and the campaign petered out against the timber blockhouses, watchtowers and fortified villages of the *Militargrenze*, whose troop numbers were growing towards the high-water mark of the 1550s when there would be 5,000 men under arms on permanent border duty.

In 1537 the Ottomans despatched a large army to the coast of Albania and landed in Italy in imitation of one of the last acts of Mehemmed II. The cavalry of this army, some 8,000 men, raided inland through Otranto and to Brindisi. The raids certainly terrified the Italians but there was now another danger erupting far closer to home for the Ottomans as in 1547 Ivan the Grand Prince of Moscow became Tsar of All the Russias. In 1552 he seized the Khanate of Kazan and in 1556 the Astrakhan Khanate. Given that the tsar was of the same division of Christianity as the Serbs, Wallachians, Moldavians and Bulgarians it was to be expected that the rising power of Russia would soon enough be brought to bear on the Ottomans' Balkan Empire. Furthermore, the growth of Ivan IV's empire was linked inextricably to missionary work by the Russian Orthodox Church. Forced conversions and rabid intolerance of the Muslim faith was a key feature of this Russian 'Crusade'. Then in 1554 King Philip II of Spain met with a Russian trade delegation while he was in England to marry Mary Tudor. Negotiations began during which he agreed to supply arms and artillery for use against the Ottomans.

The Cossacks of the Ukraine allied themselves, or rather offered their services to, the tsar and on both land and on the Black Sea they brought raiding and terror even to the mouth of the River Bosporus.

Suleiman I's diplomacy both to counter his encirclement and to distract the Habsburgs from the Balkan front centred on Francis I and the French obtained the kind of trading rights across the Ottoman Empire that the Italian maritime republics had been enjoying for some time. It was only fear of the Habsburgs' armies that kept Venice from joining the French in a pact with Suleiman I. The sultan also punished the *Voivode* of Moldavia for colluding with the Habsburgs by taking his capital Suceava.

In 1542 Suleiman I's garrison had to repulse a Habsburg attack on Pest and the sultan responded in the next year with a push to the West that gained him a few ex-Hungarian provinces and a buffer zone for Buda and Pest. Then a pattern settled down in the lands of the former Hungary as the Habsburgs ran their border possessions through a mix of Catholic and Protestant lords, with the attendant care that this required, whilst the Ottomans attempted to control sometimes truculent Hungarian vassals. Whilst 1552 saw Ottoman control spread over much of the now detached Hungarian dependency of Transylvania, the battleground of Hungary was, in fact, a drain on the resources of both sides and the Treaty of Edirne signed in 1568 is a reflection of the fact that there were concerns for both empires far away from the Balkans and Hungary. A cold war that flared hot now and again, often because of errant vassals, then began but some degree of stability of the border was realised with an agreement 'founding' a small Hungarian kingdom in the north-west under the Habsburg emperor and the division of central Hungary into Ottoman provinces.

Despite their maritime problems in the Red Sea and Indian Ocean the Ottomans still maintained an impressive Mediterranean naval threat under Grand Admiral Hayredddin Reis, or Barbarossa as he is more commonly known. Pitted against the aspirations of the Ottomans for making a *Mare Nostrum* of the Mediterranean was the Habsburg admiral, equally as gifted as Barbarossa, Andrea Doria. But what really stymied the Ottomans was the fact that the Muslim rulers of North Africa soon enough realised that they were as much at risk of being overthrown by the Ottomans as by Spain and the Habsburgs and began to act as the petty lords of the Balkans had behaved towards Hungary in the 1300s. They shunned Ottoman 'friendship' and not uncommonly looked to Habsburg Spain for support against the Turks' ships.

In 1565 there was a 'rematch' between the Ottomans and the Knights Hospitaller, who had been ejected from Rhodes and were now garrisoning Malta. This time the Ottoman siege failed and in 1571 there was a further reverse at the Battle of Lepanto, though the importance of this battle, so often viewed by Western writers as a sixteenth-century Salamis, was limited as the Ottoman fleet soon recovered both in numbers and in terms of its daring.[10]

The year 1564 saw the death of Suleiman I on campaign in southern Hungary whilst countering the energetic Maximillian II, who had succeeded Ferdinand I as Holy Roman Emperor in 1558. The harem politics that had been developing during Suleiman I's reign through his infatuation with the concubine Hurrem Sultan, or Roxelana as she has become known in the West, now came to the fore. Suleiman I broke all the harem's 'rules' when he married this freed slave; he also ignored the one-mother-one-son tradition[11] and finally allowed her to move into apartments away from the harem and adjoining the Topkapi Saray. Hurrem Sultan almost certainly colluded in the downfall and execution of Ibrahim Pasha who was, until Hurrem Sultan's emergence in Suleiman I's affections, the sultan's closest confidant. She also had a hand in the judicial murder of Mustafa, Suleiman I's eldest son by his first wife. The husband of her daughter, Rustem Pasha, amassed a fortune from bribes, the sale of offices and through manipulation of the coin and the price of grain whilst the sultan virtually retired from public affairs. Indeed, his presence with the army in 1564 was due to a final twinge of guilt over having ceased to lead it as his predecessors always had.

The rot that had set in in the empire became apparent with the accession of Selim II when a Janissary revolt in Istanbul threatened the uncrowned sultan with deposition if their accession bonus was not sufficiently impressive. Selim II's accession was eventually secured by payments to the army but even the coin it was paid in was rapidly losing value. The basic problem was that the Ottoman currency system was based on silver coinage and not gold like the *fiorino d'oro* of the Florentine Republic. The massive devaluation in silver currency value across Europe with the Spanish New World mines' overproduction in the late sixteenth century had a disastrous effect on the real buying power of Ottoman silver coinage. In 1585 there was a massive devaluation of the Ottoman *Akce*, or Asper.

After his accession Selim II spent more time in the harem than he did in the office and his successors Murad III and Mehemmed III fell completely under the influence of favourites. The role of the *valide*, the queen mother or mother of the ruling sultan, at times seemed to eclipse even that of the grand wazir. The importance of the African eunuchs of the harem also increased during these reigns and soon enough any government office could not be filled without recourse to bribery of the chief eunuch.

In 1593 Hasan Pasha, the governor of Bosnia, crossed the River Kulpa, the border between Habsburg and Ottoman Hungary. There was a furious and rapid response from the *Militargrenze*, who defended the fortress of Sisak that dominated the 'usual' invasion route to Vienna along the River Sava. Hasan Pasha was killed along with much of his force. By July the two empires were at war again. It was a war of attrition, of little movement and of thirteen long years. By 1595 the fact that the Habsburg forces could not be removed from the line of defences that extended across a long front comprised of the bastions of Nagykanizsa, Gyor, Komaron, Nove Zamky and Eger, and the economic and social crises within the empire, saw the inexperienced Sultan Murad III forced into leading his army in person by the grand wazir. The sultan was victorious in his only battle, though it was widely suggested that he had to be held firm by his grandees to prevent him fleeing the field.

Nagykanizsa and Pest were lost and regained by each side and in 1595 the Hungarian ruler of Transylvania, Sigismund Bathory, whose ancestor had fought with Vlad Dracula, defected to the Ottomans, but there was little that could disguise the fact that the war was burning itself out. Wallachia also opted for Ottoman vassalage in an attempt to prevent the war between the great powers from completely destroying the country. A stalemate finally ensued as the Habsburgs were hampered by the Protestant Reformation and the subsequent Catholic backlash it provoked; though arguably they gained the advantage of employing mercenaries and commanders schooled in the harsh conflict that rolled across the Low Countries in this period against the Ottomans. Meanwhile, the Ottomans continued to battle unrest in Anatolia and the enigmatic Shah Abbas of the Safavids.

The war also precipitated further economic crises in the Ottoman Empire. Currency manipulation and ruinous rates of interest on domestic loans (despite the Islamic ban on usury) saw more and more fiscal misery piled on to the peasantry and on to provincial troops holding small *timars*, as the government also resorted to tax-farming to balance the books.

The number of men that the Ottomans were now required to keep under arms to fight on the Iranian and Balkan fronts was draining the treasury. By 1609 there were 40,000 Janissaries on the payroll, up from 8,000 in 1527 and 13,500 in 1574. This was terrifying exponential growth and the Ottomans turned to the *reaya* just as Vlad Dracula had turned to the peasants to fuel his army. Certainly musketry had made it easier to make peasants into soldiers but the problem was that disaffected peasants when given firearms did not always employ them in the service of the state. Many times in the seventeenth century the Ottomans' peasant battalions were as likely to fire on their masters as on the enemy. In 1656 just such a revolt paralysed Istanbul as once again the coin was found to have been debased to the extent that, of the newly minted coins, 1,000 Aspers held a real market value of only 200. The Janissaries also began to use their muscle as 'king-makers' on a more and more frequent basis. The Koprulu family took advantage of the chaos to become the real first men of the empire.

The Ottoman war machine still functioned and the outbreak of the Thirty Years War in 1618 gave it an opportunity that it looked possible to exploit as the Protestant *Voivode* of Transylvania, Gabriele Bethlen, called on the sultan to protect the protestants of Eastern Europe against the Habsburgs. This threat to the Catholic position was, however, neutralised by the victory of the Count of Tilly over the Protestant King Frederick V of Bohemia at the Battle of the White Mountain in November 1620.

Inconclusive Ottoman campaigns against the Polish–Lithuanian Commonwealth and their Cossack allies followed in the 1620s, and 1657 saw the revolt of George II Rakoczi in Transylvania and the near detachment of Transylvania from Balkan affairs as Rakoczi took it into alliance with Poland in a war against the Swedes. An Ottoman force sent to bring the *voivode* back into line was swiftly defeated in 1657 but in 1658 an army under a Koprulu forced the *voivode* to flee and Moldavia was also brought back into line. The Ottoman general had to exterminate many of his own cavalry troops before and during the campaign just in order to avoid an army revolt. In 1660 George II Rakoczi was finally captured and executed. The city of Oradea was taken and the Ottomans deliberately destroyed the centrepiece of the city with artillery fire. These were four bronze statues of medieval Hungarian knights and local belief held that the city could never fall whilst these 'guardians' stood. The Ottomans took the bronze scrap that was left after their bombardment and made guns from them in Belgrade. These guns were then used against the Habsburgs and referred to with an appropriate amount of black humour and irony as the 'Gods of the Hungarians'.

The Habsburgs were content to agree to an extension of the peace of 1606 in 1642 and 1649 as they were embroiled in and then recovering from the Thirty Years War and there were successes for the Ottomans against second-rate foes, as at Crete in 1669. But the end of the seventeenth century saw the sultans fighting unwinnable wars against the Polish–Lithuanian Commonwealth and with the Habsburgs and Russia.

August 1664 saw a military disaster at Saint Gothard Abbey on the River Raba as the Habsburg General Montecuccoli, a veteran of the Thirty Years War, crushed an Ottoman army. A peace accord of twenty years was secured by a Habsburg government that was unable to exploit the victory because of its own weakness in Hungary as the counter-Reformation policies of Emperor Leopold I saw a purging and execution of many of the Hungarian nobles and numerous revolts.

In 1683 the Ottomans besieged Vienna. Initially all went well. Gyor had been bypassed and the Habsburg emperor fled Vienna at the advance of the Ottoman army. Tatar cavalry also raided extensively to the west of the city. A bombardment began on 14 July and a month later a mine breached the first line of defensive walls. Only the Polish–Lithuanian Commonwealth was bound by treaty to come to the aid of Vienna and the situation inside the city was desperate by the time the Polish–Lithuanian army of Jan III Sobieski, and the small Habsburg army of Charles of Lorraine, began to attack the Ottoman supply lines in September. There were also small contingents of Bavarian and Saxon troops making up the force of about 60,000 men.

The Ottomans had neglected the defence of the heavily forested and mountainous region to the west of Vienna as it seemed impossible to bring an army through the area and muster it. This was, however, exactly what the European commanders managed to do and after cross-ing the River Danube at Tulln they deployed to attack, taking some three days to set their positions. The Ottomans were outnumbered but could not withdraw as it seemed that the siege was close to being won. As many men as could be taken from the siege were deployed to meet the Europeans in battle. Wallachians and Moldavians fought along-side Tatars and regular Ottoman troops but in the battle that lasted from morning to evening they were swept aside and the broken army retreated to Belgrade. There were huge recriminations in the Porte as it became clear that the army had taken insufficient heavy guns to breach the vast walls of Vienna.[12] The grand wazir was executed on Christmas Day 1683.

The following year looked grim for the Ottomans as rumours of the formation of a vast league of the Europeans and Russia were heard in Istanbul. Russia was to attack through the Crimea, Polish–Lithuanian forces would take Wallachia into the Commonwealth, and Venice would re-ignite its war in Bosnia and against the islands of the eastern Mediterranean. Even France, a state that the Ottomans had done so much to cultivate relations with as a counterweight to the Habsburgs, had apparently joined the alliance. In fact, this grand league never came to complete fruition,[13] but it was certainly a time of reverses as in 1686

Buda and a large part of Hungary was lost to the Habsburgs, and in 1687 the Ottoman field army was defeated at the Second Battle of Mohacs. The army revolted against its generals after this defeat and even demanded that the grand wazir, who was leading the army, hand over the sacred standard of the Prophet Muhammad, which had been conveniently found in Damascus during a time of earlier military difficulties and which had been brought to Europe to lead the Ottomans to victory.

The sequel to the above was the loss of Belgrade in 1688, and Transylvania also came under Austrian control. There would have been further reverses if it had not been for the outbreak of the Nine Years War in 1688 between France and the Holy Roman Empire and its allies. Leopold I was unable to respond, due to simple lack of resources, to the Ottomans retaking Belgrade in 1690.

The 'victory' of 1690 could barely disguise what was happening to the Ottoman army. Mutinies had broken out in 1687 and every year since. At one point the guy ropes to the grand wazir's tent were cut whilst he was on campaign and all the army's standards were sent back to Istanbul by the troops in protest at the appalling condition of the fortresses and equipment with which they were expected to fight the *Militargrenze*. In 1688 Janissaries and a mob of civilians murdered the grand wazir in Istanbul and also entered his harem and carried off women as booty. There was also depopulation of previously wealthy areas that had produced impressive tax-revenues as Christians fled an increasingly fiscally oppressive regime for the Habsburg's lands. This was essentially a reverse of the fourteenth and fifteenth centuries, when the Turks were far more amenable overlords than the Byzantines or Hungarians. Varna lost one-third of its population in this period. There was also a new puritanical element to the previously tolerant religion settlement of the Ottoman state in this period, probably as a result of the ongoing misfortunes of the empire. Rights of Jews and of Orthodox Christians were both eroded and the Jews in particular were made scapegoats for the ongoing economic calamities of the empire over the course of the seventeenth century.

In 1691 there was a further defeat at Slankerman and by the end of the year there was a solid Habsburg presence in Transylvania. The two sides sparred over the course of the 1690s but there was no knock-out punch possible as both sides were fiscally and militarily drained.

Then in 1697 came the blow that finally sent the Ottoman Empire tumbling to become the sick man of Europe. The Ottoman army was moving towards Transylvania in an attempt to break Habsburg control over the River Danube. The campaign began with acrimonious arguments among its commanders, a misreading of the marshy land and number of rivers that would have to be traversed by the army and even a misrepresentation to the sultan of the numbers of troops under arms. One hundred and four thousand men were listed on the rolls whereas only 50,000 effective troops could be mustered.

The army reached Senta, where the Habsburg commander, Prince Eugene of Savoy, had destroyed the bridge. In the ensuing battle almost the entire Ottoman general staff were killed and the sultan fled the field. The devastation wreaked upon the imperial army was immense.

The Treaty of Karlovitz was signed in 1699 and was the direct result of this military disaster. It brought a lasting peace between the Habsburgs and Ottomans. It also became the starting point for intense Western and Russian interference in the internal politics of the Ottoman Empire as the 'captive' states of the Balkans were seen, once again, as belonging to the Christian world and not a part of an 'Eastern' empire.

The Ottoman Empire would continue to fray, under Russian pressure in the main, until its eventual extinction in 1923 and its vassal states in the Balkans, under the influence of the 1848 revolutions in Western Europe, would generate new political and cultural movements in an attempt to 're-create' nations that had been essentially lost now for some 400 years. Vlad Dracula, along with a host of other semi-mythical characters, were about to be brought back to life and placed in the service of this new nationalism.

Serbia's journey back into history to find characters on which to build a new nation, like Romania's, began with poets. In 1847 Petar Petrovic Njegos composed 'The Mountain Wreath'. A flavour of the work, which was a product of a desire to reassert a Serb national identity, is given by the chorus: 'The high mountains reek with the stench of non-Christians'. The work appears to have been based on myths constructed in the medieval period that were converted into an oral tradition; Serbia, like Romania, was a largely illiterate society in the nineteenth century.[14] The Serbian national identity that emerged in the twentieth century was distinctly anti-Catholic and anti-Muslim, and given the two empires that the Serbs had been dominated by for more than half a millennia this was not entirely surprising. The poets and early nationalists of the Serbs adopted an ideology that presented the medieval Serbian state of Tsar Stefan Uros IV Dusan and Saint Sava as a 'golden age of order and orthodoxy' and contrasted this with the disasters that befell Serbia after the incursions of the Muslim Turks and the 1389 Battle of Kosovo. As discussed earlier, the fact that this view did not meet the historical truth was not important and it survived the disasters of 1914–18 and Serbia being subsumed into the Yugoslav state. When Serbian national identity began once again to be reasserted at the end of the ethnic and cultural miasma that was the former Yugoslavia in the 1980s, the myth became even more dangerous as it identified Muslims in general as problematic to the culture of the Serbian state. This was particularly evident in attitudes towards the Kosovo–Albanians who occupied the religious 'heartland' of Nemanjic Serbia.

In 1989 Slobodan Milosevic both neatly encapsulated a Serb nationalist interpretation of Serbian medieval history, and bent it to his needs. In a speech commemorating the 500th anniversary of the first Battle of Kosovo he stated that Prince Lazar had battled to 'defend Europe from Islam' and that Serbia had continued to this day to be 'a fortress defending European culture and religion'. The contemporary media of Serbia echoed a similar message and emphasised the persecutions of the Islamic theocratic state against the Serbian aristocracy. The religious differences between the Christian 'bond servants' and their Muslim oppressors were constantly expressed. There was no mention of Skanderbeg's resistance.

The history of Bosnia under the Ottomans had been one of conversion to Islam, with many Bosnians reaching high office such as Hersekzade Ahmed Pasha. This was in spite of the Bosnians' Slav heritage and Serbian language and culture. They became, along with the Albanians,[15] one of the chief supports of Ottoman rule in the region. The post-Cold War Serbian national identity focused on the survival under Muslim occupation of the Serbian Orthodox Church. With Milosevic's leadership it was almost inevitably a short road to the horrors of Srebrenica.[16]

Croatia's bloody twentieth century was less affected by a re-animation of the ghosts of the past and rather more by the state's strong adherence to Catholicism, which had begun with Venetian colonisation, continued with Hungarian domination during the 'Hunyadi era' and been solidified by Croatia accepting Austrian–Habsburg rule in 1527. With the advent of the Second World War and Italian ambitions in the Balkans, Croatian nationalism took on a badge of ultra-Catholicism that took much from the ultra-conservatism of Franco but rather more from the Fascism of Mussolini, and later from the Nazism of Hitler.

The failure of Mussolini's Balkan campaign in 1940 was the cata-lyst for Hitler invading Yugoslavia on 6 April 1941. As the Germans entered Zagreb on 10 April, the Croat Fascists of Ante Pavelic's Ustasa party declared an independent Croatia with Hitler's approval. Italy, Hungary and Germany dismembered Yugoslavia and left Croatia as a nominally self-governing state.

The Ustasa of Croatia worked to create a 'pure' Catholic Croatia through enforced conversions, deportations and mass extermination. Serbian adherence to the Orthodox faith was viewed in ethnic and not religious terms by the Ustasa and very often conversion was actively denied to Serbs as they sought to avoid persecutions and mass murder. Jews were also part of this holocaust, most probably because of Pavelic's debt to Hitler, but oddly enough (or perhaps not so oddly given Hitler's ambitions in the Middle East) Muslims were excluded from the torment and deportations to concentration camps that the Ustasa inflicted on the Serbs and Jews.

The Ustasa started with a ban on Cyrillic script in all publications and the closing of Serb Orthodox primary and pre-schools. Then the massacres began in the spring of 1941. Two-hundred and fifty Serbian men were taken from villages in April. They were forced to dig a mass grave, and were then bound with wire and buried alive. In the town of Otocac more than 300 Serbs, along with their priest and his son, were rounded up. The priest was forced to recite prayers for the dying while the men, including his son, were hacked to death with axes. The priest was skinned alive after having his hair and beard torn off, and his eyes gouged out.[17] These were horrors which Vlad Dracula would have been proud to have inflicted.

As discussed earlier, Vlad Dracula's resurrection in the nineteenth century was largely achieved by the hands of poets. The coming of Communism in Romania following the disasters of the Second World War and occupation by Soviet Russia saw a another change in the character of the mythical Prince Vlad Dracula. His 'modern' style of conduct in government and his independence struggles were emphasised by panegyrists of the Ceausescu regime. Excusing the brutality of Vlad Dracula was important for the Ceausescu regime of the 1970s as its emphasis on internal discipline, subjugation of personal needs or rights in the service of the state and the importance of the hand of government, and the state, over and above that of the welfare of the people who actually made up the state was evident in both regimes, even though they were separated by 500 years. It was almost as if the Romanian government was on a mission to prove Benedetto Croce's maxim that 'every historical judgement gives to all history the character of contemporary history, because however remote in time events thus recounted may seem to be, history in reality refers to present needs and present situations wherein those events vibrate'. It was a pity for the Romanian people that these same writers did not take on board Croce's instruction for all historians, that the historian's task is one of 'criticism, criticism and then criticism'.[18]

In December 1976 the Romanian government celebrated the 500th anniversary of the death of Vlad Dracula. Sculptures, paintings, essays and even a play were commissioned to emphasise the *voivode*'s clear-cut political goals that justified his actions, which were never described as merely gratifying his need for cruelty. The disposal of the *boyars* strengthened his rule, and the purge of the cripples and thieves was to eradicate 'social parasitism and dishonesty'. Given that the Ceausescu regime was constantly secured by purges and that its impatient response to social problems included the infamous orphanages of the 1980s, Vlad Dracula was the perfect vehicle to excuse the crimes of the contemporary regime by reference to a 'a Prominent Personality of Our National History, Personifying the Will of the Romanian People to Live Freely Within the Boundaries of their Ancestors' Territory', and 'Vlad the Impaler, Hero of the Struggle for Freedom and Independence'.[19] Vlad Dracula was even credited with having invented 'people's warfare' long before Mao Ze Dong or Ho Chi Minh, as he had 'raised a large army, an army of all those capable of fighting, sacrificing the entire nation for the benefit of the fatherland by creating a genuine desert in the face of the invader, as well as continually engaging in skirmishes'.[20] The military achievements of this superman were placed alongside those of Stephen the Great and John Hunyadi as Vlad Dracula was remembered as being 'one of the Knights of the Cross, that is, a leader of the struggle waged by Europe against the Asiatic impact of Ottoman expansion'. The third *Athleta Christi*, Skanderbeg was as forgotten by the Romanians as he was by the Serbs[21] but the Romanian historians did remember how Vlad Dracula, like Milosevic's Lazar of Serbia, had turned 'the Romanian people into a wall protecting the West, a wall that the enemy could occasionally penetrate or leap over, but could never pull down to allow the borders of the tri-continental empire to sprawl north of the Danube, and install pashas or muezzins in Tirgoviste, Bucharest, or Suceava'. Whilst this is clearly nonsense perhaps some sympathy could, however, be given for the line, 'Christendom relied on the Carpathian countries in the struggle without ever really helping, for its aid never reached Moldavia or Walachia in time.'[22]

The obsession with social harmony and order that has run through every 'Democratic Dictatorship of the People'[23] was easy to harness to the idea of a Romanian prince 'who upheld good, strictly observed order' and who was 'an honest *voivode* of undaunted courage who would never pardon an evildoer; a knight of justice and freedom who would never forgive an oppressor of the people'. Needless to say, the oppressors of the people in this case were the Ottomans of the fifteenth century but they could equally be the countries of NATO or the Soviet Union dependent on how obsequious or independent-minded the premier was feeling at any particular time. Equally important to Ceausescu was to link Vlad Dracula to 'present-day society by working out a code of socialist behaviour'.[24] Indeed, as Secretary General of the Romanian Communist Party, Ceausescu's constantly reiterated call was for labour discipline, the maintenance of socialist morality, and civic-patriotism.[25] The fact that Ceausescu, particularly through his policy of exporting Romania's agrarian wealth whilst malnutrition stalked the country, took as little care of the Romanian people as Vlad Dracula had seems almost redundant to comment on.

Given that Ceausescu, after drawing so many parallels between his own regime and that of the Impaler, should be killed by his own people after being hounded from office, just as the tyrant Vlad Dracula's father had been, was appropriate. That he died unmourned by his contemporaries just as Vlad Dracula had been also seems entirely apposite.

NOTES

Acknowledgements

1 Count Dracula, Johnathan Harker's Journal, 8 May. Stoker, B.,
  Dracula, 1897.
2 Grousset, R., *Histoire des Croisades et du Royaume Franc de
  Jerusalem, Tome I: L'anarchie Musulmane et la Monarchie Franque*,
  Plon, Paris, 1934; *Histoire des Croisades et du Royaume Franc de
  Jerusalem, Tome II: Monarchie Franque et Monarchie Musulman
  l'equilibre*, Plon, Paris, 1935; *Histoire des Croisades et du Royaume
  franc de Jérusalem, Tome III: La Monarchie Musulmane et
  l'anarchie Franque*, Plon, Paris, 1935.

Introduction

1 Van Helsing, Mina Harker's Journal, 30 September. Stoker, B.,
  Dracula, 1897.

Chapter 1

1 From Mina Harker's Journal, 30 September. Stoker, B., *Dracula*, 1897.
2 Macrides, R., 'George Akropolites: The History, Introduction,
  Translation and Commentary', *Oxford Studies in Byzantium*,
  Oxford University Press, Oxford, 2007, 85.
3 The Genoese republic's records indicate that Genoa aimed to
  challenge the Venetians' dominance of the northern Mediterranean
  by the taking of bases in the south. The First Crusade gave them
  their first opportunity. From then on ongoing conflict with the
  Venetians was guaranteed. See Byrne, E.H., 'Genoese Trade with
  Syria in the Twelfth Century', *American Historical Review*, January
  1920, 191–219.

4   For an appraisal of just how intertwined Genoese and Ottoman interests were see Fleet, K., 'The Treaty of 1387 between Murad I and the Genoese', *Bulletin of the School of Oriental and African Studies*, University of London, vol. 56:1, 1993, 13–33.

5   Angold, M., *The Byzantine Empire: A Political History 1025–1204*, 2nd edition, Longman, London, 1997.

6   Wolff, R., *A History of the Crusades, Volume Two – The Later Crusades*, ch. 6, 1189–1311, editor Setton, K., University of Wisconsin Press, London, 1969.

7   For a superb deconstruction of how belief acted as the central pillar of secular life and how heresy or conversion was viewed by medieval communities see Sumption, J., *The Albigensian Crusade*, Faber and Faber, London, 1978, 39–42.

8   Frolow, A., 'Doctrinal Causes' in *The Latin Conquest of Constantinople*, editor Queller, D., Wiley and Sons, New York, 1971.

9   Housley, N., *The Later Crusades: From Lyons to Alcazar 1274–1580*, Oxford University Press, Oxford, 1992, 57–61.

10   Queller, D., *The Fourth Crusade*, Leicester University Press, Leicester, 1978, Introduction.

11   Riley-Smith, J., *The Crusades: A Short History*, Athlone Press, London, 1990.

12   For the pre-eminence of the Egyptian Turkish Mamluks among medieval warriors in archery, close combat, siege warfare and horsemanship see Waterson, J., *The Knights of Islam: The Wars of the Mamluks*, Greenhill Books, London, 2007, ch. 5.

13   Wittek, P., '[By 1300] Osman was predestined to attain the position of a world empire', in 'The Rise of the Ottoman Empire', *Royal Asiatic Society Monographs*, vol. XXIII, 1967, 1–33.

14   Inalcik, H., 'The Emergence of the Ottomans' in *The Cambridge History of Islam. [Part One] vol. 1A. The Central Islamic Lands from Pre Islamic Times to the First World War*, editors Holt, P., Lambton, A., and Lewis, B., Cambridge University Press, Cambridge, 1970.

15   Lindner, R., *Nomads and Ottomans in Medieval Anatolia*, Indiana University Press, Bloomington, 1983, 2–38.

16   Wittek, P., 'The Rise of the Ottoman Empire', *Royal Asiatic Society Monographs*, vol. XXIII, 1967, 1–33.

17   Barber, M., *The New Knighthood: A History of the Order of the Temple*, Cambridge University Press, Cambridge, 1994, 40–43.

18   Waterson, J., *The Knights of Islam: The Wars of the Mamluks*, Greenhill Books, London, 2007, chs 1, 2 and 4 in particular.

19   Waterson, J., *Sacred Swords: Jihad in the Holy Land 1097–1295*, Frontline Books, London, 2010, 56–120.

20 Turan, O., 'Anatolia in the Period of the Seljuks and Beyliks', in *The Cambridge History of Islam. [Part One] vol. 1A. The Central Islamic Lands from Pre Islamic Times to the First World War*, editors Holt, P., Lambton, A., and Lewis, B., Cambridge University Press, Cambridge, 1970.

21 Lindner, R., *Nomads and Ottomans in Medieval Anatolia*, Indiana University Press, Bloomington, 1983, 2–38.

22 Morgan, D., *The Mongols*, Blackwell, Oxford, 1990, 40–49.

23 Lindner, R., *Nomads and Ottomans in Medieval Anatolia*, Indiana University Press, Bloomington, 1983, 2–38.

24 Wittek, P., 'The Rise of the Ottoman Empire', *Royal Asiatic Society Monographs*, vol. XXIII, 1967, 1–33.

25 Cahen, C., *Pre Ottoman Turkey*, translated by Jones-Williams, Sidgewick and Jackson, London, 1968, 169.

26 Lindner, R., *Nomads and Ottomans in Medieval Anatolia*, Indiana University Press, Bloomington, 1983, 2–38.

27 Cahen, C., *Pre Ottoman Turkey*, translated by Jones-Williams, Sidgewick and Jackson, London, 1968, 43–45.

28 Koprulu, M., 'Life along the Border and the Founding of the Ottoman Empire' in *The Origins of the Ottoman Empire*, translated and edited by Leiser, G., State University of New York Press, New York, 1935/1992 edition.

29 Morgan, D., *The Mongols*, Blackwell, Oxford, 1990, 158–175.

30 Inalcik, H., 'The Emergence of the Ottomans' in *The Cambridge History of Islam. [Part One] vol. 1A. The Central Islamic Lands from Pre Islamic Times to the First World War*, editors Holt, P., Lambton, A., and Lewis, B., Cambridge University Press, Cambridge, 1970.

31 Koprulu, M., 'Life along the Border and the Founding of the Ottoman Empire' in *The Origins of the Ottoman Empire*, translated and edited by Leiser, G., State University of New York Press, New York, 1935/1992 edition.

32 Heywood, C., 'Boundless Dreams of the Levant. Paul Wittek, The George-Kreis and the Writing of Ottoman History' in *Journal of the Royal Asiatic Society*, 1989, 33–50. Heywood is excellent on the romanticism of previous, highly influential, historians of the Ottoman state and their requirement for a 'motive force' in Ottoman history. It seems that historians have previously followed, all too easily, the later chronicles of the early Ottoman Empire; these emphasised a *Ghazi* or Danishmendid ancestry for many families. The *Danishmendname*, for example, is explicit in its description of a holy war against the infidel Christians but must be viewed as a later romantic construction; a Western equivalent of this kind of 'history' would be taking the *Chanson d'Antioche* at face value.

33 Demetrios Kydones, in Imber, C.,*The Ottoman Empire 1300–1481*, Isis Press, Istanbul, 1990, 29. The Papacy's reluctance to aid Byzantium is not surprising given the intellectual direction of Church thinkers of the period. Phillipe de Mezieres' Crusade treatise of the fourteenth century argues the need to 'spread Catholicism to the eastern countries'.

34 Saladin was, of course, a Kurd rather than a Turk but the same system applied. For the unity he achieved in his empire and the rapid dissolution that ensued upon his death see Waterson, J., *Sacred Swords: Jihad in the Holy Land 1097–1291*, Frontline Books, London, 2010, chs 6 and 7.

35 For how the patrimonial share-out paralysed and ultimately shattered the superpower of the medieval age see Waterson, J., *Defending Heaven: China's Mongol Wars 1209–1370*, Frontline Books, London, 2013, chs 2 and 4.

36 Fletcher, J., 'The Mongols: Ecological and Social Perspectives', *Harvard Journal of Asiatic Studies*, vol. 46:1, 1986, 11–50. Reprinted in Fletcher, J., *Studies on Chinese and Islamic Inner Asia*, editor Manz, B.F., Ashgate, Aldershot, 1995. Professor Fletcher has argued that the Mongols arrived in Persia with 'attitudes nurtured in the East Asian steppe: disdain for peasants, who, like the animals that the Mongols herded, lived directly off what grew from the soil', and that 'with the steppe extortion pattern in mind, the Mongols did violence and used terror, reinforced by their ideology of universal dominion, to induce their victims to surrender peaceably'. The Ottomans appear to have had a far deeper understanding of their state's need to nurture its agrarian base and peasantry.

37 Anonymous Ottoman chronicle, in Lewis, B., *Islam from the Prophet Muhammad to the Capture of Constantinople*, Harper and Row, New York, 1974, 226–227. The Porte was the sultan's mobile headquarters.

38 The Vlachs are a distinct ethno-linguistic group, usually described as descendants of Roman colonists and Latinised natives, who at the coming of the Slavs in the sixth century sought safety from the invaders by withdrawing to upland regions of the Balkan mountains, where they commonly became shepherds and peasants.

39 Vinogradoff, P., 'Feudalism' in *The Cambridge Medieval History*, vol. 3, Cambridge University Press, Cambridge, 1924, 458–484.

40 Davis, R., *A History of Medieval Europe from Constantine to Saint Louis*, Longman, London, 1970.

41 Vinogradoff, P., 'Feudalism' in *The Cambridge Medieval History*, vol. 3, Cambridge University Press, Cambridge, 1924, 458–484.

42 Reynolds, S., *Fiefs and Vassals: The Medieval Evidence Reinterpreted*, Oxford University Press, Oxford, 1994, 17–46.

43 'Alberon, Bishop of Liege' from a *Source Book for Medieval Economic History*, editors Cave, R., and Coulson, H., Biblo & Tannen, New York, 1936 edition, 1965 reprint, 299–301.

44 Peter the Venerable vs. Saint Bernard of Clairvaux. 'On the Keeping of Serfs' from a *Source Book for Medieval Economic History*, editors Cave, R., and Coulson, H., Biblo & Tannen, New York, 1936 edition, 1965 reprint, 299–301.

45 Gibbons, H., *The Foundations of the Ottoman Empire*, Oxford University Press, Oxford, 1916, 22–23.

46 Vickers, M., *Between Serb and Albanian: A History of Kosovo*, Hurst and Co., London, 1998, 12.

47 In most Islamic states, both those preceding and those which were contemporaneous with the Ottomans' *timar* system, the basic 'fief' was called the *iqta*. For how the system was managed in the early Saljuq Empire and in the Mamluk dynasty see Waterson, J., *The Ismaili Assassins: A History of Medieval Murder*, Frontline Books, London, 2008 and Waterson, J., *The Knights of Islam: The Wars of the Mamluks*, Greenhill Books, London, 2007.

48 Inalcik, H., *The Ottoman Empire: The Classical Age 1300–1600*, translated by Itzkowitz, N., & Imber, C., Weidenfeld and Nicolson, London, 1973, 12.

49 Inalcik, H., *The Ottoman Empire: The Classical Age 1300–1600*, translated by Itzkowitz, N., & Imber, C., Weidenfeld and Nicolson, London, 1973, 12.

50 Early in the Balkan conquest, the Ottoman Empire consisted of two provinces: *Rumelia* or Europe derived from the Turkish name for the Byzantine 'Roman' Empire, *Rum*, and Anatolia.

51 Inalcik, H., *The Ottoman Empire: Conquest, Organisation and Economy*, Variorum Reprints, London, 1978, 114.

52 In Imber, C., *The Ottoman Empire 1300–1481*, Isis Press, Istanbul, 1990, 116.

53 Barton, S., 'Women on the Frontline' in *History Today*, December 2014, 3–4, and Barton, S., *Conquerors, Brides and Concubines: Interfaith Relations and Social Power in Medieval Iberia*, University of Pennsylvania Press, Philadelphia, 2015. As the author notes, this appalling feature of war persists in the crimes of *Daesh* against the Yazidi of Iraq, and those of Boko Haram against Nigerian Christians.

54 Fergusson, N., *The War of the World: Twentieth-Century Conflict and the Descent of the West*, Penguin, New York, 2007, xlix–li and 629–635.

55 Malcolm, N., *Kosovo: A Short History*, Macmillan, London, 1998, 67.

56 Inalcik, H., *The Ottoman Empire: The Classical Age 1300–1600*, translated by Itzkowitz, N., & Imber, C., Weidenfeld and Nicolson, London, 1973, 12.

57 Malcolm, N., *Kosovo: A Short History*, Macmillan, London, 1998, 81.

58 Barton, S., 'Women on the Frontline', *History Today*, December 2014, 3–4, and Barton, S., *Conquerors, Brides and Concubines: Interfaith Relations and Social Power in Medieval Iberia*, University of Pennsylvania Press, Philadelphia, 2015.

59 The Ottomans gave Vuk Brankovic's lands to their loyal vassal, Stefan Lazarevic. Despite this and Brankovic's continued and ultimately fatal resistance there is a Serb nationalist tradition of Brankovic being the 'battlefield Iscariot' at Kosovo.

60 Pryor, J., *Geography, Technology and War: Studies in the Maritime History of the Mediterranean 649–1571*, Cambridge University Press, Cambridge, 1988, 1–50.

61 Raiding, in a fragile agrarian economy such as the Balkans supports, was as likely to bring an area under control as was the winning of a pitched battle, or at least make its continued occupation by the enemy untenable. For the importance of raiding in the medieval period, see Gillingham, J., 'Richard I and the Science of War in the Middle Ages', in editors Gillingham, J., and Holt, J.C., *War and Government in the Middle Ages: Essays in Honour of J.O. Prestwich*, Boydell & Brewer, Woodbridge, 1984, 78–91.

62 Mircea I and his troops' 'desertion' from the battlefield when they saw they were on the losing side is not surprising. They knew that their lands would be the first to suffer Ottoman retribution and that they would need to return home to prepare for the inevitable punitive raids. See Rosetti, R., 'Notes on the Battle of Nicopolis (1396)', *The Slavonic and East European Review*, vol. 15:45, 1937, 629–638.

63 From the writings of Johann Schiltberger in Imber, C., *The Ottoman Empire 1300–1481*, Isis Press, Istanbul, 1990, 46; 1,500 would make more sense than the 15,000 that Schiltberger reports.

64 Marlowe, C., *Tamburlaine The Great, Part I*, c. 1590.

65 The succession in the 'one generation nobility' of the Mamluk dynasty was always complicated and interregnums were almost the norm as king makers gathered around candidates and puppets at the death of each sultan. Even the greatest of the Mamluk sultans, Baybars I, could not secure adequately the throne for his bloodline; his son was dismissed after a short reign and a pattern was set. See Waterson, J., *The Knights of Islam: The Wars of the Mamluks*, Greenhill Books, London, 2007, in particular ch. 7.

66 In Holt, P., *The Age of the Crusades: The Near East from the Eleventh Century to 1517*, Longman, London, 1986, 179.

67 In Marozzi, J., *Tamerlane, Sword of Islam, Conqueror of the World*, Harper Collins, London, 2004, 291–292.

68 Malcolm, N., *Kosovo: A Short History*, Macmillan, London, 1998, 83.

69 Marlowe, C., *Tamburlaine The Great, Part I, c. 1590*.

70 Malcolm, N., *Kosovo: A Short History*, Macmillan, London, 1998, 83.

71 Inalcik, H., *The Ottoman Empire: The Classical Age 1300–1600*, translated by Itzkowitz, N., & Imber, C., Weidenfeld and Nicolson, London, 1973, 17.

72 Imber, C., *The Ottoman Empire 1300–1481*, Isis Press, Istanbul, 1990, 69–70.

73 Imber, C., *The Ottoman Empire 1300–1481*, Isis Press, Istanbul, 1990, 73.

74 Malcolm, N., *Kosovo: A Short History*, Macmillan, London, 1998, 88.

75 Kopanski. A., 'Islamization of Albanians in the Middle Ages: The Primary Sources and the Predicament of the Modern Historiography', *Islamic Studies, special issue: Islam in the Balkans*, summer/autumn 1997, 191–208.

76 Inalcik, H., *The Ottoman Empire: The Classical Age 1300–1600*, translated by Itzkowitz, N., & Imber, C., Weidenfeld and Nicolson, London, 1973, 19.

77 'Asikpasazade's Turkish Chronicle' in Imber, C.,*The Ottoman Empire 1300–1481*, Isis Press, Istanbul, 1990, 116.

Chapter 2

1 Jonathan Harker's Journal, 8 May. Stoker, B., *Dracula*, 1897.

2 The name Szekely is derived from a Hungarian expression meaning 'frontier guard'. They remain a distinct group within southern Hungary today.

3 Moldavia was also 'under stronger steppe influence than Wallachia as indicated by the many sabres and abundant archery equipment found in its graves'. See Nicolle, D., *Hungary and the Fall of Eastern Europe 1000–1568*, Osprey, London, 1988, 38.

4 Nicolle, D., *Hungary and the Fall of Eastern Europe 1000–1568*, Osprey, London, 1988, 39.

5 Zachariadou, E., 'Ottoman Diplomacy and the Danube Frontier (1420–1424)', *Harvard Ukrainian Studies. Essays presented to Ihor Sevcenko on his Sixtieth Birthday by his Colleagues and Students*, 1983, 680–690.

6 See Waterson, J., *The Knights of Islam: The Wars of the Mamluks*, Greenhill Books, London, 2007, chs 1 and 5.

7 The *devshirme* took one child from every forty households every five years.

8 Inalcik, H., 'Ottoman Methods of Conquest' in *The Ottoman Empire: Conquest, Organisation and Economy*, Varorium Reprints, London, 1985, 105.

9 Inalcik, H., 'Ottoman Methods of Conquest' in *The Ottoman Empire: Conquest, Organisation and Economy*, Varorium Reprints, London, 1985, 105.

10 Kunt, M., *The Waqf as an Instrument of Public Policy: Notes on the Koprulu Family Endowments in Honour of Professor Menage*, editors Heywood, C., and Imber, C., Isis Press, Istanbul, 1994, 189.

11 Inalcik, H., 'The Socio-Political Effects of the Diffusion of Firearms in the Middle East' in *War, Technology and Society in the Middle East*, editors Parry, V., and Yapp, M., Oxford University Press, London, 1985, 190.

12 Petrovic, D., 'Firearms in the Balkans on the Eve of and After the Ottoman Conquests of the 14th And 15th Century' in *War, Technology and Society in the Middle East*, editors Parry, V., and Yapp, M., Oxford University Press, London, 1985, 190.

13 The Turkish word *reaya* literally means 'flock' or 'follower'; the implications of such a term being used to describe the general Turcoman populace are immense. See Inalcik, H., 'The Socio-Political Effects of the Diffusion of Firearms in the Middle East' in *War, Technology and Society in the Middle East*, editors Parry, V., and Yapp, M., Oxford University Press, London, 1985, 195.

14 Inalcik, H., 'The Socio-Political Effects of the Diffusion of Firearms in the Middle East' in *War, Technology and Society in the Middle East*, editors Parry, V., and Yapp, M., Oxford University Press, London, 1985, 211.

15 The Ottomans met the vast Turcoman confederate army of Uzun Hasan in battle near Malatya on 11 August 1473. An officer of Hasan's army cried out, 'Son of a whore, what an Ocean!' when he first spied the Ottoman army and yet Ottoman chroniclers recorded that Mehemmed II had been so worried about the size of Hasan's forces that he had called for extra prayers, fasts and religious observances to be carried out all over the empire before the battle. Uzun Hasan was reported afterwards as being happy simply to have escaped the battlefield because 'having never seen a battle with handguns and cannon he was helpless before the Ottomans'. See Imber, C., *The Ottoman Empire 1300–1481*, Isis Press, Istanbul, 1990, 217.

16 Inalcik, H., 'Servile Labour in the Ottoman Empire', *Studies in Ottoman Society and Economic History*, Variorum Reprints, London, 1979/1985, 27.

17 Kunt, M., *The Waqf as an Instrument of Public Policy: Notes on the Koprulu Family Endowments in Honour of Professor*

Menage, V, editors Heywood, C., and Imber, C., Isis Press, Istanbul, 1994, 189.

18 Inalcik, H., 'Servile Labour in the Ottoman Empire', *Studies in Ottoman Society and Economic History*, Variorum Reprints, London, 1979/1985, 26.

19 Riley-Smith, J., 'The Variety of Crusading 1291–1523' in *The Crusades: A History*, 3rd edition, Yale University Press, 2014, ch. 9.

20 Keen, M., *Chivalry*, Nota Bene, Yale, 2005, 143–161.

21 'Oh how merciful is God!' and 'Just and Faithful.'

22 Florescu, R., and McNally, R., *Dracula, Prince of Many Faces: His Life and His Times*, Back Bay Books, Boston, MA, 1990, ch. 2.

23 For both a description and illustrations of Hussite arms and armour see Turnbull, S., *The Hussite Wars 1419–36*, Men-at-Arms Series, Osprey Publishing, Oxford, 2004.

24 Turnbull, S., *The Hussite Wars 1419–36*, Men-at-Arms Series, Osprey Publishing, Oxford, 2004.

25 Turnbull, S., *The Hussite Wars 1419–36*, Men-at-Arms Series, Osprey Publishing, Oxford, 2004.

26 DeVries, K., and Smith, R., *Medieval Military Technology*, University of Toronto Press, Toronto, 2012, 148–149.

27 Tractaus de Moribus, 'Condicionibus et Nequicia Turcorum', in Imber, C., *The Ottoman Empire 1300–1481*, Istanbul, Isis Press, 1990, 117.

28 In Imber, C.,*The Ottoman Empire 1300–1481*, Isis Press, Istanbul, 1990, 118.

29 Tuleja, T., 'Eugenius IV and the Crusade of Varna', *The Catholic Historical Review*, vol. 35:3, October 1949, 257–275.

30 In Gill, J., *The Council of Florence*, Cambridge University Press, Cambridge, 1959, 290.

31 In Imber, C.,*The Ottoman Empire 1300–1481*, Isis Press, Istanbul, 1990, 122.

32 'The Chronicle of the Holy War' in Imber, C., *The Ottoman Empire 1300–1481*, Isis Press, Istanbul, 1990, 124.

33 Vladislaus III may also have been swayed by the praise that was coming from every corner of the Catholic world for his leadership of the two states that were perceived of as being the 'Wall of Christendom' against the barbarian Turks. The Italian humanist Francesco Filelfo wrote flatteringly to the king on 5 November 1444 to wish him well in the Crusade: 'All the nations and kings of Christendom pray God this day for your health and victory … Thou art a bulwark for the whole Christian Commonwealth.' See Knoll, P., 'Poland as "Antemurale Christianitatis" in the Late Middle Ages', *The Catholic Historical Review*, vol. 60:3, October 1974, 381–401.

34 Housley, N., *The Later Crusades: From Lyons to Alcazar 1274–1580*, Oxford University Press, Oxford, 1992, 89.

35 Housley, N., *The Later Crusades: From Lyons to Alcazar 1274–1580*, Oxford University Press, Oxford, 1992, 89.

36 Housley, N., *The Later Crusades: From Lyons to Alcazar 1274–1580*, Oxford University Press, Oxford, 1992, 89.

37 France, J., *Victory in the East: A Military History of the First Crusade*, Cambridge University Press, Cambridge, 1994, ch. 2.

Chapter 3

1 Mina Harker's Journal, 30 September. Stoker, B., *Dracula*, 1897.

2 Inalcik, H., *The Ottoman Empire: The Classical Age 1300–1600*, translated by Itzkowitz, N., & Imber. C., Weidenfeld and Nicolson, London, 1973, 11.

3 There is some evidence that Skanderbeg's fatal delay in joining with Hunyadi on the battlefield of Kosovo was partly related to protracted negotiations with the Venetians to bring his conflict with them to an end. He had promised Hunyadi 20,000 men for the campaign early in September but he did not conclude the Treaty of Lezhe with the Venetians until 4 October 1448.

4 Malcolm, N., *Kosovo: A Short History*, Macmillan, London, 1998, 90.

5 It could be argued that the extension of the *devshirme* was also required simply because of the extensive and increasingly far-flung borders that the Ottoman army now had to fight on. Of course, enslavement of Muslims was 'technically' illegal under Sharia law, but then so was the enslavement of Christians or Jews as both are 'people of the book'. The theological-legal argument extended by the Ottomans to justify the *devshirme* may have been 'justified on the grounds of custom and analogy' and as an evolution of the fifth of all booty that each Holy War leader was entitled to under Sharia law. See Wittek, P., 'Devshirme and Sharia', *Bulletin of the School of Oriental and African Studies*, University of London, vol. 17:2, 1955, 271–278.

6 In Nicolle, D., *Constantinople 1453: The End of Byzantium*, Osprey, Oxford, 2000, 11–12.

7 Ehrenkreutz, A., 'The Place of Saladin in the Naval History of the Mediterranean Sea in the Middle Ages', *Journal of the American Oriental Society*, April–June 1955, 100–16, and Waterson, J., *Sacred Swords: Jihad in the Holy Land 1097–1295*, Frontline Books, London, 2010, 109–138.

8 White, L., 'The Crusades and the Technological Thrust of the West', in *War, Technology and Society in the Middle East*, editors

Parry, V.J., and Yapp, M.E., Oxford University Press, 1975, 97–112.

9 Waterson, J., *The Knights of Islam: The Wars of the Mamluks*, Greenhill Books, London, 2007, ch. 8.

10 The Greek Church would much later become a singular point of resistance to Ottoman rule but in 1453 Orthodox adherents certainly preferred the turban to the Cardinal's hat. See Geanakoplos, D., 'The Council of Florence (1438–39) and the Problem of Union between the Greek and Latin Churches', *Church History*, vol. 24:4. December 1955, 324–346.

11 Runciman, S., *The Fall of Constantinople 1453*, Cambridge University Press, Cambridge, 1954, 120.

12 In Nicolle, D., *Constantinople 1453: The End of Byzantium*, Osprey, Oxford, 2000, 77–79.

13 Apparently Mehemmed II, on his triumphal entry into the city, 'as a trial of his strength ... shattered with his iron mace the under-jaw' of one of the three intertwined serpents of the famous Delphic column that had stood in the Hippodrome since the time of Constantine. To the rustic Turks these monsters were the daunting idols or talismans of the city. Mehemmed II's destruction of them is probably apocryphal but sums up the victory for the rational arm of central government over the traditions, beliefs and ways of the distant Turkic steppe that the fall of Constantinople heralded. See Menage, V., 'The Serpent Column in Ottoman Sources', *Anatolian Studies*, vol. 14: 1964, 169–173.

14 Blair, S., and Bloom, J., *The Art and Architecture of Islam 1250–1800*, Yale University Press, London, 1994, 231–232.

15 Inalcik, H., 'Servile Labour in the Ottoman Empire', ch. 7 in *Studies in Ottoman Society and Economic History*, Variorum Reprints, London, 1985, 25–26.

16 Imber, C., *The Ottoman Empire 1300–1481*, Isis Press, Istanbul, 1990, 183.

17 Imber, C., *The Ottoman Empire 1300–1481*, Isis Press, Istanbul, 1990, 158.

18 Inalcik, H., 'The Hub of the City: The Bedestan of Istanbul', ch. 9 in *Studies in Ottoman Society and Economic History*, Variorum Reprints, London, 1985, 1.

19 Inalcik, H., 'The Policy of Mehemmed II toward the Greek Population of Istanbul and the Buildings of the City', ch. 6 in *The Ottoman Empire: Conquest, Organisation and Economy*, Variorum Reprints, London, 1970/1985, 236.

20 Imber, C., *The Ottoman Empire 1300–1481*, Isis Press, Istanbul, 1990, 199.

21 Imber, C., *The Ottoman Empire 1300–1481*, Isis Press, Istanbul, 1990, 208.

22 Imber, C., *The Ottoman Empire 1300–1481*, Isis Press, Istanbul, 1990, 217.

23 In Nisbet-Bain, R., 'The Siege of Belgrade by Muhammad II, July 1–23, 1456' in *The English Historical Review*, vol. 7:26, April 1892, 235–252.

24 See Florescu, R., and McNally, R., *Dracula, Prince of Many Faces: His Life and His Times*, Back Bay Books, Boston, MA, 1990, 113–114.

25 Richard II of England, another isolated monarch, created a special bodyguard named the Cheshire Archers in the late 1390s. By the autumn of 1398 he had more than 300 of these men grouped into seven watches. The similarities between the way in which Vlad Dracula and Richard II tried to rule are striking, as are the speed and character of their respective falls from power. See Gillespie, J., 'Richard II's Cheshire Archers', *Transactions of the Historic Society of Lancashire and Cheshire*, vol. 125, 1974, 1–39.

26 The brutality of the *devshirme*, or 'tribute of blood', cannot be, I feel, overstated. Dr Basilike Papoulia has made the best summary of its callous nature; the *devshirme* was 'the forcible removal, in the form of a tribute, of children of the Christian subjects from their ethnic, religious, and cultural environment and their transplantation into the Turkish-Islamic environment with the aim of employing them in the service of the Palace, the army, and the state, whereby they were on the one hand to serve the sultan as slaves and freedmen and on the other to form the ruling class of the State'. Vlad Dracula's rejection of the *devshirme* would undoubtedly have created a groundswell of support among the peasant class. See Menage, V., 'Some Notes on the 'devshirme', *Bulletin of the School of Oriental and African Studies*, University of London, vol. 29:1, 1966, 64–78.

27 Vorsino, M., 'Dracula: From Historical Voievod to Fictional Vampire', Master's thesis, University of Texas at Arlington, 2008, 34–35.

28 One consistently sees historians writing how the volume of killing undertaken in medieval accounts of massacres by invading armies is untenable since the people could have simply run away whilst awaiting murder. This notion is faintly ridiculous as the obvious question in an agrarian society tied for its survival to its crop production is – run where? The numbers given in the sources undoubtedly relate not just to those killed by sword or arrow but those who died as a result of the obliteration of cities and the agrarian infrastructure around them during assaults and reprisals. See Waterson, J., *Defending Heaven*, Frontline Books, London, 2013, Introduction and 216, note 2.

29 Florescu, R., and McNally, R., *Dracula, Prince of Many Faces: His Life and His Times*, Back Bay Books, Boston, MA, 1990, ch. 4.

30 This is not to suggest that the 'Reformation' or even the evangelism that would split the church most drastically in the time of Martin Luther had already begun but rather that the independent ideas of the Hussites (and the idea of independent churches) and the political and financial ambitions of the German princes and emperors in this period allied to an increasingly disparaging opinion of the morals and actions of the Papacy meant that there was a stolid resistance to any pope who tried to project power over the Alps, or even beyond the papal lands. The Bull *Execrabilis* of January 1460, in which Pius II condemned all appeals from the decisions of the Pope to an ecumenical council, is symptomatic of the Papacy's increasing loss of power and reaction to conciliarism (18 January, 1460). See MacCulloch, D., *Reformation: Europe's House Divided: 1490–1700*, Allen Lane, London, 2003, 35–42.

31 The origin of 'Dracula' has been suggested as being derived from the Romanian word for devil, *Dracul*, but this is clearly wrong as no prince would allow such an epithet to be applied to themselves in their lifetime. Vlad Dracula signed his letters of 1475 to the citizens of Sibiu as 'Dragulya', and he is recorded in contemporary documents as Drakulya. What is far more likely is that Vlad wanted to keep the relationship of his family with the illustrious Order of the Dragon alive so he signed as Drakuglia as a derived form of his father's title. Multiple spellings of the same word were, of course, common before the advent of printing. See Nandris, G., 'A Philological Analysis of "Dracula" and Rumanian Place-Names and Masculine Personal Names', *The Slavonic and East European Review*, vol. 37:89, 1959, 371–377.

32 This practice was not peculiar to the Ottomans. In 1260 Qutuz, the Mamluk sultan, cut Hulegu Khan's envoys in half in the horse market, and placed their heads on the gates of Cairo after Hulegu sent them to him with an insulting letter and demands for his surrender. The Mamluks retained many of their steppe traditions despite being an urban caste and so did the Ottomans. See Waterson, J., *The Knights of Islam: The Wars of the Mamluks*, Greenhill Books, London, 2007, ch. 4.

33 Florescu, R., and McNally, R., *Dracula, Prince of Many Faces: His Life and His Time*, Back Bay Books, Boston, MA, 1990, chs 4 and 6.

34 Florescu, R., and McNally, R., *Dracula, Prince of Many Faces: His Life and His Time*, Back Bay Books, Boston, MA, 1990, chs 4 and 6.

35 The Golden Horde used the bodies of *dead* plague victims as biological weapons by firing them into the Genoese slaving and trading centre of Caffa on the Black Sea in the late 1340s. It has

been suggested that the Black Death then entered Alexandria via
the Black Sea trade and spread rapidly across Egypt in 1347. I
can only think of one other possible recorded episode of perhaps
deliberate 'live' subject transmission of a debilitating disease and
that would be the 300 in every 1,000 US troops who were infected
with gonorrhoea in Vietnam in 1963. See Rasnake et al. 'History
of U.S. Military Contributions to the Study of Sexually Transmitted
Diseases', *Military Medicine*, 170, 4:61, 2005, 61–65.
36 In Florescu, R., and McNally, R., *Dracula, Prince of Many Faces: His
Life and His Times*, Back Bay Books, Boston, MA, 1990, chs 4 and 6.

Chapter 4

1 Mina Harker's Journal, 30 September. Stoker, B., *Dracula*, 1897.
2 Even the Crusaders, who were at least *in* Asia, if only on its
extreme western coast, could not coordinate effectively with the
Mongol Ilkhanate of Iran and Iraq against Mamluk Syria. Medieval
communications, despite some notable exceptions such as the *yam*
postal system of the Mongols and the *barid* messengers of the
Mamluks, were not up to the strain of much beyond the carriage
of news. See Waterson, J.,*The Knights of Islam: The Wars of the
Mamluks*, Greenhill Books, London, 2007, ch. 7.
3 Freedman, L., *Strategy: A History*, Oxford University Press, Oxford,
2013, xii.
4 Freedman, L., *Strategy: A History*, Oxford University Press, Oxford,
2013, xii.
5 Shakespeare, W., *The Life and Death of Richard the Second*, Act 3,
Scene 2.
6 Tout, T., *The Administrative History of Medieval England*,
Manchester, 1937, 133–138, quoted in Prestwich, J., 'The Military
Household of the Norman Kings', *The English Historical Review*,
vol. 96, no. 378, January 1981, 1–35.
7 Gibbon, E., *The Decline and Fall of the Roman Empire*, Everyman
Edition, London, 1776/1910, chs III, V and XIII.
8 Riley-Smith, J., *The Crusades: A Short History*, Athlone Press,
London, 1990, 73.
9 Riley-Smith, J., *Further Thoughts on Baldwin II's Etablissement
on the Confiscation of Fiefs in Crusade and Settlement*, editor
Edbury, P., University College Cardiff Press, Cardiff, 1985, 176.
10 Of all the lords of the medieval age who were 'rebranded' as
precursors of the ideal Communist by the Balkan socialist republic
polities of the Cold War era, Skanderbeg was probably the most
truthfully drawn. He seems to have had an understanding of, and
empathy for, the peasantry that Vlad Dracula and any of his other

contemporaries among the higher lords were completely lacking in. 'Although a feudal lord [he] understood better than others of his class in Albania and abroad that for as long as the Ottoman enemy stood at the gates of the Homeland, not his narrow personal feudal and class interests, but the interests of the entire Albanian society must be placed, first,' 'Legendary Hero of the Albanian People', New Albania, 1, 1985. In Banac, I., 'Political Change and National Diversity', Daedalus, Winter 1990, 141–159.

11 Scriven, G., 'The Awakening of Albania', *Geographical Review*, August 1919, 73–83.

12 In Albanian, *Dragua* is the epithet for heroism. However, Skanderbeg is not given this appellation by the Albanian texts of the period. He is described as the *Kulshedra* of Albania. The *Kulshedra* is a large and powerful eel that lives in the mud of rivers and which terrified the subconscious of the Albanian peasantry. The metaphor is based on the sheer terror that he spread among the Ottoman ranks in the fifteenth century. One legend claims that the day Skanderbeg was born his mother dreamt of a *Kulshedra* whose body covered the entire territory of Albania with its head reaching down to the border of the Ottoman Turkish lands, where it devoured all its enemies with a vast bloody mouth. See Doja, A., 'Mythology and Destiny', Anthropos, 2005, 449–462.

13 Even in the early twentieth century Skanderbeg was remembered through both the customs and dress of Albanians. 'Skanderbeg jackets', short black homespun coats with thick epaulettes and long fringes of black wool, were commonly worn in mourning for the prince. See Ryan, M., 'Some Impressions of Albania', *Studies: An Irish Quarterly Review*, June 1939, 293–302.

14 Petry, C., *Twilight of Majesty: The Reigns of the Mamluk Sultans al-Ashraf Qaytbay and Kansawh al-Ghawri in Egypt*, University of Washington Press, Seattle, 1993, 170.

15 Translator Michael, M., *The Annals of Jan Dlugosz: Annales seu cronicae incliti regni Poloniae*, an English abridgement, IM Publications, Chichester, 1997, 589.

16 In Florescu, R., and McNally, R., *Dracula, Prince of Many Faces: His Life and His Times*, Back Bay Books, Boston, MA, 1990, ch. 6.

Chapter 5

1 A note from Van Helsing to John Seward, MD, 27 September. Stoker, B., *Dracula*, 1897.

2 The Tatars of the Golden Horde would have taken at least three and up to five horses with them into any war. They had to because a small steppe pony of 300kg cannot carry more than 17 per cent

of its own weight effectively and a Tatar trooper tilts the balance to well over this point. A steppe pony could therefore only maintain battle for eight to ten minutes maximum before needing to be changed. For the khan to return from Moldavia with only *one* pony things must really have gone awry. See Smith, J., 'Mongol Society and Military in the Middle East: Antecedents and Adaptations' in *War, Technology and Society in the Middle East*, editors Parry, V., and Yapp, M., Oxford University Press, London, 1975, 256–258.

3 There was certainly a degree of 'trophy taking' in the display of Vlad Dracula's head to the people of Istanbul but there was also the problem of producing proof of death for any bête noire of a medieval state. The Mongols would send heads of traitors on tours of their lands to ensure that everyone knew the danger had been extinguished. They also sent body parts and organs on circuits around the provinces but that had much more to do with intimidating than informing the populace.

4 In Florescu, R., and McNally, R., *Dracula, Prince of Many Faces: His Life and His Times*, Back Bay Books, Boston, MA, 1990, ch. 7.

5 Mehemmed II seems to have had highly detailed information on Italy and its military science and capabilities right from the outset of his second reign. See Babinger, F., 'An Italian Map of the Balkans, Presumably Owned by Mehmed II, the Conqueror (1452–53)', *Imago Mundi*, vol. 8, 1951, 8–15.

6 A *waqf*, or endowment for religious and charitable purposes, could be made by an Ottoman aristocrat, and his executors and family managed the endowment and thereby ensured their own (comfortable) livelihoods. This is not to suggest that the essential idea of the *waqf* was corrupt. Some of the most wonderful religious monuments in Ottoman lands were erected as a result of *waqf* endowments and any number of *maristans* or hospitals owed their origin and maintenance to the *waqf* of sultans and great *beys*. See Oktay, O., 'Limits of the Almighty: Mehmed II's "Land Reform" Revisited', *Journal of the Economic and Social History of the Orient*, vol. 42:2, 1999, 226–246.

7 An estimate of the Ottoman army in 1475 suggests 6,000 Janissaries were in the service of Mehemmed II. By the time of the Siege of Vienna in 1683 the Janissaries made up over a quarter of the total invading army. A Janissary's early 'career' after capture as a young boy involved being hired out for five to seven years as a labourer for Turkish families to learn Turkish, basic military skills and the Muslim faith. When a training corps vacancy became available the young man would then undergo at least six years of barracks training under strict discipline. He was trained to use a variety of weapons, including the bow, musket, javelin and sword.

8   For Mehemmed II's contribution to the arts through pastronage and also his own sketches and efforts in drawing, see Raby, J., 'A Sultan of Paradox: Mehmed the Conqueror as a Patron of the Arts', *Oxford Art Journal*, vol. 5:1, 1982, 3–8.

9   A contemporary Greek chronicler went to the trouble of 'computing' the total number Mehemmed II's victims, and obtained the number eight hundred and seventy-three thousand persons who were executed on the sultan's direct orders. These included prisoners of war, Janissaries who deserted in the face of the enemy and 'heretic Turks'. Needless to say, the number is too accurate not to arouse our suspicions, and the last two groups could have expected very little from any other contemporary state or indeed almost any other state at any time or provenance in history. See Marinesco, C., 'L'état et la Société Turcs a L'époque de Mahomet II a Propos d'un Ouvrage Récent', *Revue Historique*, vol. 214:1, 1955, 35–47.

10 The question of ethnicity is always a tricky one but time and again, even when wars are supposed to be about cultural divides, political allegiance, religious persuasion and class, they collapse into genocidal struggles. Ethnic wars also always seem to be the most brutal as they can only, by definition, end with the annihilation of the 'other'. This must, 'logically', go far beyond the battlefield and the destruction of the enemy's army and requires ethnic-cleansing of civilians too. See Fergusson, N., *The War of the World: Twentieth-Century Conflict and the Descent of the West*, Penguin, New York, 2007, introduction.

11 See ch. 2 'End and Means in War', in *On War*, Von Clausewitz, C., translator Graham, J., 1874 edition, Project Gutenberg, London.

12 'War therefore is an act of violence intended to compel our opponent to fulfil our will.' See ch. 1 'What is War?' in *On War*, Von Clausewitz, C., translator Graham, J., 1874 edition, Project Gutenberg, London.

13 In Florescu, R., and McNally, R., *Dracula, Prince of Many Faces: His Life and His Times*, Back Bay Books, Boston, MA, 1990, ch. 7.

14 In Florescu, R., and McNally, R., *Dracula, Prince of Many Faces: His Life and His Times*, Back Bay Books, Boston, MA, 1990, ch. 7.

15 The earliest historical work in Slavonic relating to the history of Wallachia is the *Skazanije o Draculeav voievodea* (The Story of Prince Dracula) based on events during the reign of Vlad Dracula. The account may have been originally composed in Transylvania in Middle Bulgarian in 1486 but the surviving manuscripts are Russian copies, the earliest dating from 1490. Slavonic was of course almost exclusively restricted in its use to scribes and churchmen. Many of the 'tales' of Vlad Dracula therefore existed only in the oral tradition. See Deletant, D., 'Slavonic Letters in

Moldavia, Wallachia and Transylvania from the Tenth to the
Seventeenth Centuries', *The Slavonic and East European Review*,
January 1980, 1–21.
16 Cocteau, J., *Journal d'un inconnu*, Grasset, Paris, 1953.
17 From *Ion Bogdan, Vlad Tepes si naratiunile germane si rusesti
asupra lui* (*Vlad the Impaler and German and Russian Descriptions
of Him*), Bucharest, 1896.

Chapter 6

1 Johnathan Harker's Journal, 5 May. Stoker, B., *Dracula*, 1897.
2 Menage, V., 'Mission of an Ottoman Secret Agent in France in
1486', *Journal of the Royal Asiatic Society of Great Britain and
Ireland*, October 1965, 112–132.
3 Rosetti, R., 'Stephen the Great of Moldavia and the Turkish
Invasion (1457–1504)', *The Slavonic Review*, vol. 6:6. 1927,
86–103.
4 One argument for the 'rise' of the West and the hegemony that
Western nations have exerted on the world in the modern period
is that the devastating impact of the Black Death in China and
the reorientation of the Ming Dynasty to China's north rather
than to the traditionally seagoing south meant that despite the
achievements of Admiral Zheng He the South China Sea was
essentially abandoned by the Ming, along with active sea trade, and
that this allowed the Portuguese, Dutch and English to create a new
world trade and geopolitical system. See Abu-Lughod, J.L., *Before
European Hegemony: The World System, A.D. 1250–1350*, Oxford
University Press, Oxford, 1989. For the journeys of Zheng He and
the Ming Dynasty's isolationist policies see Dreyer, E., *Zheng He:
China and the Oceans in the Early Ming Dynasty, 1405–1433*,
Longman, London, 2006.
5 Finkel, C., *Osman's Dream: The Story of the Ottoman Empire
1300–1923*, John Murray, London, 2005, 99–105.
6 Zarinebaf-Shahr, F., 'Qizilbash "Heresy" and Rebellion in Ottoman
Anatolia during the Sixteenth Century', *Anatolia Moderna VII*,
1997, 1–15 in Finkel, C., *Osman's Dream: The Story of the
Ottoman Empire 1300–1923*, John Murray, London, 2005, 105.
7 In 1530 Charles V would be crowned as Holy Roman Emperor
by a chastened pope in Bologna's cathedral. This was of course
after the 1527 sack of Rome. The emperor also made his desire
for a uniformly Catholic world very explicit by his crowning as
the sole representative of 'their' empire. The coronation also very
strongly implied a claim on the seat of the last Roman emperor –
Constantinople.

8 Francis I's words to his mother in a letter, '*de toutes choses ne m'est demeuré que l'honneur et la vie qui est sauve ...*', are an apposite farewell to the days of wistful medieval knight-errants. It would be hard to imagine any monarch of the early modern era mentioning the retention of their honour when recounting the loss of a battle and their own capture on the field.

9 This constant readiness was in stark contrast to the time it took to raise an army comprised of feudal contingents which, at a minimum, was forty days, and more than 400 days in the case of the Holy Roman Emperor Henry VII when he called for troops to accompany him to Rome in 1309.

10 More important than the Battle of Lepanto was the Treaty of Le Cateau–Cambresis. The settlement of differences between France and the Holy Roman Empire effectively reoriented Europe away from power-plays over Central Europe and towards the Atlantic Ocean. Spanish gold from the New World funded European ambitions and hastened its overtaking of the economies and polities of the East. The Ottomans would become helpless bystanders to their own decline. See Labib, S., 'The Era of Suleyman the Magnificent: Crisis of Orientation', *International Journal of Middle East Studies*, vol. 10:4, November 1979, 435–451.

11 Peirce, L., *The Imperial Harem: Women and Sovereignty in the Ottoman Empire*, Oxford University Press, New York, 1993, 38–39.

12 Stoye, J., *The Siege of Vienna*, Birlinn Ltd, Edinburgh, 1964, 150–173.

13 It could be suggested that the Holy League that was formed in 1684 with Habsburg Austria, Poland and Venice as participants was almost the last major representation of Europe as 'Christendom', indeed the Treaty of Utrecht (1714) was the last European treaty to refer to the *Respublica Christiana*. The continued presence of the Ottoman Turks in the Balkans was one factor in the forging of an early modern era notion of 'Europe'. See Yapp, M., 'Europe in the Turkish Mirror', Past & Present, vol. 137, *The Cultural and Political Construction of Europe, November 1992*, 134–155.

14 Vickers, M., *Between Serb and Albanian: A History of Kosovo*, Hurst and Co., London, 1998, 12.

15 Kopanski, B., 'Islamization of Albanians in the Middle Ages: The Primary Sources and the Predicament of the Modern Historiography', *Islamic Studies*, vol. 36:2/3, *Special Issue: Islam In The Balkans*, 1997, 191–208.

16 Anzulovic, B., *Heavenly Serbia: From Myth to Genocide*, New York University Press, New York, 1999, and Malcolm, N., *Kosovo: A Short History*, Macmillan, London, 1998, 67.

17 Falconi, C., *Il Silenzio di Pio XII. Papa Pacelli e il Nazifascismo*, Sugar, Milan, 1965.

18 In Croce, B., *La Storia Come Pensiero e Come Azione*, Bibliopolis, Naples, 1938/2002, 2.

19 From articles by Cazanisteanu, C., *Scinteia*, December 1976, and Pavelescu, I., *Romania Libera*, December 1976. Material prepared for the use of editors and policy staff of Radio Free Europe, 1977. http://osaarchivum.org/files/holdings/300/8/3/text/52-5-181.shtml

20 Giurescu, C., 'Gallant and Dreaded Vlad the Impaler', *Magazin Istoric*, vol. 3:84, March 1974, 3–12.

21 Oddly enough Skanderbeg was not forgotten by Karol Bogumil Stolzman, an artillery captain who took part in the Polish rising of 1830–31. His treatise on guerrilla warfare is a superb 'do it yourself' guide to insurrection, and includes advice on how to produce explosives in one's own kitchen and exactly how much gunpowder is required to produce landmines. He claimed Skanderbeg as a major inspiration and suggests him as one of the fathers of modern partisan warfare. See Laqueur, W., 'The Origins of Guerrilla Doctrine', *Journal of Contemporary History*, July 1975, 341–382.

22 Sanziana Pop, 'Eight Years for Eternity', *Luceafarul*, 1 December 1976. In Cioranescu, G., *Vlad the Impaler: Current Parallels with a Medieval Romanian Prince*, Material prepared for the use of editors and policy staff of Radio Free Europe. 1977. http://osaarchivum.org/files/holdings/300/8/3/text/52-5-181.shtml

23 For the mechanism of how the 'will' of the masses outweighs the rights of those who stand in any form of opposition to the dictatorship of the 'people', see Mao Ze Dong, 'On The People's Democratic Dictatorship'. Speech in Commemoration of the Twenty-eighth Anniversary of the Communist Party of China. *Selected Works of Mao Tse-Tung* (sic), vol. I, Foreign Languages Press, Beijing, 30 June 1949.

24 From the Code of Principles and Standards Governing the Work and Manner of Living of Communists, and of Socialist Ethics, Scinteia, Bucharest, 20 December 1974.

25 Ceausescu, N., Speech at the RCP CC Plenum of 2–3 November 1976, Scinteia, Bucharest, November 1976.

FURTHER READING

Obviously the referenced works are the starting point for any reader interested in further reading about the Ottomans, Hungarians, Serbs, Wallachians, Moldavians, Venetians, Western and Eastern Crusaders, and other clans and individuals who have graced us with their presence in this slim volume. For those readers who wish to pursue their studies a little further the following works are suggested. Most are readily obtainable, but some of the studies of the medieval Balkans and the Ottomans and their foes in Asia could be considered 'specialist'.

Allen, W., *Problems of Turkish Power in the Sixteenth Century [XI]* (London: Central Asian Research Centre, 1963).

Atiya, A., *The Crusade of Nicopolis* (London: Methuen and Co., 1934).

Boyar, E., *Ottomans, Turks and the Balkans: Empire Lost, Relations Altered* (London: Tauris Academic Studies, 2007).

Carmichael,C., *Ethnic Cleansing in the Balkans: Nationalism and the Destruction of Tradition* (London: Routledge, 2002).

Cazacu, M., *L'histoire du prince Dracula en Europe centrale et orientale (XV e siècle)* (Présentation, édition critique, traduction et commentaire. Genev. Librairie Droz, 1988).

Clark, J., *Serbia in the Shadow of Milosevic: The Legacy of Conflict in the Balkans* (New York: Tauris Academic Studies, 2008).

Cossuto, G., 'I Musulmani di Romania e Il Nuovo Corso Politico: Note sull'attuale Situazione Sociale e Culturale', *Oriente Moderno, Nuova Serie*, Anno 13:74:7/12 (Luglio-Dicembre, 1994), pp. 203–18.

Fisher, S. 'The Foreign Relations of Turkey 1481–1512', *Illinois Studies in the Social Sciences*, vol. 30:1 (Urbana: Illinois University Press, 1948).

Florescu, R. and McNally, R., *Dracula: A Biography of Vlad the Impaler, 1431–1476* (New York: Hawthorn Books, 1973).

Halecki, O., *The Crusade of Varna: A Discussion of Controversial Problems* (New York: Polish Institute of Arts and Sciences, 1943).

Hankin, J., 'Renaissance Crusaders: Humanist Crusade Literature in the Age of Mehmed II', *Dumbarton Oaks Papers*, vol. 49, *Symposium on Byzantium and the Italians, 13th–15th Centuries*, 1995, 111–207.

Hupchick, D., *The Balkans from Constantinople to Communism* (New York: Palgrave, 2001).

Inalcik, H., *Mehmed the Conqueror (1432–1481) and His Time* (Chicago: University of Chicago Press, 1960).

Irwin, R., 'Gunpowder and Firearms in the Mamluk Sultanate Reconsidered', in Winter, M. and Levanoni, A. eds, *The Mamluks in Egyptian and Syrian Politics and Society* (Leiden: E.J. Brill, 2004).

Kortepeter, C., *Ottoman Imperialism during the Reformation: Europe and the Caucasus* (New York: New York University Studies in Near Eastern Civilization, 1972).

Locke, G., *The Serbian Epic Ballads: An Anthology* (London: ASWA, 2002).

Mackay, A. and Ditchburn, D., *Routledge Atlas of Medieval Europe* (Routledge, 1997).

Mihailovic, K., *Memoirs of a Janissary, translated by Benjamin Stolz, historical commentary and notes by Svat Soucek* (Michigan Slavic Translations No. 3, Ann Arbor, Department of Slavic Languages and Literatures, University of Michigan, 1975).

Nandris, G., 'The Historical Dracula: The Theme of His Legend in the Western and in the Eastern Literatures of Europe', *Comparative Literature Studies*, vol. 3:4, 1966, 367–396.

Nicol, D., *Byzantium and Venice: A Study in Diplomatic and Cultural Relations* (Cambridge: Cambridge University Press, 1988).

Okey, R., *Taming Balkan Nationalism: The Habsburg 'Civilising Mission' in Bosnia 1878–1914* (Oxford: Oxford University Press, 2007).

Pamuk, S., *A Monetary History of the Ottoman Empire* (Cambridge: Cambridge University Press, 2000).

Rich, E., and Wilson, C. (eds), *The Cambridge Economic History of Europe, Volume V: The Economic Organization of Early Modern Europe* (Cambridge: Cambridge University Press, 1977).

Roudometof, V., *Collective Memory, National Identity, and Ethnic Conflict: Greece, Bulgaria, and the Macedonian Question* (Connecticut: Praeger Publishers, 1964/2002).

Schwartz, S., *Kosovo: Background to a War* (London: Anthem Press, 2000).

Sghevill, F., *A History of the Balkans from the Earliest Times to the Present Day* (New York: Dorset Press, 1991).

Shepard, J. (ed.), *The Cambridge History of the Byzantine Empire c.500–1492* (Cambridge: Cambridge University Press, 2008).

Stephenson, P., *Byzantium's Balkan Frontier: A Political Study of the Northern Balkans, 900–1204* (Cambridge: Cambridge University Press, 2000).

Todorova, M., *Imagining the Balkans* (Oxford: Oxford University Press, 2009, updated version).

Treptow, K., *Essays on the Life and Times of Vlad Tepes*, no. 323 (Boulder, Colorado: East European Monographs, 1991).

INDEX

The
History
Press   The destination for history
        www.thehistorypress.co.uk

Made in United States
North Haven, CT
19 August 2022

22893205R10150